Parks, Plants, and People

Parks, Plants, and People

Beautifying the Urban Landscape

Lynden B. Miller

W. W. Norton & Company

New York • London

This book is dedicated to the memory of
William Hollingsworth (Holly) Whyte (1917–1999)
for his love of cities and people,
and for all he taught us about good public space.

All photographs by Lynden B. Miller unless otherwise credited.

For information about permission to reproduce selections from this book, write to
Permissions, W. W. Norton & Company, Inc., 500 Fifth Avenue, New York, NY 10110

For information about special discounts for bulk purchases, please contact
W. W. Norton Special Sales at specialsales@wwnorton.com or 800-233-4830

Manufacturing by KHL Printing Co. Pte Ltd
Book design by Jonathan Lippincott
Production manager: Leeann Graham

Library of Congress Cataloging-in-Publication Data

Miller, Lynden B.
  Parks, plants, and people : beautifying the urban landscape / Lynden
B. Miller. — 1st ed.
     p. cm.
  Includes bibliographical references and index.
  ISBN 978-0-393-73203-0 (hardcover)
  1. Landscape gardening—New York (State)—New York. 2. Urban
parks—New York (State)—New York. 3. Public spaces—New York
(State)—New York. 4. Urban beautification—New York (State)—New York.
I. Title.
  SB470.54.N6M55 2009
  712.09747'1—dc22

                                      2009004536

ISBN: 978-0-393-73203-0

W. W. Norton & Company, Inc., 500 Fifth Avenue, New York, N.Y. 10110
                    www.wwnorton.com
W. W. Norton & Company Ltd., Castle House, 75/76 Wells Street, London W1T 3QT

0 9 8 7 6 5 4 3 2 1

Contents

Acknowledgments

A number of years ago, I was speaking to the Horticultural Society in Charleston, South Carolina, about my efforts to beautify New York through public garden design. After my talk, Charleston's mayor, Joseph P. Riley, Jr., asked me if I could give him a book with my recommendations and experiences so that he could pass it along to his associates. I realized then that I needed to redirect some of my efforts toward getting my thoughts on paper in order to share what I had learned over the years about reinvigorating parks and gardens.

Reading Robert Caro's *The Power Broker* was a galvanizing moment for me when it appeared in 1974. Learning about Robert Moses and his destruction of neighborhoods and open space in New York helped open my eyes to the importance of parks and green spaces that respond to people's needs. Bob Caro, along with Rick Darke, Paula Deitz, Dan Hinkley, Deborah Needleman, and Helen Pratt, encouraged me in the writing of this book.

In my work, I have been inspired by many people: the lives and work of Beatrix Farrand and Frederick Law Olmsted, and the accomplishments of Mayor Richard M. Daley of Chicago, who has done so much to transform his city. My life has been enriched by knowing and working with Drew Becher, Dan Biederman, Amanda Burden, Ann Buttenweiser, David Emil, Don Elliott, Marion and Andrew Heiskell, Penelope Hobhouse, Shirley Strum Kenny, Gregory Long, Christopher Lloyd, Danny Meyer, Bette Midler, Philip Pitruzzello, Elizabeth Barlow Rogers, and Beth Straus. David Rockefeller shares my commitment to the beautification of city life, as did the late Mary Todd Rockefeller, a serious gardener and an early contributor to my work.

My colleagues here in New York have generously shared their expertise with me: from the Central Park Conservancy, Doug Blonsky, Matthew Brown, Neil Calvanese, and Andrea Hill; at New Yorkers for Parks, Christian DiPalermo, Sheelah Feinberg, Cheryl Huber, and Maura Lout; from Battery Park City, Eileen Calvanese and Eric T. Fleisher; and at the New York Botanical Garden, Jessica Arcate, Margaret Falk, Todd Forrest, Peter Kukielski, and Karl Lauby. Working for many years with Diane Schaub, the matchless curator of the Conservatory Garden, has been a joy.

Besides those mentioned in the text, many people involved with cities, parks, and horticulture graciously shared knowledge and information with me: Jen Bruler in Wilmington, Delaware; Sherrie Cochran in Tupelo, Mississippi; Geoffrey Dyer and Cathie Cox in Toronto; Barbee Crutcher and Monte Powell in Seattle; Linda Jonash and Lucia Droby in Boston; Nancy Gronowski and Gloria Lee in Portland, Oregon; Randee Humphrey and Frank Robinson in Richmond, Virginia; Jim Lowden in Vancouver; Patti McGee in Charleston, South Carolina; Louis Appell, Genevieve Ray, and Brian Tate in York, Pennsylvania; and Alison Strickler in Chicago.

I have enjoyed collaborating over the years with landscape architects Tom Balsley, Marc Boddewyn, Bradford Greene, Faye Harwell, Ken Smith, and Michael Van Valkenburgh; architects John Belle, Fred Bland, Harry Buttrick, Hugh Hardy, Neil Kittredge, Jean Phifer, Jaquelin Robertson, and Kevin Roche; and enlightened university administrators Marc Burstein and Emily Lloyd.

My students at New York University, where I have taught since 2006, were a great help in researching the Internet as I was gathering material for this book, especially Lindsey Nelson and Ajay Patel. My thanks go to Joseph DeSciose and Sara Cedar Miller for their wonderful photographs.

I have been blessed with a splendid editor, Nancy Green, at Norton, and I am most grateful to Sarah Carter Roberts for sharing her remarkable horticultural expertise and her passion for plants.

A million thanks to my associate, Ronda Brands, who entered my life just when I most needed both her design assistance and her prodigious editing skills. She worked with me for countless hours fine-tuning this manuscript.

The unfailing support of my husband, Leigh Miller, has kept me going through the many years of my career and the sometimes tortuous but ultimately rewarding process of writing this book.

Introduction

In the 1980s, New York City had become the symbol of urban decay, and Bryant Park, six acres located behind the Public Library on 42nd Street, was a prime example. Surrounded by a wall and fencing, the park was cut off from the street, making it a haven for drugs and crime—one of the first places to be nicknamed "Needle Park." In 1987, after a drug-related murder, it was closed to the public.

At ten o'clock on a warm summer evening ten years later, about ten thousand people from all over the city spread out blankets and unpacked picnics on Bryant Park's expansive green lawn to watch *The Wizard of Oz* on an outdoor movie screen. Just blocks away from the honking horns and neon lights of Times Square, tall trees and long flowering borders were just visible in the dark. When Judy Garland sang "Somewhere Over the Rainbow," the crowd spontaneously joined in—a magical moment.

The transformation of Bryant Park from a frightening, drug-infested jungle to a well-tended oasis is just one of many dramatic turnarounds in the restoration of New York City's public spaces, a transformation I have been privileged to be part of for over twenty-five years. If it can be done in New York, it can be done anywhere. In this book I show you how high-quality, imaginative year-round plantings can soften and civilize city life, and how to evaluate, design, fund, and maintain lushly planted and inspiring public spaces.

Good parks have the power to transform city life, changing the way people feel about themselves and their city. Photo by Joseph De Sciose.

Anyone who loves cities and plants can be part of this. City dwellers, city planners, philanthropists, civic activists, public officials, developers, architects and landscape architects, gardeners, horticulturists, and environmentalists—everyone should be aware of the exciting possibilities of planting for people. Beautifying your city brings environmental, social, and economic benefits. But to create successful public spaces you need energy, determination, and above all a belief in the powerful connection between people and nature.

When office workers step outside and find themselves surrounded by life-affirming natural elements—changing seasons, tall trees, wide lawns, flowers, birds, bees, butterflies—something positive happens to them. People respond to beautiful surroundings by respecting and protecting these places and by sharing this beauty with one another. Two tourists in the restored Bryant Park once told me, "When we came to New York in the 1980s, it was ugly in the city and people were disagreeable. Now it is beautiful and everyone is so nice." I know there is a connection.

For two decades, from 1960 to 1980, New York City lurched from one fiscal crisis to another. City services were cut to save money. Mounds of garbage and abandoned automobiles lined the streets. Graffiti covered the walls and windows of subway cars. Rising crime statistics were cited every day in the papers, and New Yorkers of different backgrounds or from different neighborhoods became afraid of one another. Previous generations of New Yorkers could escape the streets in the city's 29,000 acres of parks, where they could walk, play, or just sit on benches. The Parks Department once had a big budget and lots of dedicated employees to care for its parks and plantings. But when budgets were slashed in the early 1970s, park maintenance was one of the first items to be cut.

In Central Park, the 843-acre oasis in the heart of Manhattan that has always been New Yorkers' beloved backyard and a favorite destination of visitors, budget cuts were particularly obvious. Frederick Law Olmsted, who, along with Calvert Vaux, created the park's wonderful naturalistic design in the 1850s, believed strongly in the power of parks. Olmsted wrote that the chief purpose of a park is to produce an effect "like that of music . . . that goes back of thought and cannot be fully given in the form of words."[1] He hoped that Central Park would provide people of all classes and races with a much-needed contrast to the city streets. And for more than a hundred years, it did.

But by the late 1970s, what had once been elegant and beautiful had become ugly and dangerous, and the crowds whose presence had kept

In the 1980s, as a result of budget cuts in park maintenance, much of the public space in New York looked like this mall at Broadway and 135th Street. Such depressing sights and associated crime affected everyone's morale.

Central Park's Sheep Meadow was full of trash and empty of people in the late 1970s. Photo courtesy of Central Park Conservancy.

After its restoration by the Central Park Conservancy, the Sheep Meadow is filled with people. Photo by Sara Cedar Miller.

City streets have also been beautified. On 42nd Street, you can sit on a bench and read your newspaper or make a phone call next to planter boxes and hanging baskets filled with flowers.

the park safe began to avoid it. Benches were broken, paths flooded, lawns strewn with trash, shrubs overgrown, and buildings burned out. Central Park had become, in the words of one Parks Department employee, "a municipal embarrassment." Eventually Elizabeth Barlow Rogers, a visionary city planner and writer who was appointed Central Park's first administrator in 1979, had had enough. Rogers attacked the problem by appealing to New Yorkers' pride in their city and their love for its best-known park.

Rogers began the Herculean task of restoring Central Park, a task that would end up taking two decades and costing over $500 million. She realized that finding additional city funds to restore the park was a lost cause, and that private dollars would have to be raised. In 1980 she formed the Central Park Conservancy, at that time a unique public-private partnership, to work with the New York City Parks Department to restore the city's best-loved park. The Conservancy's board of trustees includes civic and business leaders who seek private support from individuals, corporations, and foundations. New Yorkers, for all their reputed cynicism, are fundamentally proud of their city and very fond of it; they have shown incredible generosity in supporting the renovation and restoration of many important public institutions, from museums to libraries to parks.

The restoration of Central Park was, to borrow Malcolm Gladwell's phrase, the "tipping point" that galvanized the private sector and brought about renewed interest in the quality of life of the city's public spaces. Since then, New York has gradually but dramatically become a more civil city. Its major buildings, such as the main branch of the Public Library and Grand Central Terminal, have been restored. Not only parks but also streets have been beautified; thousands of flower-filled planter boxes now flourish on the sidewalks amid the chaos of comings and goings. Millions of visitors from all over the world come to enjoy the many pleasures of New York City life.

Since 1982, I have had the great good fortune to direct the restoration or design of a number of public gardens and parks, many of which had been virtually abandoned. A painter and gardener, I had the opportunity first to discover and then to prove my conviction that beautiful outdoor spaces, maintained to the highest standard, contribute greatly to the quality of life in a city. I have seen firsthand the power of a well-planted, well-maintained place to transform city life and the way people behave and feel about their city.

One of my first projects was the Conservatory Garden, then a secluded, overgrown formal garden in a long-neglected northern section of Central Park. Back in the 1970s, Betsy Rogers and I had walked in Central Park together, dreaming of great vistas opened up, underbrush cleared, compacted earth once again green and lush. On summer afternoons, while watching our children play, we talked about plants and parks. She knew that I was a painter who had a passion for plants. I had studied horticulture at the New York Botanical Garden and in English gardens extensively while living in London. My abstract landscape collages had been exhibited in SoHo, but I wasn't sure that I wanted to go back to the art world.

In 1982 Rogers, in her role as administrator of Central Park and head of the Central Park Conservancy, told me, "I have a project for you. I want you to restore the Conservatory Garden up in the northern end of the park." Astonished at such a daunting idea, I asked, "Are you out of your mind? I wouldn't know how to do that!" "Well," she replied, "I want an artist's eye up there. I'll help you. And by the way, not only do I want you to restore the plantings and raise the money to do it, but you also will have to find a way to bring the people back." My life would never be the same again.

Because the Conservatory Garden lacked gardeners and received no maintenance, trash flew about on the September day when I went to have a look. The six-acre garden at 105th Street and Fifth Avenue was deserted. Far from the prestigious apartment buildings to the south, this part of Central Park abutted East Harlem, at that time a neighborhood of crowded tenements, vacant lots, and run-down housing projects. The city was polarized, socially and economically, and many New Yorkers perceived the northern part of Central Park as a dangerous place. But even in its overgrown state, the Conservatory Garden was beautiful and I fell in love with it.

I spread out the 1937 plans of the garden on my kitchen table and realized that I would have to rely on my experience as both a painter and a gardener to revivify the garden. I felt something should be in bloom from early spring to late fall, and that evergreen shrubs, interesting bark, and berries would give life to the winter landscape. Little did I realize that I had inadvertently stumbled on a key to successful public space: a planting design for four seasons. My ideas at the time were about beautiful plants and combinations, not about low maintenance.

The Conservatory Garden in Central Park was neglected, overgrown, and forgotten in 1982.

The Conservatory Garden, restored, on a beautiful day in early May. Photo by Joseph De Sciose.

Some people I approached for funding were skeptical about high-quality gardening in a depressed section of the city, but Betsy Rogers supported me from the start.

One day after the restoration (described in the next chapter) was well under way, I took a taxi to the garden from a meeting downtown. It was about four o'clock in the afternoon, and the driver, unshaven and cross, told me I was definitely his last fare of the day. When we came to 105th Street and I asked to be left off on the park side of Fifth Avenue, he turned around and said loudly, "Lady, you can't go into the park looking like that. You'll get killed in there." I noticed an empty parking space right in front of the garden entrance, so I handed him a coin for the meter and suggested he come in and see this dreadful place. After some persuading, he agreed and we started down the steps.

It was early May. The crabapples were in full bloom, the color of raspberry ice cream. The lawn was green and smooth, with a fountain in

The Conservatory Garden is an oasis for people to enjoy nature and one another.

the distance. The driver's mouth fell open. By the time he saw the thousands of daffodils, tulips, and blue grape hyacinths, he was in shock. "My God," he said, "I've got to go home to Queens and get my wife. She'll never believe this."

I have noticed that after their initial shock that such a place could exist in a big city, first-time visitors always want to share the garden with someone they care about. You can see the magic of the experience on people's faces. Whether they come to an old garden in Central Park, a community garden in the Bronx, or a spectacular flower display in Chicago, people simply feel better about themselves and their city when they are surrounded by beautiful plants. In an article in the *New York Times* in 1987, Enid Nemy suggested that taking a friend to see the Conservatory Garden could give "more pleasure than a wildly expensive material gift"; more important, she continued, it " confers . . . a mood of serenity."[2] A visitor once told me that she didn't think you could have a cross thought in such a place.

Human beings have always needed a relationship with nature, oases of green escape. In many religions Paradise is envisioned as a garden. One spring afternoon as I was leaving the Conservatory Garden, I saw a young man leading a pretty girl dressed in a flowered dress and a straw hat. This would not have been remarkable except that her eyes were closed; she appeared to be blind. He carried her down the steps; I continued on my way. But when I reached a place on the street with a view down into the garden I stopped to watch the couple. He spoke to her and she opened her eyes. She looked at the garden and then threw her arms around him. The next day I asked the garden curator if she had noticed them. "Oh yes, of course. He made her keep her eyes closed until they got into the garden," she said. "That was the guy who called last week to ask what was going to be in bloom because he was going to bring his girl to ask her to marry him."

People call the Conservatory Garden "the Secret Garden" for the charming bronze statue (by New York City sculptor Bessie Potter Vonnah) of two characters from the children's classic of that name by Frances Hodgson Burnett. The statue has overlooked the little pool in

A statue of the young characters in *The Secret Garden* is dedicated to the children of the city of New York. Just as the garden in the book had magical effects, the Conservatory Garden has transformed many lives.

the garden's south section since 1937, with a plaque dedicated to the children of New York in honor of Burnett. In *The Secret Garden*, Mary, Colin, and Dickon are three young children whose lives are transformed by the experience of restoring a garden. Like the garden in the book, the Conservatory Garden was neglected and forgotten, with only a few valiant roses still managing to bloom, and its restoration has transformed many lives—hundreds of volunteers, the wonderful staff, and most important, the residents of East Harlem and the wider city as well.

At the dedication of the Conservatory Garden in 1983, Johnny Colon of the East Harlem School of Music, who provided salsa music for the ceremony, said "You have made it possible for the children of East Harlem to have a look at flowers of different colors in their natural state. Many of these children would not otherwise have the opportunity to experience such a joyful and inspiring sight."

∽

By 1986, when it had become clear that the Conservatory Garden's restoration was a success, other organizations and nonprofit institutions around the city came to me. If I could do that in East Harlem, maybe they should get me to their site, they said. I began to design plantings and gardens for other public places that had been neglected and underfunded; each project led to others, some restorations, some new parks.

Based on my knowledge and love of plants, I have consistently tried to use plants that enhance visitors' experience of the place and the city. Adding plants to the city landscape in a sustainable way means choosing varieties that are adaptable, appropriate to the conditions of the specific site, and maintainable over the long term so that they can continue to contribute to the enrichment of city life and the greening of the urban environment.

Big cities like New York are made of concrete and steel; city lights often outshine the moon and stars. Plantings that are carefully conceived for seasonal change give city dwellers a reason to keep returning: to see what has happened since the last visit, to experience the transformations that nature brings. People who can't tell a *Thalictrum* from a *Lamiastrum* respond to the patterns and rhythms of nature. Even teenagers, so full of restless energy, will come into a garden, look around, and actually sit down. In a beautiful, well-maintained place where they feel safe, people behave in a civil and pleasant way, and by extension they feel pride in themselves and in their city. It is not necessary to be rich or well educated to love a flowering place where you are made to feel welcome. The subtle unspoken message is "We did this for you and you are worth it." People hear that message and rise to the occasion. They pick up their trash and they are courteous to one another.

Gardens have beneficial, even healing effects. Across the street from the Conservatory Garden is a hospital that cares for both children and adults. Some years ago a woman named Gertrude Fensterstock brought her wheelchair-bound husband, who had been a distinguished judge before his debilitating stroke, to the garden. He could no longer speak, but he could nod and shake his head. As he watched us doing our gardening chores, his face would light up. For about a year, the couple came frequently, and we became enormously fond of them and looked forward to their visits. When the mayor of New York came to a ceremony in the garden in 1985, Mrs. Fensterstock introduced her husband and said that the garden was keeping him alive. Then they failed to come. I learned that the judge had been transferred somewhere else; a few months later, Mrs. Fensterstock called to tell me that he had died shortly afterward. She believed that he had lost the life-sustaining pleasure of those garden visits.

Being able to see trees from their windows helps hospital patients get well more quickly. Healing gardens are being planted all over the country. Community gardens provide pleasure—and food—for urban neighborhoods. Workers who fill their offices with houseplants know the pleasures of watching plants grow. Airlines know that pictures of nature will soothe their passengers as they wait to take off.

Dr. Frances E. Kuo and Dr. William Sullivan founded a multi-disciplinary research laboratory at the University of Illinois at Urbana-Champaign to explore the relationship between people and the physical environment. To examine the impact of natural features such as trees, grass, flowers, and green spaces on urban life, they studied the residents of a Chicago housing project consisting of twenty-eight identical 16-story buildings, and their published findings demonstrate that greening can positively affect urban neighborhoods.[3] They showed that residents who lived with even a few straggly trees and a little bit of grass experienced less violence in their homes and more community spirit among their neighbors than those who lived in buildings within the same project that had no connection to nature. To their initial surprise, the scientists discovered that trees and grass brought people together, and that in turn deterred crime. Dr. Kuo later remarked, "I think that through this research I have become convinced that trees are a really important part of a supportive, humane environment. Without vegetation, people are very different beings."[4]

Planting in cities is not only good for the soul and the environment but also good for the wallet. Before New York's Park Avenue was lined with beautiful islands of trees, shrubs, and flowers, it was just a street along the railroad tracks. Now it is one of the city's most desirable places to live. Before Central Park was built, Frederick Law Olmsted predicted that the real estate value of the surrounding areas would rise, and it did. In Boston, real estate skyrocketed near parkland proposed as part of the Big Dig project even before the parks were built. People everywhere prefer to live near parks and green space, and they will pay for it. Many studies around the country have shown that just as homeowners who invest in good landscaping enjoy increased resale value for their properties, good parks and public gardens cause neighborhood real estate values to rise dramatically. Good parks and gardens also become popular tourist destinations; Central Park is the second most visited site in New York City after the Empire State Building.

Nowhere has all of this been more apparent than in Chicago over the last twenty years. Mayor Richard M. Daley, who has done so much to make Chicago one of the most beautiful cities in America, has said: "I

With gardens and parks like this one, Mayor Daley has made Chicago a great place to live and work and an example for other cities.

Sunshine on the hollyhocks in Bryant Park brightens a visitor's afternoon. Photo by Joseph De Sciose.

believe very strongly that the cities that pay attention—really pay attention—to quality of life will be the cities that thrive in the twenty-first century. . . . Trees, flowers, a small park, even a sidewalk bench can soften the rough edges of a city, calm your nerves and make you feel a little more in control of things. . . . [Parks] are essential building blocks of strong neighborhoods."[5]

The general public, professional urban designers, architects, landscape architects, and city governments need to realize the tremendous importance of beautification to the health and economic welfare of cities. Outdoor spaces with ivy and a little grass to mask the concrete are not enough. Beautiful parks and gardens in the city are not a frill; they are essential to the well-being of its citizens. I hope that my experiences in New York and what I have learned about people all over the country who are taking steps to improve their cities will inspire you to create more of these oases where you live.

All Over Town

The Conservatory Garden and Other Projects

It is far easier, simpler to create spaces that work for people than those that do not—and a tremendous difference it can make in the life of a city.
—William H. Whyte, The Social Life of Small Urban Spaces

After eighteen years as a painter, my career as a public garden design-er began unexpectedly in 1982 with the restoration of the Conservatory Garden in Central Park. This project led me to other commissions, large and small, in New York and the surrounding area. I do not design private gardens because I so strongly believe in what gardens and plantings in public places do for city people that I want to keep that as my focus. My work is both about horticulture and about improving city life through beautification. In this chapter, I introduce some of the projects I have worked on through the years, more or less chronologically, and explain what I have learned from each about plants and people.

The Conservatory Garden

In September 1937 the Conservatory Garden at 105th Street and Fifth Avenue in Central Park opened to front-page fanfare in the *New York Times*. It was designed by the aptly named M. Betty Sprout and her col-league Gilmore Clarke, landscape architects working with the New York City Parks Department. Created many years after Frederick Law Olmst-ed and Calvert Vaux's splendid naturalistic design for the rest of the park, this fine formal six-acre garden in the park's northern end was one of the early New York City projects of the Work Projects Administration

An overhead view of the formal six-acre Conservatory Garden at 105th Street and Fifth Avenue in Central Park. The garden, which has three sections, opened in 1937. Photo by Joseph De Sciose.

(WPA), the program established in 1935 under President Franklin Delano Roosevelt to create jobs during the Great Depression. The Conservatory Garden takes its name from the complex of large glass conservatories (greenhouses for floral display) built on the site in 1899 and taken down in 1934 because of their high maintenance costs. Under the direction of Robert Moses, parks commissioner from 1934 to 1968, the garden was built in their place. Moses hired hundreds of gardeners to work for the Parks Department—many of them Italian immigrants who had lost their jobs at the great estates around the city during the Depression—and some of them worked in this formal garden.

Betty Sprout divided the Conservatory Garden into three sections, each inspired by a different European design tradition. She designed the North Garden, rather French in feeling, to have two spectacular seasonal displays, one in spring and one in fall. The Italian-flavored Central Garden, with its large rectangular lawn and clipped yew hedges, is elegant and green all year except for one week in May, when double pink-flowering crabapples bloom. The South Garden was designed to display mostly perennials and annuals, and it resembles an English garden in style.

Such an elaborate design required a great deal of maintenance, and for the first several decades of its life, fourteen Parks Department gardeners were assigned to the garden. They installed and maintained the seasonal displays and kept the hedges trimmed, the trees pruned, and the lawn mowed. The garden had many visitors. But in the 1970s, when park upkeep came to be considered an unnecessary expense, the gardeners were let go. On my first visit in the fall of 1982, I could see the dramatic results of this neglect.

As I passed through the tall black iron gates adorned with ornate scrollwork, I knew I was entering a very special place. A battered sign said that the gates had been made in Paris in the nineteenth century and given to the city in 1939. I looked in at a shabby rectangle of lawn, allées of overgrown crabapples, and some large yew hedges. It was a beautiful day, but no visitors were present. One of the few Parks Department gardeners, a young man named Bill Steyer, came to the gates to escort me through the deserted garden.

In the distance stood an iron pergola completely overgrown with vines and an empty fountain. Graffiti covered the steps and walls leading up to the pergola. Shopping carts lay overturned among the plants. The bluestone paving was broken, bicycle tracks broke through the hedges in places, and old socks and beer cans were strewn under the

6 acres, Formal
14 gardeners

Sad conditions in the Conservatory Garden in early 1982 included a shabby rectangle of lawn, allées of overgrown crabapples, and some large yew hedges. Photo courtesy of Central Park Conservancy.

overgrown shrubs. Most unnerving of all were the tall, unkempt hedges that blocked the view, creating a sinister, forbidding atmosphere. Nevertheless, the garden was a magical place with a fine underlying design. The birds were singing, and the busy, noisy streets seemed far away.

The Conservatory Garden attracted few visitors when it was full of graffiti and broken bottles. Photo courtesy of Central Park Conservancy.

The large flowerbeds in the South Garden were a jumble of overgrown foliage. I recognized the leaves of irises, peonies, and butterfly bushes, and I saw some cheerful blue and yellow annuals blooming among the weeds, courtesy of volunteers from the New York Committee of the Garden Club of America. Although most of the club's members lived outside the city, they had adopted the garden and worked energetically on its behalf for several years, arriving each spring with station wagons full of flowers and returning in fall to plant bulbs. But the garden received little or no maintenance between the Garden Club's visits. The North Garden was in better shape: Korean chrysanthemums first planted in 1943 were still being grown from seed by Parks Department staff, who also planted tulips there every spring. Five Parks Department gardeners headquartered in the garden did their best, but they were also responsible for 150 other parks around Manhattan.

I could see that the first thing we needed to do was to cut down the hedges to open sight lines, then remove everything from the overgrown beds, analyze the soil, and redesign the plantings.

But to do all this we needed money. I had been given no budget and no funds. I had no fund-raising experience, and since the Central Park Conservancy had its hands full raising money for the rest of the park, I would need to find my own donors, and a lot of them. I took pictures of the Conservatory Garden that fall, and over the winter months I showed them to a number of friends who were passionate New Yorkers. I set up an old portable home movie screen in their living rooms and showed them slides of some of the worst conditions in the garden; then I showed them luscious photos of magnificent English gardens, such as Hidcote, Sissinghurst, and Great Dixter, taken when I lived in England and was educating my eye to great garden design. I told them that if they would donate funds, I would try to bring the Conservatory Garden back to life inspired by these models. Although the contrast was great, the slides also showed that despite the garden's current squalor, the underlying design was fine. This potentially lovely oasis in the city deserved restoration.

Fortunately for the Conservatory Garden, New York is full of generous people who love Central Park. By appealing to their civic pride, I found many people who responded enthusiastically and referred me to others. Interest in gardening was burgeoning at this time, and that too helped bring in donations.

Fund-raising with the Central Park Conservancy continued through the winter of 1982–83 while I worked on the redesign of the overgrown beds in the South Garden. When donations of $25 came in, we were thrilled; $100 was cause for elation. When a check for $10,000 arrived, we broke out a bottle of champagne. By spring, we had the princely sum of $26,000 in hand to order new plants and to hire a seasonal worker. For the first time in decades, the Conservatory Garden would have a gardener whose only job was to attend to its needs.

I studied Betty Sprout's 1937 overall design, most of which had stood the test of time. But I thought her use of perennials in the South Garden was rather rigid—sixty feet of catmint in straight lines, for instance—and I found that her planting plans were based primarily on blooms, with little attention paid to foliage. Sprout's design was also very high-maintenance, with three distinct, complete changes each year in each section—bulbs and spring pansies, summer annuals, and autumn chrysanthemums. This was out of the question in the 1980s. Adding shrubs, I knew, would not only lower the maintenance requirements but also give structure to the garden in winter.

I had to think big; the South Garden had five beds fifteen feet wide and between seventy-five and ninety feet long, intended for perennials. Since wide bluestone walking paths bordered both sides, I designed a spine of flowering shrubs down the middle with an occasional ornamental grass as an exclamation point. Then I added the perennials, with bulbs for spring and annuals for summer.

At quarter-inch scale, the plans covered my kitchen table, so I took over a small storage room in the back of our apartment and furnished it with a telephone, a typewriter, and plant catalogs by the hundreds. A friend of mine, Lalitte Scott Smith, determinedly not a gardener, came to visit one day. "Okay," she said, "I'll help you get this off the ground. I'll answer the phone and work on the lists but, for God's sake, don't teach me any of those stupid Latin plant names." She stayed to run the volunteer program for many years, and she designed the logo and the beautiful signs we installed in the garden. And she *did* learn all those Latin names, and became an accomplished alpine garden expert as well. Such is the influence of a wonderful garden.

To the garden's great benefit, Pepe Maynard, a knowledgeable garden designer and plantswoman, joined the team for a number of years, culminating with her design of the first woodland plantings on the southeast slope of the garden in 1984. We began with the South Border in 1982, together contacting nurseries, describing our plans for the border, and asking for their help. Many wholesale nurseries were generous, giving me good prices even though I had not worked with them before; some got caught up in the excitement of the project and even donated plants. We ordered 2,500 shrubs and perennials, some in containers and some bare-root.

That spring, I drafted a group of accomplished gardeners and friends to dig up all the overgrown perennials from the big beds, and we gave the plants to community gardeners in the area. Then we had to address the condition of the soil. When the Central Park Conservancy began in 1980, the leaves from 26,000 trees were being raked and trucked out of Central Park at taxpayers' expense. The Conse[rvancy began a] program to compost those leaves for use in the park. As [luck would have] it, the composting area was right next to the garden, s[o we were able to] incorporate six inches of beautiful "black gold" into [the beds.] Then we cut back many of the shrubs that blocked vi[ews of the garden;] they looked awful for a while, but soon recovered.

[...] pink saucer magnolias were blooming [...] n rich black compost was worked into [...] empty beds. In the background are the [...] med hedges that had previously blocked [...] ws of the garden.

The beds were clean and empty; the soil was d[ark and rich. On a] cool gray day in April, we had a ceremony to mark the [rebirth of the] South Garden. The two old pink *Magnolia* x *soulan*[giana (saucer mag]nolias) from Betty Sprout's original plan were in bloom. The little bronze statue of Mary and Dickon from Frances Hodgson Burnett's *The Secret Garden* had been restored. Some of the magnolia blossoms had fallen to the ground, and Betsy Rogers and I put them into Mary's basket. Everyone was there—the valiant Garden Club ladies, the Parks Department gardeners who had tried to save the garden from ruin, representatives from the neighborhood, and Carolyn Maloney, our city councilwoman. Rogers and Parks Commissioner Henry Stern spoke, and the East Harlem School of Music played salsa music.

On the following Friday, some of the plants we'd ordered were scheduled to arrive, but we couldn't begin planting until Monday morning. There was no one to take delivery in the park, so I arranged for nearly a thousand bare-root perennials to be delivered to the only place I could think of: my apartment building. I live only six blocks from the garden, and the superintendent reluctantly agreed to let me keep the plants in the outdoor courtyard for the weekend. The Parks Department was scheduled to pick them up Monday morning and take them to the garden. In the meantime, a few stalwart volunteers and I sorted perennials into five different sections for the five big perennial beds. One person opened the boxes and checked off the plants. Then people called back and forth: "I need thirty-two *Alchemilla*." "Over here!" With time out for sandwiches, it took us about seven hours. At five o'clock, everyone went home, leaving the carefully sorted piles of plants in open cardboard boxes marked with the bed numbers for the planting on Monday.

About an hour later, I heard the weather report for the weekend: heavy rain and gusty wind. I knew the plants couldn't sit in the courtyard all weekend; the cardboard boxes would fall apart. We didn't have a choice. After covering the furniture in our apartment with plastic bags, my husband and I, along with our two teenage sons, trudged down to the courtyard to rescue the perennials from the weather. Boxes and boxes of plants came up in the elevator, to the astonishment of my neighbors. We stashed them wherever we could, spoiling the painstaking system of the afternoon. Then we threw open the windows for air circulation and hoped for the best. On Monday morning, back down in the elevator they went.

Then the planting began. Following my plan, I marked out the areas for each plant by shaping long strands of white string on top of the soil. A volunteer placed a label in the center of each area identifying the name and number of plants, and then we laid them out for planting. (Using labels in this way remains a useful tool for me in design layout.) It took about ten days to finish the beds; in subsequent jobs of this scale, I hired professional contractors with experienced workers, and the work could be done in one or two days.

That spring, enough rain fell and soon everything began to grow and fill in. It didn't take long for the city to start coming back to the garden. One morning, as I was on my hands and knees checking on the new plants, I looked up to see an elderly woman watching me with great interest. I said hello and she explained with a sweet smile that she lived nearby, in a building that looked down on the garden. Her name was Mrs. Russell; she loved the garden and had been very worried about it. She was pleased that someone was finally taking action. After that, every Sunday she and Mr. Russell came into the garden after church, sat on a bench by the newly planted beds, and kept watch. Mrs. Russell brought a whistle and a pad and pencil with her. Mr. Russell beamed fondly as she explained that if anyone got out of hand, she would blow her whistle and pretend to write down their names. I made them the garden's honorary godparents.

To correspond with the plan, areas were marked out with white string and labeled.

Visitors began to return to the restored garden. A local couple arrived every Sunday after church to keep order.

The design of the South Garden borders was based on my experience as a gardener and as a painter. I used a mix of ornamental shrubs, both flowering and evergreen, enhanced by large groupings of perennials complemented by smaller groups of annuals and bulbs. Though some skeptics advised me to provide just ordinary annuals, I found that my combination of plants for all seasons pleased and attracted visitors.

The key plants I use in my designs are described in further detail in chapter 3, but among the shrubs I placed in the South Garden long ago that are still thriving there are *Hydrangea quercifolia* (oakleaf hydrangea), *Cornus alba* 'Elegantissima' (red-stemmed variegated dogwood), *Berberis thunbergii* f. *atropurpurea* 'Rose Glow' (a noninvasive barberry cultivar), and *Cotinus coggygria* 'Royal Purple' (purple smoke bush). Important perennials included *Miscanthus sinensis* cultivars (maiden grass), *Alchemilla mollis* (lady's mantle), *Echinacea purpurea* (purple cone flower), *Heuchera* 'Plum Pudding' (coral bells), *Hibiscus moscheutos* (hardy hibiscus), *Salvia* x *sylvestris* 'Blauhügel' ('Blue Hill' sage), and *Helleborus* x *hybridus* (Lenten rose). The annuals and bulbs change from year to year. The mixed borders, with their clipped evergreen hedges of *Ilex crenata* (Japanese holly) and *Euonymus kiautschovicus* 'Manhattan' (spreading euonymus), give the public something to enjoy not just in spring and summer, but also in fall and winter.

People came in greater and greater numbers as word got out, and I found myself very moved by the effect that the plantings had on visitors.

In the Conservatory Garden, mixed borders planted with a combination of shrubs, perennials, annuals, and bulbs provide a constantly changing display.

Winter can be a beautiful season in a well-planted garden.

A rich assortment of colors and textures makes fall a great season for visiting the Conservatory Garden.

Children in a nearby school made a birthday banner for the Conservatory Garden's fiftieth birthday. The garden's most enduring present was an endowment for its long-term maintenance.

Their astonishment and delight in the garden as it changed from week to week and their respect and care for it kept me from ever returning to my painting studio as I had intended. I have been the garden's director for more than twenty-five years.

The garden is very different in design from the plan that Olmsted and Vaux created for the rest of Central Park. I know that Olmsted would have hated the formality of the Conservatory Garden's design, but because he was a great believer in the healing aspects of parks and plants for city dwellers, I know too that he would have loved what people experience there every day, all these years later.

The Conservatory Garden was fully restored in time for its fiftieth birthday in 1987. As a special birthday present, the garden received a large endowment from a generous New York family to pay for maintenance (see chapter 8, on private funding, for more about this).

In 1986, when it became clear that the Conservatory Garden was a success, I was approached by the New York Botanical Garden, the Central Park Zoo, and Bryant Park, three great New York spaces all experiencing hard times and needing help to attract visitors and private financial support. It was at this point that I decided to start my own business to work officially and exclusively on public garden design.

The New York Botanical Garden

Founded in 1891 on the model of London's Kew Gardens, the New York Botanical Garden (NYBG), located in the Bronx, is both a world-renowned scientific institution for exploration and research and a 250-acre public garden. By the 1980s, the grounds and gardens were in bad shape, and many people avoided going to the Bronx. Like other cultural institutions facing cuts in city funding, NYBG was forced to raise private funds, but most of the money was allocated to the science programs. When Gregory Long became its president in 1989, the Botanical Garden's renaissance began. In subsequent years, he raised the private support that became more and more necessary, directing new funding to the horticulture programs and staff and in the process attracting hundreds of thousands of happy visitors to the garden.

In 1986, however, the Irwin Perennial Garden—supported with donations from the Watson family in memory of their sister, Jane Wat-

A painting by Janet Ross from the early 1990s shows the Enid A. Haupt Conservatory and the Irwin Perennial Garden at the New York Botanical Garden after restoration. Janet C. Ross, artist. Photo courtesy of the New York Botanical Garden.

son Irwin—had deteriorated to such an extent that the family asked that the plaque with their name on it be removed. Beth Straus, an active member of the NYBG board, had seen my work in the Conservatory Garden and thought I might be able to revive the area, please the donors, and attract visitors again. The job was a great thrill for me because I had been a student in NYBG's horticulture program for a number of years in the 1970s.

NYBG's half-acre Perennial Garden runs parallel to the front of the great Enid A. Haupt Conservatory. When I undertook the project, the garden's design and the use of plants were incoherent. Its paths had no focus, the beds were lined with railroad ties, and the paving materials looked as though they had been salvaged from a high-school cafeteria.

Under a lovely tall white pine tree was a group of chemurgic plants, as they are called, ungainly specimens of interest to science and industry but not aesthetically pleasing, to say the least. We moved them elsewhere and improved the soil with organic material. The area lacked any enclosure to give it an identity, so I introduced yew hedges around the perimeter. When the hedges were tightly clipped at a height of about four feet, they blocked the view of the road, defined the space, and created a geometric backdrop for the ornamental shrubs and perennials.

Though it is called a perennial garden, I knew that using only herba-

The Perennial Garden had deteriorated so badly that in 1986 the original donors asked to have their plaque removed.

In 1987, the family allowed the plaque to be reinstalled after I redesigned this area. We call it the Cool Section because of its pastel color scheme: hostas, astilbes, pink azalea, and the red foliage of the purple-leaf sand cherry.

Across the path is the Hot Section, with reds, yellows, and oranges. Blues, such as *Perovskia atriplicifolia*, complement the hot colors, and the tropical *Cordyline australis* in the foreground provides drama.

ceous perennials would mean leaving the area bare and uninteresting to the public for five months of the year. I chose shrubs that had been successful in the Conservatory Garden, such as *Hydrangea quercifolia* (oakleaf hydrangea), *Cotinus coggygria* 'Royal Purple' (purple smoke bush), and a variety of ornamental grasses down the middle of the beds. We called this newly redesigned area the Cool Section because I chose plants whose flower or foliage colors were from the cool side of the spectrum: blues, pinks, purples, and grays, with rich tones of contrasting dark red foliage that enhanced the beauty of flowering plants such as *Phlox paniculata* (garden phlox) and *Thalictrum rochebruneanum* 'Lavender Mist' (meadow rue) in summer and *Anemone hybrida* 'Robustissima' (grapeleaf anemone) in fall. For the shady areas we chose perennials such as ferns, *Helleborus* (hellebore or Lenten rose), *Hosta* (plantain lily), *Heuchera* (coral bells), and *Astilbe* (false spiraea), concentrating on foliage and form as well as bloom.

We installed the Cool Section in the spring of 1987. During that first summer, Jane Irwin's sister, Helen Buckner, who was a keen gardener herself, visited and decided to restore the Perennial Garden's plaque. Two years later, we created a Hot Section. The names of the plants tell you what kind of impression they make in the garden: large groups of *Crocosmia* 'Lucifer' (montbretia), with bold straplike foliage that contrasts

Another section showcases plants that are at their best in fall, such as Korean chrysanthemums and monkshood.

beautifully with its delicate fiery red flowers, lots of *Kniphofia* (red hot pokers), and many spurges, such as *Euphorbia griffithii* 'Fireglow', along with masses of elegant bright scarlet *Hemerocallis* 'Poinsettia' (one of the many excellent daylily hybrids developed at NYBG by Dr. Arlow B. Stout in the 1930s). These bright colors were grounded by good strong blues, including several sages (*Salvia*, both annual and perennial), *Platycodon grandiflorus* (balloon flower), and gray-leaved *Perovskia atriplicifolia* (Russian sage). And again, plenty of dark red and gray foliage for contrast. As in the rest of the Perennial Garden, many shrubs, both deciduous and evergreen, provided the backdrop. In addition to the cool and hot areas is a section displaying plants that look particularly wonderful in the fall season and another for plants at their best in the height of the summer heat.

More recently, in 2000 I designed a display of so-called half-hardy plants on the Ladies' Border, a large sheltered area about three hundred feet long and thirty feet wide along the south side of the Conservatory. The name, still in use, honors a 1920s display garden funded by the Women's Auxiliary Council and originally laid out by the great garden designer Ellen Biddle Shipman. Her work there had since disappeared. I wanted to use the Ladies' Border to show visitors plants that nobody thought could grow in the New York City area, emphasizing plants for winter and early spring. Like all gardeners, my NYBG colleagues and I love to experiment. We have used different varieties of camellias, crapemyrtles, magnolias, and unusual plants normally associated with areas warmer than ours. A gorgeous paperbush shrub, *Edgeworthia chrysantha*, which I brought back in a pot on an airplane from the West Coast, has been undeterred by predictions that it would not survive in the Bronx; it has thrived on the Ladies' Border, and its fragrant yellow flowers are a winter treasure in late February each year. Some of our experiments have worked and some haven't. Each year we add new and unusual plants to this area, making it of particular interest to plantspeople.

One of the main purposes of a botanical garden is to teach people about the importance and complexity of the plant world. NYBG is a teaching institution, and these gardens are showcases for nature's diversity, demonstrating garden design and plant selections that visitors might use in their own gardens. A colleague with whom I worked for many years on this project used to say with good humor, "If it looks good, we are artists. If it doesn't, we're educators." We always wanted to be both.

Among the myriad pleasures of working at a great botanical garden

The Ladies' Border at the New York Botanical Garden is a display of plants not usually thought to be hardy in the New York City area. Here it is in all its winter beauty.

A garden full of beautiful and interesting plants can teach people of all ages to appreciate nature.

is having knowledgeable colleagues and a wide variety of available plants. Because the Conservatory Garden has no greenhouse space, all plants must be ordered from a nursery, but NYBG is able to grow many unusual plants in its own greenhouses for use in the Perennial Garden, and plants are well labeled in order to help visitors learn about them.

I have continued my involvement with the New York Botanical Garden in many different ways beyond design consultation, joining the Board of Managers in 1996. NYBG has always been one of the finest institutions for scientific exploration and research, but now, thanks to the leadership of Gregory Long and the efforts of so many people, it is once again one of the most beautiful places in the country to visit and learn about plants and gardens.

The Central Park Zoo

The Central Park Zoo, at 64th Street and Fifth Avenue, was designed in the late 1930s, at about the same time as the Conservatory Garden, and was once one of the most popular places in Central Park. But by 1983 the zoo was run down. The animals looked miserable and the cages stank. The Parks Department decided to close the facility and relinquish authority for it to the New York Zoological Society, which runs the world-famous Bronx Zoo. The animals went to much better permanent homes in the Bronx. Architect Kevin Roche of Roche, Dinkeloo and Associates in New Haven, Connecticut, redesigned the facility, retaining some aspects of the old zoo, such as the charming stone bas-reliefs of animals, the Delacorte Clock with its bronze bears circling round and striking the hours, and four stone eagles at the entrances to the seal pool. The pool itself was reconstructed with artificial rocks that looked convincingly real, and there were plans for a garden surrounding it. Birds, monkeys, polar bears, and penguins would soon follow.

The renovation of the zoo was my first experience as part of a team on a huge construction project. I began work there in 1986, and my job within Roche, Dinkeloo's overall plan was to design the Central Garden area in four quadrants around the Seal Pool. The site still had a number of lovely old crabapples left from the 1930s. To preserve them, I planned paths to give their roots plenty of space yet leave enough room for visitors and for many shrubs and perennials. After a number of discussions about the width of paths, the soil, the paving and edging, the placement

After many years of neglect, the Central Park Zoo was closed for restoration in 1983.

One of my early design drawings for the zoo's garden.

of benches, and the irrigation, Kevin Roche and I made a presentation to the zoo's director for approval to proceed with the garden area. The director turned to Kevin and said, "I don't want any itsy-bitsy gardens here." I drew myself up to my full five feet three inches and replied, "I don't do itsy-bitsy gardens." That didn't come up again.

This was the first garden I designed that would have as many visitors in winter as in summer, so the plantings had to be attractive in all seasons. I researched dwarf evergreens (called "dwarf" because they have a slow growth habit) and visited the wonderful display of them at the National Arboretum in Washington, D.C. As a result, I placed a very choice specimen dwarf evergreen in the center of each quadrant, along with a dark red *Acer palmatum* var. *dissectum* 'Garnet' (Japanese maple) for its foliage and handsome winter form, then added shrubs, grasses, sedums, and astilbes, emphasizing foliage that has presence in winter. I specified the very best plants and soil available, and fortunately, because there were sufficient funds, I didn't have to raise the money to buy them.

I ordered soil with high organic content, to sustain the plants and retain moisture, and a pH of 6.5, a level hospitable to most plants. The soil was installed in 1987, about eight months before the plants. Then the great challenge was to keep the construction crew from driving heavy equipment over the new soil and the roots of the old crabapples. Though they had reluctantly erected wooden barriers around the trees, I had to visit the site frequently to keep the backhoes and huge slabs of bluestone from reappearing regularly in the beds.

In the early spring of 1988, the animals were brought to their new homes and we planted the garden. I arrived to meet the planting crew one morning when it was still dark. I looked at the rocks in the Seal Pool and suddenly, as the sky lightened, the rocks began to move. The seals, sleeping on top of one another on the rocks, were waking up to the early morning sun.

The new Central Park Zoo opened in late May. Visitors poured in to see the animals, Kevin Roche's attractive buildings and covered walkways, and the garden. The opportunity to create a fine public space for the city was wonderful, but I learned, sadly, that my vision for the garden could not be sustained because I had no ongoing relationship with those who maintained it. The plantings began to change almost immediately; in less than a decade, almost all the plants I had chosen were gone, replaced by banana trees that had to be wrapped in burlap for the winter and a large number of assorted roses, a combination that seems quite awkward to

In 1991, each quadrant of the zoo's garden still had mixed plantings—a dwarf Japanese maple along with phlox, sedums, asters, and a few annuals, and many benches for visitors. It looks much different than this today.

me. I had worked for the architect, not the zoo, and the zoo gardeners felt no obligation or connection to me or to my design. The lesson for me was that in order to sustain a design, I would need a contract for a long-term relationship with my clients and with the gardeners, a goal I have subsequently been able to achieve in most of my projects.

Bryant Park

By the mid-1980s, Bryant Park, a six-acre park behind the New York Public Library at Fifth Avenue and 42nd Street, had become a festering sore in the center of midtown Manhattan. Drug dealers took advantage of the overgrown site to establish a base and drive other visitors away. The Conservatory Garden had seemed dangerous, but Bryant Park really was. Its fate was tied to that of the adjoining library, and as civic leaders and philanthropists began the library's renovation, they realized that they couldn't restore one without the other. They formed the Bryant Park Restoration Corporation under the leadership of the brilliant and energetic Dan Biederman. They also founded the country's first Business Improvement District (BID) dedicated to maintaining a park; all businesses owning real estate surrounding the park had to make a contribution, based on the square footage of their property, to pay for services that the city was not providing, thus making the businesses stakeholders in the park's future. (More about this in chapter 8.)

Bryant Park is six acres of green space behind the New York Public Library at 42nd Street in busy midtown Manhattan. Photo by Joseph De Sciose.

Because the park was barely maintained by the city in the 1980s, it became a haven for drug dealers, and in 1987 it was closed. Courtesy of OLIN.

The Restoration Corporation hired architect Hugh Hardy and landscape architect Laurie Olin. The wall around the park was removed, the large fountain was restored, food kiosks were built, the park was reconfigured, and the statue of William Cullen Bryant—the poet and great nineteenth-century New York City leader who helped create Central Park—was refurbished. After the two-acre lawn was removed, fifty thousand square feet of underground stack space connected to the library was built and the lawn was replaced on top. Few visitors to the park are aware of what is beneath their feet. The Restoration Corporation also added one thousand light metal chairs like those at the Tuillerie Gardens in Paris.

Meanwhile, in 1987 Dan Biederman asked me to design plantings for two 300-foot-long flower beds to be created along the balustrade walls flanking the two-acre lawn. Since this was not part of the original scheme for the park and therefore not part of the budget, he also asked me to raise the money. By great serendipity, the same family that had so generously underwritten the most important aspect of the Conservatory Garden's future—its maintenance—owned a building facing Bryant Park. The Weiler-Arnow family agreed to give $350,000 to the Restoration Corporation to build the gardens, and the Greenacre Foundation donated my design fee.

One of the display beds on the sunny side is seen here in 1997. The plants include *Buddleja davidii* 'Nanho Blue' and *Rosa* 'Betty Prior'.

Openings were cut into the balustrade wall on each side of the lawn so that people could traverse the park from north to south as well as east to west. Between these openings on both sides were six thousand square feet of planting beds, predominantly sunny on the north side, shady in the south. Laurie Olin and I added benches recessed into these six beds so that visitors could sit surrounded by flowering plants. I began designing the long beds with the same type of mixed planting that had proved so successful in the Conservatory Garden, but emphasizing winter, with a variety of *Ilex* (hollies), *Prunus laurocerasus* (cherry laurel), *Skimmia japonica* (Japanese skimmia), and *Rhododendron* 'Boule de Neige'. Roses and sun-loving shrubs and perennials filled the beds on the north side, and, of course, my beloved *Hydrangea quercifolia* (oakleaf hydrangea) was repeated on both sides. The shady southern side is particularly rich in foliage combinations and textures.

Because visitors would walk alongside the beds, I also installed a series of tall vertical evergreen yews (*Taxus cuspidata* 'Capitata') every

The south side of Bryant Park, mostly in shade, features the foliage of oakleaf hydrangeas, hostas, and astilbes, with built-in benches and movable chairs. Photo by Joseph De Sciose.

On Bryant Park's opening day in April 1992, five thousand 'Pink Impression' tulips came into bloom in the big display beds alongside shrubs and perennials. A progression of vertical yews runs down the back of each bed.
Photo by Lisa Miller.

twenty feet on each side to carry the eye down the border and to echo the vertical windows in the back of the library building. The yews provide a transition between the tall plane trees on the sides of the park and the huge horizontal green lawn in the center. In my planting designs, the blooms were of secondary importance to the form and structure of the various plants. I chose a combination of evergreen and deciduous shrubs and large ornamental grasses, with large drifts of perennials and small pockets of bulbs followed by annuals.

In the fall of 1990 (a year and a half before the park opened), while construction continued all around us, contractors filled the beds with about 750 cubic yards of soil made to my specifications, with good drainage and plenty of organic matter. The following fall, a Long Island landscape contractor, his crew, and a number of volunteers from the Conservatory Garden helped place and install the plants. I assigned each volunteer to one of the six beds and gave each a clipboard with the bed's design and a list of the plants on it. At six-thirty in the morning, when the trucks pulled up loaded with 363 shrubs and 2,500 perennials, the volunteers helped the landscape crew get the right plants to the right beds and place them according to my design. I went from one bed to another checking everything and making adjustments before planting began. (As everyone who designs gardens knows, the design is just a vehicle for getting the right number of plants. When you see the size and quality of what actually arrives, you inevitably make some adjustments.) I added five thousand 'Pink Impression' tulips in the long beds, choosing this particular tulip so that people who looked down on the park from the surrounding buildings the next spring would notice the very large pink flowers and come down to see what was going on.

After five years of hard work, hundreds of public meetings, and the expenditure of $9 million in federal, state, city, and private funds, the grand reopening of Bryant Park was scheduled for April 1992. Although the specific date wasn't announced until a few days before, on the appointed day, just in time for the crowds and the speeches, those tulips decided to bloom! It was a colorful symbol of the renaissance of this great and much-needed public space.

Almost immediately, Bryant Park became a favorite public gathering place for millions. A few days after the opening, I watched a well-dressed young man do a cartwheel on the big green freshly planted lawn. He said that he had not believed that Bryant Park would work, but he was thrilled that it had.

Bryant Park after its restoration is always full of people, which helps keep it a safe place.
Photo by Joseph De Sciose.

The gardens in Bryant Park quickly became an integral part of the programming of the park, attracting a constituency of regular visitors who enjoyed the progression of the seasons and asked questions about the plants. Tours of the gardens showed people what they could grow at home. Visitors told me that they would go out of their way to visit the park so they could sit on the benches, surrounded by hollyhocks, roses, and butterflies. One woman confided that she had been offered a job in another part of the city with a small salary increase, but she wasn't taking it. "They don't have Bryant Park there," she said. A young horticulturist who later worked in the Shakespeare Garden in Central Park recalled that seeing the gardens and coming in every day to learn the plants in Bryant Park was what inspired her to change careers and take up horticulture.

Dan Biederman always understood the importance of horticulture in Bryant Park and in the city. Before the rest of the city caught on and followed his example, he began adorning the streets around the park with lush planter boxes and hanging baskets. At first, the only money available to maintain the Bryant Park gardens came from the grant from the Weiler-Arnow family, but gradually garden maintenance became part of the park's yearly budget. The Business Improvement District provided security and general maintenance. Worries about security were voiced at first; the shrubbery in the gardens was said to be wired to prevent theft. That wasn't true, but the story was publicized to deter anyone who coveted our gorgeous plants (and none of the plants was touched). As crowds came in at all hours, the drug dealers simply disappeared; if you make a park attractive for the "good" people, the "bad" ones will leave. Crime was no longer a problem.

Once Bryant Park was made beautiful and was visibly cared for, visitors felt comfortable there. On a sunny day in any month of the year, lunchtime brings crowds to the park. Sometimes it's hard to see the grass because so many bodies are on it, and the lawn has to be closed after rains to let it recover. In the shady allées of London plane trees, areas wired not for security but for computers are set aside, with special chairs designed for laptop users. Many tables have been added beside the movable chairs for eating or working. Visitors can enjoy chess tournaments, jazz concerts, and comedy performances; food kiosks, a restaurant, and an outdoor café; a carousel for children; free movies during the summer; and a popular skating rink installed over the lawn each winter.

When the park was in bad shape, its problems spread to the neighboring streets and buildings. It was an area, not just a park, to avoid. But from the day the newly designed and refurbished park opened, it had a dramatic effect on nearby businesses and real estate. Within a week, a large long-vacant office space in one of the surrounding buildings was sold. Shops began to reopen, sidewalks were repaired, and eventually the elegant Bryant Park Hotel opened across the street. A study conducted in 1999 found that real estate values had skyrocketed. (More about this in chapter 8, on private funding.)

I learned two important things in Bryant Park. First, gardens are ephemeral. I was involved with the design and maintenance of horticulture in the park and the two long beds at the front of the New York Public Library on Fifth Avenue for ten years, but eventually the demands of other projects made it impossible for me to continue. The mixed borders in front of the library were subsequently replaced with a static seasonal display of annuals and bulbs, and the gardens in Bryant Park have changed as well, with an emphasis now on displays of annuals and bulbs rather than mixed plantings for year-round interest.

Second, and much more important, I learned that gardens and plants are good not only for people but also for neighborhoods and businesses. Although it sometimes seems that almost *too* much goes on in Bryant Park, whether bustling or serene, the restored park is a much-loved oasis that helps revive a city dweller's soul.

Wagner Park

When Battery Park City—the spectacular ninety-two-acre complex of apartments, houses, businesses, and schools built out into the Hudson River on landfill from the building of the World Trade Center—was established by Governor Nelson Rockefeller in 1968, a third of its acreage was set aside by law for parks and open spaces. A permanent entity, the Battery Park City Conservancy, was created to maintain the landscape as part of the joint city-state project. The complex as a whole is run by the Battery Park City Authority (BPCA), a state-regulated agency that collects money from lease-holders for the area's maintenance.

The wide esplanade along the Hudson River running the full length of Battery Park City is lined with trees, attractive plantings, and many different large and small parks and artworks. The BPC Conservancy and its large work force, including many horticulturists, do an outstanding job maintaining the thirty-six acres of parks. The BPCA has a long history of inviting artists to work on public spaces within the complex. South Cove, for example, is a brilliantly designed waterfront park created by artist Mary Miss with landscape architect Susan Child. But in 1988, another artist's proposed design for a garden in the lower end of Battery Park City stirred controversy: the plan called for a number of small garden rooms with tall hedges and a high wall along the edge; the hedge walls would prevent residents and visitors from enjoying access to river views, and the projected maintenance cost of the design was astronomical (many times more than that of the much larger Conservatory Garden).

In the fall of 1991, after a fair amount of publicity, Governor Mario Cuomo brought the project to a halt, citing community opposition, and announced plans for a competition to redesign the three-and-a-half-acre space. In early 1992, the BPCA created a three-pronged design team of Boston-based architect Rodolfo Machado, landscape architect Laurie Olin, and me. I was the only New Yorker, and I provided the horticulture component. We worked together on this project for four and a half years.

David Emil, president of the BPCA at the time, made it clear from the start that they wanted a garden on the site that would be open and welcoming, and in the many public hearings and community meetings I attended, the public agreed. The design collaboration produced something for everyone: a lovely open landscaped park with planting beds, fine trees, and two distinct gardens, one on either side of two brick buildings. We designed the site to celebrate the views of the Statue of Liberty and Ellis Island. Wagner Park opened in October 1996.

The two new gardens are between allées of *Acer rubrum* (red maple trees) and the wide lawns leading to the river, and they include many benches and seating walls. Slightly lower in grade than the rest of the park, the gardens are surrounded by yew hedges, sheltering the spot on this windy site, especially in winter, and allowing me a little more range as to what plants would survive so near the water. My plant choices were those I used habitually because they work well for the public, but I try always to add something special in each garden. In Wagner Park, I used more *Buddleja davidii* 'Nanho Blue' (butterfly bushes), *Picea pungens* 'Globosa' (blue spruce balls), *Chamaecyparis pisifera* 'Golden Mop' (a low-growing yellow-foliaged false cypress), and *Centranthus ruber*

Wagner Park's three acres are designed to celebrate views of the Hudson River and the Statue of Liberty. There are two formal gardens in this landscaped park. Photo by Joseph De Sciose.

Wagner Park is located close to where the World Trade Center once stood. The South Garden blooms with a profusion of pinks and blues, including roses, *Gomphrena*, *Perovskia atriplicifolia*, and *Solenostemon* 'Red Carpet' in the foreground. Photo by Joseph De Sciose.

The South Garden has a pastel color scheme in beds of varying heights and shapes, with lots of seating areas and benches.

(valerian). Because roses are so beloved by the public, I included them throughout the design.

The two gardens have different color schemes: the South Garden is pastel, with pinks, purples, and grays, while the North Garden's flowers and foliage are warm reds, yellows, and oranges. In contrast to the Irwin Perennial Garden at NYBG, where I used different color palettes in two adjoining sections of one garden, these are two large separate gardens, each devoted to a color palette. To unify them, I gave both gardens repeated elements of dark red, such as *Acer palmatum* 'Bloodgood' (Japanese maple) and *Prunus* x *cistena* (purple-leaf sand cherry); ornamental trees, such as *Cornus kousa* (kousa dogwood) and vertical evergreen *Thuja occidentalis* 'Smaragd' (emerald arborvitae); many shrubs, such as *Hydrangea macrophylla* 'Nikko Blue', 'Mariesii Variegata', and 'Blue Wave' (bigleaf hydrangea), *H. quercifolia* (oakleaf hydrangea), and *Spiraea thunbergii* and its yellow-leaved cultivar 'Ogon' (meadowsweet);

and a variety of ornamental grasses. The roses vary in flower color: pink *Rosa* SIMPLICITY, *R.* CAREFREE BEAUTY, and *R.* 'Betty Prior' in the cool South Garden and bright red *R.* 'Trumpeter' in the hot North Garden. The annuals and bulbs are planned to go with the color schemes: pink/blue in the south, red/yellow/orange/blue in the north. One visitor who enjoyed the bright color combinations in the North Garden pronounced it "a fiesta."

The North Garden's color scheme is "hot": oranges, yellows, and reds, with lots of blue. Red tulips bloom here in spring.

Again, the resulting mix is a four-season combination of ornamental trees, shrubs, perennials, annuals, and bulbs intended to give pleasure through the year. Wagner Park and its gardens draw residents, tourists, and workers from the Wall Street area, who come for the plantings, the views, and the small restaurant with outdoor tables and umbrellas.

Thanks to the Battery Park City Conservancy, maintenance here has never been a worry. I continue to act as a consultant and advise on the choice of annuals and bulbs and any necessary changes to the design. Two dedicated, accomplished gardeners have worked with me, and the gardens still look very much as they did when I designed them.

Visitors come all year to enjoy the plant combinations at Wagner Park. A potted papyrus rises from the pool next to *Rosa* SIMPLICITY and *Gomphrena* 'Lavender Lady'.

Madison Square Park

A 6.2-acre park in midtown Manhattan between Fifth and Madison avenues, Madison Square Park is in an area known as the Flatiron District, named for the building that overlooks it. The original Madison Square Garden was located next to it until 1925. In those days, the park was in good condition, but, as with so many other New York parks, by the 1980s it was in bad shape. Except for the tall stately trees, some more than a hundred years old, Madison Square Park was a bare, cheerless place, frequented mainly by squirrels, rats, and pigeons and often used as a refuge by the homeless. It was the same old story: lack of city funds for park maintenance. Although there were plenty of shops and office buildings in the area, few people visited the park, even on a fine day.

The restoration of Madison Square Park began in 1996 under the direction of the City Parks Foundation, a nonprofit arm of the Parks Department. Danny Meyer, a successful restaurant owner who had begun a turnaround of Union Square Park (near his very popular Union Square Café) some years before, had recently opened several restaurants in the Madison Square Park area. In the *New York Times* in

Lack of maintenance left Madison Square Park a bare, sad place virtually empty of people.

Visitors can see the Empire State Building from six-acre Madison Square Park.

Now replanted with twenty thousand shrubs and ground covers, Madison Square Park is full of visitors.

November 1998, Danny was quoted as saying: "The park is part of our décor, part of our ambience. We want to take a page out of the Bryant Park playbook."[1]

In addition to the City Parks Foundation, important local businesses, including MetLife, New York Life, and Credit Suisse, participated in the effort to restore the park to its original grandeur, raise an endowment, and hire full-time staff to maintain it. The landscape architecture firm Abel Bainnson Butz oversaw the path renovations, repairing the cracked asphalt and broken benches and realigning the statues in the park. The horticultural aspects of the landscape—the plants—were left for last, as is so often the case. This was especially ironic because the park was designed originally by Ignatz Pilat, a noted horticulturist who had worked with Frederick Law Olmsted in Central Park.

I began the landscape plantings in the fall of 1999, just six months before the park was due to reopen. I considered a wide variety of shrubs and perennials that would bring year-round vitality to the park. Many of them were the usual suspects, but because tall trees provided a fair amount of shade, the conditions were perfect for large numbers of hydrangeas and hollies. The idea was to design not a garden but a park with many planting areas, so I used perennials in large groupings as ground covers under the shrubs, with very few annuals except at the entrances. With no time to make the usual detailed plans, we ordered huge numbers of plants and then placed them around the park as they arrived. That fall and early the next spring, I worked with Kelco, a Long Island landscaping firm, to improve the soil as best we could and plant the twenty thousand shrubs and perennials called for in the design.

Because we never knew which plants were going to come in on any given day until they appeared at about seven o'clock each morning, we used large sticks—like giant tongue depressors—with the name and number of the plants in each grouping marked in indelible ink. I worked out the design by instinct each day, grateful for my prior experience with big plantings. My associate Kristi Stromberg Wright held the master list, noted the daily count, and reminded me of what hadn't arrived yet. If we wanted to plant a good combination of *Athyrium niponicum* var. *pictum* (Japanese painted fern) next to dark-red *Heuchera* 'Plum Pudding' (coral bells) around a group of *Hydrangea macrophylla* 'Nikko Blue' (bigleaf hydrangea), but one of those plants hadn't come in that day, we would plant the ones we had on hand and leave space for the latecomer, marked by a stick bearing its name. Keeping all this in mind at once proved an exciting challenge. I never cease to be amazed that in the end the plantings turn out looking as I imagine them in my head. I think my experience as a painter helps me to visualize the plants, the combinations, and the overall design.

Hollies, hydrangeas, and red-stemmed variegated dogwoods do particularly well in Madison Square Park.

One Friday in May, Kelco crews delivered the last group of plants—about 250 gorgeous big hostas, blue-green *Hosta sieboldiana* and yellow-green *H.* 'Sum and Substance', in two- and three-gallon pots. The foreman told the crew that if they worked really fast, they could have Saturday off, so they literally ran after Kristi and me with the plants in wheelbarrows. We would place them among the shrubs and perennials; another crew would follow with shovels and spades and put them into the ground. We were all laughing at the pace, and I thought that I had never had such fun making a park look rich and full. People leaned over the fence saying, "We love it—when can we come in?" The last and very important step was to mulch all the planting beds with straight compost instead of the usual garden mulch in order to enrich the soil.

The park opened in June 2001. The Madison Square Park Conservancy was formed the next year to raise money and to oversee and maintain the park under a board of directors drawn from representatives of many of the surrounding businesses. This conservancy, like the Central Park Conservancy, has a ten-year renewable contract with the city to run the park and raise money to fund it. Madison Square Park's popular food kiosk, movable chairs and tables, playground, and many events and art installations attract people twelve months of the year, and the gardener and staff, aided by several volunteer groups, keep the plantings vibrant and lush.

I stayed on as a consultant for several years after the opening to train the gardener and advise on the plantings. Now I just visit the park and enjoy it along with other New Yorkers.

Madison Square Park is beautiful in winter. In the snow the branches in the urns look like flowering plants. Photo by Joseph De Sciose.

The Broadway Malls

The Broadway Malls, a series of twenty-two-foot-wide green median strips running down the middle of New York's Broadway for five miles between 60th and 168th streets, were built after the Civil War; lined with trees, they amount to ten and a half acres of parkland. By the 1970s, many of them were dismal and overgrown, infested with rats and frequented by drug dealers. The nonprofit Broadway Mall Association (BMA) was established in 1980 to work with the Parks Department and other organizations to improve the malls for neighbors and nearby businesses and turn them into places where people can meet and sit together in good weather. With funding from the Lincoln Square Business Improvement District, for example, the malls between 60th and 70th streets have been beautifully transformed by the designs of Mary Riley Smith.

In the late 1990s, while I was working on projects for Columbia (see below in this chapter), the university hired me to work with the BMA on the malls from 112th to 116th streets, adjacent to the campus. These were no garden oases; they lacked both water sources and any recent city maintenance. Tangled tree roots and compacted soil resulted in dead or dying plants that accumulated trash, and the rat holes made the malls dangerous—if you weren't careful when walking around, you could end up with a sprained ankle. The 116th Street mall also had a huge concrete area with subway ventilation grates.

I called on a landscape contracting firm, Town and Gardens, Ltd, to help me with this project, because they were used to landscaping challenges—they work on terraces high in the sky, lifting plants there with cranes. We had worked together on a number of jobs over the years. (I once telephoned Don Sussman, an owner of the firm, to ask him a question about one of our projects; he answered calmly that he could discuss it more easily later in the day because he was thirty feet up in the air pruning a tree on Park Avenue.)

At my direction, Town and Gardens' crew removed the dead plants on the malls and added lots of compost to improve the soil, enabling it to retain more rainwater. I assembled a list of tough shrubs and perennial ground covers for the areas under the trees, using large groups of each so passersby and traffic speeding past see and appreciate the different forms and textures rather than an apparently random distribution of plants. We added thousands of the indestructible *Euonymus fortunei* 'Coloratus' (purple wintercreeper euonymus), with its green shiny leaves in the warm months that turn an interesting dark red in winter, and we

Broadway Malls are the medians on this famous street. Many were inhospitable sites with no city maintenance, no water sources, and very bad soil.

planted thousands of daffodils to come up through the euonymus in spring—a combination I knew would succeed because the daffodils and sixty thousand euonymus plants I included in the restoration of Verdi Square on 72nd Street and Amsterdam Avenue some years before had held up well. In the square raised beds at each end of the malls, behind the benches, I chose the same blue and white color scheme of perennials and annuals that I was using on the Columbia campus nearby so that visitors would know who was responsible for the changes to come.

Less than a week after we completed the installation, the city's Department of Transportation decided to begin construction work on the 116th Street mall; they erected horrible orange plastic fencing and street barriers and killed all the plants. When they were done, we had to plant the strip all over again. Why is it that as soon as you finish planting, whether by a building, in a courtyard, or on a median strip, someone will suddenly decide that now is the perfect time to power-wash the building, put up scaffolding, or take up the sidewalk? I can only speculate that an improved landscape inspires people to do things they have been putting off for years!

In the late fall of 2006, commissioned by the Broadway Mall Association and working with Town and Gardens again, we landscaped a long mall area at 135th Street, just above where the subway tracks disappear into the ground. Here I used colorful *Cornus sericea* (red and yellow twig dogwood), along with the ubiquitous euonymus, for winter interest in the center of the mall. At each end, red *Berberis* (barberry), red Knock Out shrub roses, and the wonderful variegated *Yucca filamentosa* 'Color Guard' provided year-round color. Daffodils were planted for spring and bold annuals for the summer months. The BMA calls this planting the avenue's "gateway to Harlem."

After we improved the soil with lots of compost, we planted shrubs and perennials behind the benches. Here, for example, *Taxus* x *media* 'Densiformis' and *Prunus* x *cistena* flank a butterfly bush and an annual sweet potato vine called 'Margarita'.

Even large subway grates and hydrants can be softened by the addition of raised planters with *Euonymus fortunei* 'Coloratus'.

Tribute Park, Rockaway, Queens

The small community of Rockaway in the borough of Queens sits on a narrow piece of land between the Atlantic Ocean and Jamaica Bay. The streets are lined with houses with porches, and flowers are everywhere. Though technically part of New York City, it feels very far away. In 2003 the residents of Rockaway decided to build a memorial park to the many firefighters and police officers from their community who were killed in the World Trade Center disaster.

Tribute Park on Jamaica Bay in Rockaway, Queens, is a memorial to the many firefighters lost from this small community on 9/11. The view looks back at the city where the World Trade Center once stood.

Nadia Murphy, a passionate and knowledgeable gardener who lives nearby and whose fireman husband was wounded on 9/11, became the driving force behind the project. I worked with her, the Rockaway Chamber of Commerce, and the Parks Department on the little park, a triangular piece of land about a third of an acre in size, sandwiched between the main street and the water and adjacent to a drugstore parking lot. We erected a high wall to block this commercial distraction. The site looks west to where the twin towers had once been clearly visible, and has wonderful open views of the water, with Manhattan in the distance and the boats passing by.

The Chamber of Commerce commissioned three special elements

for the park, all made by a local artist: a memorial *tempietto* (small temple), a concrete and mosaic circular sculpture, and a large rock with a firefighter's hat and the names of those who died. I designed wide paths that led from the entrance gate around the mosaic disc to the water and around the triangular site. Along the paths next to the walls were eight-foot beds for plantings, with benches all around. On those paths, the community installed bricks, each inscribed with the name of one of the many park donors.

Local residents help maintain Tribute Park.

I looked for tough plants suitable to this exposed site and took advantage of Nadia Murphy's knowledge of plants that would thrive in Rockaway on the bay. We chose colorful shrubs and perennials, saving the toughest ones, such as *Rosa rugosa* (rugosa rose), for the areas along the water's edge. Hydrangeas, pink and blue rose of Sharon, different cultivars of low-growing junipers, and the blue vertical *Juniperus scopulorum* 'Wichita Blue' were all part of the mix. I knew from my experience with Wagner Park that perennial hibiscus does well by the water, so we used pink *Hibiscus moscheutos* 'Lady Baltimore' (hardy hibiscus) here, along with 'Betty Prior' roses, yellow-leaved *Spiraea thunbergii* 'Ogon' (meadowsweet), and my favorite perennial sage, *Salvia* × *sylvestris* 'Blauhügel' ('Blue Hill' sage). Large areas of yellow *Achillea* 'Moonshine' (yarrow) and the tiny blue-leaved *Sedum cauticola* 'Lidakense' (stonecrop) were placed in the center, with red-berried *Crataegus viridis* 'Winter King' (green hawthorn tree) for shade. Matthew DiVittorio, from the Parks Department's Landscape Construction division, tagged the plants I had requested in Long Island nurseries, and we all worked together with a landscape crew on a blistering hot day in September 2005 to install the plantings in the park. Despite my fears about the effect of the heat on the newly planted park, all went well.

New York's mayor, Michael Bloomberg, dedicated the memorial park a few weeks later in a ceremony attended by many neighbors, with a band, bagpipes, and fireboats spouting out on the water. Since then, a volunteer group, Friends of Tribute Park, has been formed to help care for the space, and the Parks Department does its best to support their efforts. Twice a year, in fall and spring, the Friends hire a landscape contractor for a cleanup; every August, they hold a fund-raiser with chamber music and a reception. Neighborhood parks like Tribute Park are vital to the health of a city and can be a great asset to the community, a source of civic pride and enjoyment.

Pier 44 Waterfront Garden, Red Hook

In the fall of 2003 I got a call about a piece of land in Red Hook, along the Brooklyn waterfront, that belonged to Greg O'Connell, a developer who wanted to create a landscape for the public. I was intrigued by someone willing to make his own property available to the public, so I headed to Red Hook by water taxi, a ferry service whose small yellow and black checkered boats remind old New Yorkers of the beloved long-gone Checker taxicabs. Because many parts of Red Hook cannot be reached easily by mass transit, it has remained a unique part of the city—a working waterfront with old houses, cobblestone streets, big warehouses, and a lot of truck traffic.

O'Connell's long, thin, overgrown piece of land along the water's edge was sandwiched between a tiny, stony beach and a parking lot full of trucks and machinery. Nearby stood a number of beautiful nineteenth-century brick pier buildings, also owned by O'Connell. The spectacular view of the Statue of Liberty, the seabirds, and the smell of seawater enchanted me.

O'Connell did not fit the image I had of most developers: wearing striped overalls, he drove up in a battered light blue pickup truck. We hit it off immediately. His assistant, Debbie Romano, was involved right from the beginning; she would eventually take on the important job of maintaining the landscape we produced. O'Connell and his son Michael wanted to do a lot of the work themselves, and they said that if I would design a bicycle path and a boardwalk with plantings, they would build it.

Some of the land jutted out into the harbor; O'Connell wanted me to plant that area thickly to prevent it from becoming a haven for illicit activities. I told him that my experience was the opposite: the way to make it safe was to open up the space and invite people to use it. He looked skeptical but agreed to try. I made a simple plan that included two paths, intending to amplify it later, and left it with him. The next thing I knew, he and Michael had built the paths from my sketch, leaving space between them and along the parking lot's fence for planting, as I had suggested. I could see I had to work fast, so I quickly drew up a planting plan with large informal groups of shrubs and perennials that would withstand the harsh conditions along the water's edge, including junipers, bayberries, hollies, and the beautiful blue *Vitex agnus-castus* (chastetree), with large drifts of purple cone flower, daylilies, grasses, variegated yuccas, and catmint. After O'Connell had cleared "the point," as we decided to call it, I chose four *Celtis occidentalis* (hackberry) to give

This desolate stretch of empty waterfront in Red Hook, Brooklyn, belonged to a developer who decided to landscape it and open it to the public. I created a planting design for all four seasons.

Lush plantings along the beach attract local residents. The two water towers become very large garden ornaments.

some shade there. These trees, though not ornamentally spectacular, can withstand salt spray and wind. After improving the soil with compost, we planted the garden in June 2004.

I love the process of finally installing a garden, making decisions on the spot about plant combinations that I might not have thought of in advance but that come to mind when I see the actual plants. The excitement of the installation is the reward for the work of designing the project, attending meetings, and sourcing the plants. But the Pier 44 garden was unlike any other project I had done: while my associate Catherine Redd and Debbie Romano were placing the plants, Michael O'Connell was driving a backhoe around to show me nearby trees and shrubs that were too close to the water and asking if I would like to use them. The next thing I knew a large crabapple was sitting in the bucket and we added that. We also moved several rugosa roses, a large fat Japanese holly, large clumps of German iris, a tall arborvitae, and a curly willow, and found places for them all. One of the shrubs Michael wanted to give us couldn't be moved until later in spring because it harbored a nest with baby birds in it.

A large black iron bollard once used to tie boats to a pier was hidden in the bushes by the water. I asked if we could use that. "Why not?" was the answer, and soon it too was hanging from the bucket. We placed it in the middle of the point that jutted out into the water. At the end of the day, all the plants were in the ground thanks to O'Connell's crew of

A bicycle path and a boardwalk flank waterside plantings in Red Hook. *Echinacea purpurea*, *Perovskia atriplicifolia*, and *Hemerocallis* 'Happy Returns' are in bloom in summer.

workers. Pointing to the Statue of Liberty in the harbor, I said to Michael, "Now, if you really wanted this project to be a success, you would go get her with your backhoe and we'd put her in here. I think she would be a great addition."

When I told O'Connell how important seating was, he immediately produced about fifteen benches, and we placed them strategically, along with trash cans. We also added some large boulders from the side of his parking lot as seating, and he dedicated one of them to me.

The plants loved Red Hook as much as I did. They bloomed and bloomed. Goldenrod, sedums, and asters flowered as the grasses waved back and forth in the salt air. The *Myrica pensylvanica* (bayberry) and other evergreens came through that first winter well. The Pier 44 Waterfront Garden officially opened on a gray rainy day in May 2005, with Brooklyn officials, neighbors, and friends enjoying a picnic lunch in the Red Hook Maritime Museum, a former working barge that is permanently attached to the shore near the garden. We ate key lime pies made by one of O'Connell's tenants from Pier 41.

Since that first planting, we have added many more plants to an adjoining area and parking lot next to a huge pier building now occupied by a Fairway market, where O'Connell has also built apartments looking out onto the water (see chapter 8 for more on this project). We hope to be able to extend this landscape further along the waterfront in Red Hook.

97th Street "Pocket Park"

For years I walked by a small abandoned park space near my home. Situated between 96th and 97th streets on Park Avenue, it was a grim and unpleasant hangout for pigeons and rats; the attractive, well-landscaped parts of Park Avenue stopped at 96th Street. Just above the park, the tracks for trains coming and going from Grand Central Terminal emerge from underground. They go by frequently, and children love to look down at them; just before the train disappears into the tunnel, the engineer will look up, and, if there is a child there, he will wave and sound the whistle.

In 2006, after much lobbying by community activists, the 6,100-square-foot park received capital funds allocated by a local councilman and was nicely redesigned by the Parks Department. At my suggestion the Parks Department eliminated lawn areas (who would mow them?) and added benches and other seating.

I was asked to redo the plantings for this block-long park when the Parks Department's landscape construction division discovered that the contractor had failed to provide any drainage or irrigation in the beds and that many of the plants specified in the construction documents were wrong for the site—plants requiring sun with dry conditions, like *Santolina* (lavender cotton), for example, had been specified for full shade in a bed with no drainage. Little maintenance had been planned for this park, although workers from a local organization that employs the homeless occasionally water the plants and pick up the trash, and a neighbor volunteers to help with gardening chores like cutting back the *Nepeta* (catmint) in spring. It was imperative that I use the right plants. While I have made it a long-standing rule to avoid working on public spaces that receive no maintenance, I made an exception for this job because it was so badly needed.

After twenty-five years of designing public plantings in New York, I had developed a reliable list of tough plants for tough places. (See chapter 5 for a discussion of the low-maintenance plants I chose for this park.) I called on these dependable performers and they succeeded in adorning this now much-enjoyed little park, providing color and welcome twelve months of the year.

Other Parks and Plantings

I have had the opportunity to work on many other design and restoration projects in the New York City area, including Verdi Square at 72nd Street and Broadway, Bridgemarket at 59th Street and First Avenue, Bowling Green Park at the lower end of Broadway, Union Square Park at 14th Street, Hunter College and the plantings at their 68th Street subway entrance, the Olmsted Bed in Central Park, the Park Avenue Armory at 67th Street, Tappan Park on Staten Island, and consultation for the plantings in the sculpture garden of the Museum of Modern Art. Each project in its own way has been both a horticultural and sociological challenge for me, as I have tried to design in ways that respond to each neighborhood's unique needs.

Train tracks emerge just above the small park on 97th Street. *Nepeta racemosa* 'Walker's Low' is a spring companion to *Rosa* 'Radrazz' Knock Out, which blooms for seven months with little care.

This little green space on Park Avenue was created in 2006 for the community that lives above 96th Street.

People enjoy this much-needed green oasis. Tough plants include *Hydrangea quercifolia* 'Snow Queen', *Yucca filamentosa* 'Color Guard', and *Berberis thunbergii* 'Crimson Pygmy' in the foreground.

Columbia University's upper Manhattan campus was designed by McKim, Mead & White in the Beaux-Arts style.

In 1996 Columbia's central campus did not present a good image to the public; the unkempt plantings were in need of restoration.

In 1997 I was given the chance to redesign two central display beds at Columbia. Students and staff stopped to say they felt complimented that the university had done this for them.

College Campuses

Although campuses are not cities, the positive changes that good plantings can produce in people's lives are the same: bringing people together, making their lives more pleasant, and giving them a connection with nature. My campus work began at Columbia in the 1990s and has expanded to include two other exciting campus landscapes outside the city.

Columbia University

In 1996 the landscape architect Thomas Balsley invited me to join him on a planning group considering architectural and landscape improvements and community issues for the Morningside campus of Columbia University on the Upper West Side of Manhattan. This study was the brainchild of Emily Lloyd, then Columbia's executive vice president for administration. The university had a history of difficult relations with its neighbors and a campus with a critical need for more space. The issues were complex. Beyer Blinder Belle, the distinguished architecture, preservation, and planning firm that restored Grand Central Terminal and Ellis Island, were the architects in charge. We met regularly for two years, eventually creating a document called *A Framework for Planning* that established principles, guidelines, and standards for the university's future growth.

Many years of neglect had left campus plantings in a sad state, and this had a negative effect not only on Columbia's image with its neighbors and prospective students but also on the morale of the students, faculty, and administration. I found unpruned hedges, half-dead shrubs, compacted lawns, and the random inappropriate addition of annuals around the base of tall stately elm trees. Sometimes my colleagues from Columbia were surprised to learn that these depressing conditions actually existed; the landscape had been that way for so long that people had stopped seeing it.

I urged Emily Lloyd to let me demonstrate the difference a planting improvement could make. The central complex of buildings on Columbia's campus, designed by McKim, Mead & White in 1897, opens unexpectedly onto one of the most splendid expansive landscapes and striking architectural spaces in the city. But it was hard to enjoy the beauty under the effects of neglect. At the time, the two planting beds in the center along the balustrade wall below the main east-west crossing called College Walk had only a bunch of weedy irises and a number of ill-chosen annuals surrounded by a dilapidated picket fence. A beautiful bronze bas-relief was obscured by some straggly shrubs. Columbia and its distinguished urban space deserved better than this, but I was told firmly that the students would destroy any plants we put in. Considering how bleak and run-down the landscape plantings were, I thought it was asking a lot of the students for them to *know* that these plantings should be respected. Emily Lloyd decided to give me a chance.

In the spring of 1997 I arranged for a local landscaping contractor to remove two feet of bad soil from the two beds. We replaced it with good rich soil full of compost. Then we planted a backdrop of shrubs fronted with large groups of perennials and spaces reserved for annuals. My design emphasized the Columbia colors of blue and white, accented with the dark red foliage of *Prunus* × *cistena* (purple-leaf sand cherry). Low box hedges sat at the inside corners of each bed, along with several white 'Seafoam' roses and blue German irises. For spring, we planted *Alchemilla mollis* (lady's mantle), dark red *Heuchera* 'Plum Pudding' (coral bells), and *Salvia* × *sylvestris* 'Blauhügel' ('Blue Hill' sage), whose dark blue flowers bloom in spring and again in fall (a perfect campus plant). For summer blooms, there are white-flowered *Hydrangea quercifolia* (oakleaf hydrangea), white *Phlox paniculata* 'David', blue *Hydrangea macrophylla* 'Nikko Blue' (bigleaf hydrangea), and for fall bloom blue *Aconitum carmichaelii* (monkshood) and white *Anemone* × *hybrida* (Japanese anemone or windflower). We always add a swath of blue and white pansies for Columbia's graduation.

Despite the predictions, none of the students touched a leaf of these plantings. They were deemed a success and christened the Centennial Beds as part of a celebration of Columbia's 1897 move to the uptown campus. The university was so inspired by how the landscape improvements were received that they removed an ugly metal container building from the southeast corner of the old campus and replaced it with a lovely courtyard, called Lion's Court, comprising a long seating wall on one side backed up by plants, a rectangular lawn, and tables and chairs for dining outside one of the dormitory buildings.

A Framework for Planning proved to be a successful document for the development of the campus and its landscape. Columbia staff involved with the beautification of the campus regularly consult it; many of its recommendations regarding site furniture, paving, hedging, and other features have been followed carefully.

I have gone on to design landscape renovations for almost the entire Morningside campus, working with Columbia's assistant vice president

Students too love beautiful public space: despite predictions of vandalism, they appreciated the landscape improvements. Photo by Joseph De Sciose.

of campus operations, Don Schlosser, whose commitment to the beautification of the university's landscape has been unflagging. We have enhanced the handsome McKim, Mead & White buildings with a wide variety of ornamental trees, flowering and evergreen shrubs, perennials, and ground covers. Hundreds of benches and attractive black trash cans with Columbia's crown logo dot the campus. Hardware, bollards, window guards, and wheelchair ramps have been painted a uniform and elegant high-gloss black. On a windy and previously inhospitable rooftop plaza on the more modern East Campus, the university has added large planters of trees and flowers, chairs, tables, and umbrellas, transforming it into a pleasant place to be. In the 1990s Columbia spent next to nothing on its landscape; now it has a substantial annual budget for landscape maintenance and improvements. The university has also spent a considerable amount on street trees and other beautification efforts, such as window boxes and planters at the buildings it owns in the neighborhood around the campus, and people from the surrounding community have noticed and appreciated the change.

Parents and prospective students have a better impression of Columbia's campus life now that the landscape is flowering, green, and well cared for. I have heard people say that they felt complimented. "I can't believe that Columbia did this for us," they would say. The most heartwarming endorsement of my work came as some students passed Butler Library one afternoon. One young man pointed to the plantings and said to the others, "Hey guys! Have you noticed how awesome this campus is?"

Stony Brook University

In 1999, John Belle and Fred Bland, two partners of the architectural firm Beyer Blinder Belle, called me. They had been hired by Shirley Strum Kenny, the president of Stony Brook University, to improve the campus (Stony Brook is one of the campuses of the State University of New York, referred to as SUNY). Dr. Kenny said that there was not enough money to fix the buildings, but she hoped landscaping could help. Because of my work at Columbia, I was invited to join the project.

Nothing could have been less like Columbia's now well-planted campus at 116th Street, with its handsome Beaux-Arts buildings. Most of the thousand-acre Stony Brook campus was covered with concrete, with only a few straggly trees that failed to hide the hideous "Brutalist"

Stony Brook University on Long Island was built in the 1960s with acres of concrete.

Before landscaping and building improvements, the Javits Lecture Center resembled a concrete bunker.

Since 2001, twelve acres at Stony Brook University have been revitalized with trees, lawns, and more than a hundred thousand shrubs and perennials.

buildings hailing from the 1960s. In my opinion (and I know I am not alone in this), they deserve the name their designers gave them: the concrete architecture is cold, ugly, and, after forty years, dingy and shabby. The main auditorium building, the Javits Lecture Center, resembled a huge World War II–era bunker.

The plan was to transform two acres around the administration building by removing the concrete paving to create a beautiful central space. The architects and I planned a fountain, huge green lawns, large areas of colorful planting beds, and benches all around an open mall, with an allée of red maple trees underplanted with ground cover and bulbs. These were not gardens; this was not enclosed space. It was a challenge, and I had to develop a new way of approaching the landscape. After the paving was removed, we added 3,500 cubic yards of special soil—some with more organic matter for plantings, and some with less, for lawns. That is a *lot* of soil. Then we laid 80,000 square feet of sod and planted 20,000 trees, shrubs, and perennials.

The area had to be fenced for a long time while we worked, and a number of students, faculty, and campus visitors complained. But when the fences came down and they saw the new paths, benches, expansive lawns, and plantings, everyone was pleased. Great sweeps of grasses, sedums, yellow false sunflower, and catmint spread out along the paths.

Big landscapes need big sweeps of shrubs and perennials. Red *Imperata cylindrica* 'Rubra' echoes the reds in the architecture.

By surrounding the Javits Center with plants, we made a silk purse from a concrete sow's ear.

Stony Brook University feels that the landscape improvements have changed the public and private experience of campus life.

Large groups of the excellent noninvasive wine-red-flowered *Persicaria amplexicaulis* 'Firetail' (mountain fleece) run alongside ribbons of my favorite red *Berberis thunbergii* 'Crimson Pygmy' (barberry) with blue-flowered *Vitex agnus-castus* (chastetree). *Jasminum nudiflorum* (winter jasmine) hangs over walls, along with *Cotoneaster horizontalis* (rock-spray cotoneaster) for contrast. The red, dinner-plate-sized flowers of the perennial *Hibiscus moscheutos* 'Lord Baltimore' (hardy hibiscus) can be seen from afar, and these have become the signature plant for the Stony Brook landscape. The fountain sprays water that flows downhill into a pool. This "stony brook" is planted with grasses, dark red sand cherries, and barberries, with the perennial *Salvia* × *sylvestris* 'Blauhügel' ('Blue Hill' sage) alongside. Students can walk across in places or put their feet in the water.

Since 2000, Beyer Blinder Belle and I have landscaped another ten acres at Stony Brook, adding plantings around the library and performing arts center, in the woodland as a memorial for Stony Brook's 9/11 victims, and along a new quarter-mile entrance driveway, which has sixty *Metasequoia glyptostroboides* (dawn redwood trees) along with 500 shrubs and 26,000 mostly native perennials in the median strip. (The perennials were planted as small plugs rather than in larger containers to economize; they filled in, and many of them bloomed before the season was out. A cautionary note: when using plugs, do not overwater them.) Some eight years after we started, we had the opportunity to soften the harsh outlines of the bunkerlike Javits Center by planting thickly all around it with flowering and evergreen trees and shrubs and hundreds of perennials—a great improvement to a very difficult piece of architecture.

President Shirley Strum Kenny's commitment to our projects and her understanding of the benefits of improving the landscape have been unfailing. Stony Brook's dean of admissions told me that the appearance of a campus is a major decision-making factor in selecting a college or university, and that Stony Brook's enrollment has continued to increase each year since our work began. At my suggestion, the university created a new staff position to manage and protect the landscape. At a campus ceremony celebrating the new landscape improvements, President Kenny said, "The warm and inviting environment generated by the landscape has helped to build community by providing an incentive for people to come together socially."

Princeton University

When Mark Burstein, with whom I worked at Columbia, left to join President Shirley Tilghman at Princeton University as executive vice president, he invited me to be the garden design consultant on the beautiful landscape there. As seven generations of my family have attended Princeton, this appointment had special meaning for me. One of the greatest pleasures has been working in collaboration with the dedicated landscape staff at Princeton, particularly Jim Consolloy, the wonderfully knowledgeable grounds manager, who knows and loves every plant on the 380-acre main campus and beyond. Since 2004, we have worked together to design new gardens to enrich the areas under Princeton's stately trees with a variety of shrubs, ground covers, and plant combinations.

I was particularly excited about restoring a 1941 garden initiated by my heroine, the great landscape designer Beatrix Farrand. Farrand believed that the beauty of the campus contributed to the mental growth and well-being of students and faculty. She worked on the Princeton campus for thirty years, and toward the end of that time she turned her attention to the Wyman garden, a walled area at the Graduate School. Although the archives contained a drawing of the space with the outlines

Beatrix Farrand's drawing of Princeton's Wyman Garden, made in the 1940s, shows the outlines of a walled garden on the left. Princeton University Archives. Department of Rare Books and Special Collections. Princeton University Library.

In 2005, I reinterpreted this garden at the Graduate School at Princeton.

In keeping with Mrs. Farrand's sketch, the new garden has four vertical evergreens (*Thuja occidentalis* 'Smaragd'), and a sundial was moved to the center of the beds. I added *Juniperus squamata* 'Blue Star', Knock Out roses, Siberian iris, and *Geranium* 'Rozanne'.

of a garden, with a few vertical evergreens visible, there were no real plans, and little remained of her original design.

After removing some straggly tea roses, I designed a garden with beds of perennials and shrubs, and four vertical *Thuja occidentalis* 'Smaragd' (emerald arborvitae) at the center, surrounding an old sundial that I rescued from under some shade trees nearby. In this peaceful, sunny spot, I used the newly developed shrub roses called Knock Out that bloom all summer and fall and, I believe, would have greatly interested Farrand had they been around in her time. These were combined with rounded box balls of *Buxus* 'Green Velvet' and low-growing shrubs such as *Juniperus squamata* 'Blue Star' (blue star juniper). *Iris sibirica* (Siberian iris) provided vertical foliage. The juniper's blue color was echoed by *Helictotrichon sempervirens* (blue oat grass). Blue flowers were supplied by the long-blooming *Geranium* 'Rozanne' (perennial geranium) and dark red accents by *Heuchera* 'Plum Pudding" (coral bells) and the annual *Cordyline australis* (tropical cordyline). The garden was constructed and planted by Princeton's landscape staff. For visitors' enjoyment, we added a number of teak benches, some in the sun and others under a small pergola.

I also designed gardens for the Alumni Association around lovely old Maclean House, built in 1756 and used for many years as the home of Princeton's presidents. The front of the house, facing Nassau Street, had become nearly hidden by overgrown shrubs, which we removed and replaced. Under the shade of several huge elms surrounding the house, we created a number of planting beds, sitting areas, and places for small events. The space presents a constant challenge because the roots of several very large old elms prevent us from establishing plantings that are quite as lush as I would like. To complement the pale yellow house, I chose a number of plants with white or pale yellow flowers and green and white foliage. The mix in the gardens includes green and white *Ilex aquifolium* 'Aurea Marginata' (golden variegated holly), green and white *Cornus alba* 'Elegantissima' (red-stemmed variegated dogwood), white fall-blooming *Camellia*, and white summer-blooming *Impatiens*. The *Edgeworthia chrysantha* (oriental paperbush)—so successful in the Ladies' Border at NYBG—has fragrant early spring flowers in a shade of yellow that just matches the house.

Princeton has a large popular display garden at Prospect House, which is used for events and weddings. The restaurant and meeting rooms overlook the garden, which has for many years been a showcase

The garden at Prospect House is full of color all summer; orange *Impatiens* and *Canna* 'Pretoria' contrast with the blue of *Perovskia atriplicifolia*.

for spring bulbs and summer annuals. But the garden lacked any formal structure and looked bare in the winter months. I added hedges of *Buxus* 'Green Velvet' (boxwood), vertical evergreen arborvitae, variegated yuccas, and *Spiraea japonica* 'Goldflame' (Japanese spiraea)—all providing a backbone for the flower displays and a new dimension to the space through the year. Wanting to have plenty of orange, which is one of Princeton's colors, I suggested new varieties of annuals, such as *Tithonia rotundifolia* 'Fiesta del Sol' (Mexican sunflower) and *Begonia* 'Bonfire', along with a number of dark reds (which they hadn't used before), such as *Cordyline australis* 'Red Sensation' (tropical cordyline) and *Euphorbia cotinifolia* (red spurge), both a huge success. Another key change I made to this colorful annual display was the addition of blue: annual blue sages, *Browallia americana* (Jamaican forget-me-not), *Scaevola aemula* (fanflower), and *Tibouchina urvilleana* (princess-flower); these blues make the many different oranges more vivid. I helped lay out the blocks of colors with strong combinations and repetitions for added form and structure.

Other projects at Princeton have included a garden for Lowrie House, where Princeton's president now lives, and two little enclosed landscapes brought back to life near the library. Jim Consolloy, the landscape staff, and I continue to work together to enrich the Princeton landscape for students, staff, and visitors.

All of these experiences over many years have taught me to think about what constitutes good and bad public space and which kinds of designs work for people and which do not. I have consistently tried to emphasize the importance of people's connection with nature. Cities need beautiful spaces, whether large or small, designed with plants that enhance life for city dwellers in all four seasons. The following chapters explore the many elements I try to consider in creating successful public space—from plant choices, design principles, soil, and maintenance to volunteers, advocacy, and funding—with the hope that you will find my experience helpful as you work to beautify your own city.

Elements of a
Successful Public Space

The goal of a good public space should be to promote the widest possible use and enjoyment. —William H. Whyte, report to the Rockefeller Brothers Fund on Bryant Park, 1979

In the second half of the twentieth century, the urban planner William Hollingsworth Whyte did for urban public open space what his contemporary Jane Jacobs did for city streets and city planning: he observed how people actually use their public space so that we could design with the public in mind. Whyte, always known as Holly, was a thin man with a wry sense of humor and a great love for people. Beginning in 1970, he and his sociology students at Hunter College went out into New York City's parks and plazas to document on film what visitors did—where they sat, how they moved around—and what the elements of successful and unsuccessful space were. No detail was too small for his attention. He figured out the ideal height for seating walls. He saw that people are attracted to food and like to eat outdoors. He realized that people like to claim a small space for themselves, even if only by moving a chair a few inches. Whyte observed that women know instinctively when a place is not safe and stay away, so he concluded that the proportion of women to men in a public space is an important indication of its success: "The most-used places also tend to have a higher than average proportion of women."[1]

The architecture critic Paul Goldberger said of Whyte: "He taught all of us, more than anything, to look, to look hard, with a clean, clear mind, and then to look again—and to believe in what you see."[2] Other vintage Whyte truths are: "People sit where there are places to sit"; "The street is the river of life of the city"; "What attracts people in the city is other peo-

A successful public space is an oasis for everyone. One of William H. Whyte's important observations was that women know instinctively when a place is not safe and stay away.

Whyte studied, admired, and learned from tiny Paley Park at 53rd Street and Madison Avenue, with its movable chairs. It is still one of the most successful public spaces in New York.

ple"; "Blank walls proclaim the power of the institution and the inconsequence of the individual."[3]

The 4,200-square-foot Paley Park, designed by landscape architects Zion and Breen in 1967 and located on 53rd Street between Fifth and Madison avenues, had, and still has, all of Whyte's essential elements of a good public space. Financed by William S. Paley and named for his father, Samuel Paley, the park has been a much-visited city spot since the day it opened. It has no hiding places. It has a focus to draw you into the space—a waterfall that drowns out the sound of nearby traffic. Food is sold in a little recessed kiosk. There are movable chairs. Trees provide shade, ivy climbs the east and west walls, and there are pots of seasonal plants year-round. Though it is a small public space and is always filled with people, it never feels crowded. Whyte studied it, admired it, and learned from it.

In 1979, long before the restoration of Bryant Park began, Whyte wrote a report for the Rockefeller Brothers Fund about how to bring visitors back to the derelict park. With characteristic good humor, he observed, "Even the dope dealers are helping. If you went out and hired them you couldn't get a more villainous crew to show the urgency of the situation."[4] He recommended removing walls to open access to the street

Thanks to Whyte's advice, the design of Bryant Park works. The park is always full of people enjoying themselves.

and surrounding neighborhood, planning special events to draw people into the park, selling food, improving maintenance and security, and providing lots of places to sit.

Largely because of Holly Whyte, when Bryant Park reopened in 1992, it had no hiding places; there were food kiosks, lots of events, and—to everyone's initial astonishment—a thousand movable chairs. The drug dealers disappeared. Inspired by Bryant Park's tremendous success, other parks around New York incorporated Whyte's ideas, though he did not live to see the results.

I first became aware of Whyte through my work in Bryant Park. It turned out that unbeknownst to me he and his wife, Jenny Bell, had been early contributors to the Conservatory Garden. I read his books and spent some wonderful hours talking to him about our shared passion for what people need and deserve in public places. At that time he did not particularly believe in the power of plants in public planning design, but he liked what I had done in Bryant Park and treated me as a kindred spirit.

Whyte noticed that when public places have an external sight to draw visitors' attention—like mimes performing on the steps of the Metropolitan Museum, or a view of the Statue of Liberty—strangers talk as if they knew one another. He called this positive effect "triangulation." In my own work I had noticed that vibrant plantings had exactly this effect. I overheard strangers say, "My grandmother had that plant, do you know what it is?" or "Did you see that hummingbird?"

On a lovely warm May day a year or so before his death, when he was severely crippled with Parkinson's disease and needed a wheelchair to get around, I asked Holly to come with me to the Conservatory Garden. I knew how much he loved to watch people using a public space. I wheeled him into the garden where we sat together. As he looked out over thousands of flowers blooming, mothers sitting with their babies, lovers strolling, office workers having lunch, and school groups passing through, he took my hand. "Lynden," he said, "I should have thought of horticulture when I made my list of elements for successful urban places. You must make it part of the mix from now on." It was a wonderful moment for me and, along with the other things I learned from Holly Whyte, I have tried to make it part of "the mix."

❧

When you create or restore a public space, consider the answers to the following key questions to help you determine your own list of elements for success.

Whyte came to see the Conservatory Garden during a crowded lunch hour and realized that good plantings are also important elements of a successful public space.

Every city has sterile, cold public places like this that are usually empty.

Will the Space Meet Visitors' Needs?

Designing for the public is a sacred trust, and it must be done for the people who will use it. Designers must think about who will use the space and how they will use it. Will people pass through on their way somewhere else, or will it be a destination? What will they enjoy seeing and doing there? Will it be for active (recreational) or passive use, and if both, in what proportion? Is it in a residential or commercial neighborhood? What is its relationship to the surrounding neighborhood, to the street? Imagine yourself in the space as you are designing it. (This holds true whether you have a private client or your client is the public.) To attract visitors, any public space must offer something to them. Otherwise, even the most extravagantly designed places can become depressing and even dangerous.

The best and most successful public places have been created after consulting with the people who will use them. Try to meet with all those who have an interest in the space—regular visitors, community groups, surrounding businesses, nearby schools or churches—and ask them what they want. Meetings with community groups and civic organizations went on for years before Bryant Park finally opened; in the course of designing Wagner Park and Hudson River Park, we held many planning sessions. Listening to the community early on is essential, even if you are not able in the end to do everything they ask for. People like to feel that they have had their day in court.

A small park I won't name, located between a high school and a home for the elderly, was designed apparently without a thought to the people who would be most likely to use the space. Students at the high school are not allowed to play on the rectangular lawn in the middle of the park, and paths around the lawn are too narrow for anyone to pass an accompanied person in a wheelchair. The metal benches are uncomfortably hot in the sunny spots; a structure added when there were complaints about lack of shade is unusable because there is nowhere to sit under it. This little park is not of much use to its neighbors.

Ballplayers, runners, and school athletic programs are often vocal constituencies. Playgrounds and sports fields are important elements in many park designs, and they attract visitors. At the same time, it is essential to provide sufficient passive space for the public—benches, lawns, and planted areas, including gardens. A poll taken by the Central Park Conservancy found that the overwhelming majority of visitors used the park for such passive purposes as sitting on a bench reading the newspaper or taking a walk with a friend. Any successful design should reflect this.

Dog owners, like recreational groups such as baseball leagues and playground parents, can be valuable advocates for parks. Consult them if you are planning a park or running one. Many gardens do not allow dogs, but when I began the restoration of the Conservatory Garden, I wondered: should we let people bring their dogs into the garden? We needed visitors, and given the problems associated with the overgrown garden, those visitors might feel safer if they could bring their dogs with them. It has worked out pretty well over the years, because visitors generally leash their dogs and pick up after them, in accordance with New York City's laws.

A designated dog area or dog run is one way to accommodate dogs and their owners. In Central Park, "preferred dog areas" are rotated to avoid damage to the landscape from overuse. The Conservancy has a very successful program that works with dog owners through a group called PAWS (People Acting with Sense). A core committee meets once a month with the Conservancy to discuss dog-related issues and communicates with more than five thousand dog owners who regularly bring their pets into the park. Chicago also has dog runs in its parks; community members are required to raise funds and help maintain them. Leash laws, however, are often difficult to enforce.

A designated area for dogs can be a useful addition to a city park. This dog run is in Union Square Park.

Will the Space Be Safe?

Having eyes and ears in a public space is important, as Jane Jacobs observed in *The Death and Life of the Great American City*. She was referring to safety on the streets, but the same goes for parks. Can people see in? Can they see out? One of Whyte's first recommendations for Bryant Park was to remove the walls, fences, and overgrown hedges that made the park a magnet for bad happenings. There is a delicate balance between providing enclosure and creating discomfort. A public park should not be isolated, and the view into and out of the park should not be blocked. Do not create or allow any pockets or tall hedges that prevent people from seeing the whole space and everyone in it. If you can't see what someone else is doing, it breeds fear and distrust. If such barriers exist, they should be removed. The first thing we did when beginning the restoration of the Conservatory Garden was to cut down the overgrown hedges.

On the other hand, gardens are traditionally enclosed in some way (*garden* means "enclosure" in many languages), and they need to be protected for maintenance. See-through fencing is a good solution, and a wrought-iron fence is a worthwhile investment. For example, the six acres of the formal Conservatory Garden are set off from Central Park's naturalistic landscape by a tall wrought-iron fence that emphasizes the garden's difference from the surrounding park. The fences, cleared of underbrush, do not block the view in and out of the garden. When you pass through the tall, elegant gates to enter the Conservatory Garden, you know you are in a special place.

When I was brought in to do the landscaping in Madison Square Park it was suggested that I include an evergreen hedge all the way around the park inside the low wrought-iron fence. Because of my experience in both the Conservatory Garden and Bryant Park, and thinking of what Whyte's horrified reaction would have been to this, I objected and the idea was dropped. The point was to invite people back into the park, not to place a barrier in their way. The most important thing is that the space be visible, welcoming, and easily accessible. (Other options for fencing to protect plantings are discussed in chapter 5.)

When parks are in bad shape and seldom visited, people understandably worry about security. Homeless people frequenting the area may make them apprehensive. Whyte said emphatically that the so-called undesirables are not the problem: "It is the actions taken to combat them that is the problem."[5] He was referring to ugly barriers, lack of seating, spikes that make walls unusable for sitting. Whyte's solution was to make parks attractive to as many people as possible, and my experience has confirmed this: the more people use a park, the safer it becomes. Drug dealers tend to disappear overnight; they don't like a lot of company. So the point is to bring visitors in, not to keep "undesirables" out. You may post rules prohibiting sleeping on benches, as in Bryant Park, but all comers should be welcome.

Some of the many ways to bring people into a park and make it safe are to provide events, plenty of seating, access to food, and vibrant plantings.

Gates and fences suggest that a place is special and should be respected. The main gate at the Conservatory Garden was made in Paris in the nineteenth century. Photo by Sara Cedar Miller.

Whyte urged the presence of food to attract people. Even a small push-cart selling soda and ice cream in the park helps. Invite nearby restaurants to put tables and chairs on the sidewalk so patrons can keep an eye on the park, which should attract business for the restaurants as well.

Charles A. Lewis, who created gardens in New York City housing projects in the 1960s, was amazed to see the effects of plants on people. He wrote a wonderful book about his research and findings on this subject, *Green Nature/Human Nature: The Meaning of Plants in Our Lives*, in which he describes gardens as restorative environments: "The garden is a safe place, a benevolent setting where everyone is welcome. Plants are nonjudgmental, nonthreatening, and nondiscriminating."[6]

Several German studies have found that beautiful places are the safest places in cities. Dr. Gerhard Pirner, who participated in such a study at Saarland University, told me that the study demonstrated that "vandalism happens mostly in places which seem to belong to nobody, places nobody cares about."[7] If parks are well planted, well maintained, and well populated, security officers seldom have anything more exciting to do than walk around and answer people's questions. Real security in most places comes from having lots of visitors—at all times of the day and through the year.

Routine maintenance also helps convey the message that a park is safe. Adam Schwerner of the Chicago Parks Board told me that in Chicago, when their parks are well maintained, they are respected. The presence of maintenance staff provides a measure of security. In the Conservatory Garden, the first regular gardener we hired not only helped with the plants, but made people feel comfortable. I bought him a T-shirt imprinted with "The Conservatory Garden" so that visitors would know who he was and he could get to know them. This was the first "security" we had for the garden, and it worked. However, it was not his job to police the garden, and gardeners should *never* be expected to function as security guards.

Consulting with local police may be helpful in a high-crime area; they will help distinguish between places that are not safe and those that just appear dangerous because they are deserted and filled with litter and graffiti. Defaced park equipment and structures are ugly, but they are also a security problem; the presence of graffiti, like litter, makes people uneasy and discourages use. Since an empty space invites graffiti, you can reduce the problem by attracting more visitors. You should also remove graffiti as rapidly as you can, preferably within

People like to eat outdoors in a park. Both Madison Square Park and Bryant Park (the latter shown here) offer food, attracting lots of people and making them safe places to be.

The best park security is prevention. If parks are full of people, security officers will have little to do. This officer enjoys a conversation with a young visitor at the Conservatory Garden.

The presence of regular maintenance staff helps to keep public places safe. A first-rate gardener is the best thing that can happen to a public space. The gardener at Union Square Park has provided excellent care for the plantings for many years.

Graffiti should be removed within twenty-four hours. Photo courtesy of Central Park Conservancy.

twenty-four hours, as has been done since the earliest days by the Central Park Conservancy.

There are other creative approaches to the problem of graffiti. Get to know the people who use your park. Across the street from the Conservatory Garden was a junior high school, and at lunchtime the kids, bursting with pent-up energy, would pour noisily into the garden. I made friends with them and figured out that just a few were responsible for some of the graffiti. Pretending ignorance, I recruited those kids to help me clean up with scrub brushes. Then I made them tour guides for students. Soon the graffiti and the noise disappeared. Some of the kids who came in actually sat down. Another imaginative way to deal with graffiti was shared with me by Kim Mulcahy of the New York Department of Transportation, who has been landscaping highways around the city for years. He says that planting vines on walls is a great deterrent, even in winter, because the vines blur the wall surface and make it undesirable as a canvas. While waiting for the vine to fill in, he sometimes stencils leaves on the wall.

Plant theft is usually a problem only at the beginning of a project. Several factors increase the risk. Sometimes it's the plants themselves: at the Conservatory Garden, I planted about fifty *Ruta graveolens* (rue), an herb with beautiful blue-gray foliage, and within days they were all gone. I planted more; they disappeared again. I asked a friend who worked in a nearby community garden if she knew why. "Of course," she said immediately, "didn't you know? Some members of the East Harlem community use rue as a disinfectant and to keep away evil spirits, among other things, and it is much more powerful if stolen from someone else's garden!" I never replanted rue. We also lost rue at the New York Botanical Garden, so we don't plant it there anymore. In many cultures, there are plants with this kind of intense attraction, so it pays to be familiar with your neighborhood. At certain times of the year plants like azaleas or roses, especially if they are in bloom, can be under greater threat. For a number of years, police staked out the Conservatory Garden over Mother's Day weekend.

Other thefts of beautiful plants are the work of greedy landscapers helping themselves to specimen plants, as happened at both the Conservatory Garden and around Central Park. Once a few are caught, plant theft virtually disappears, except where there is no security presence or routine maintenance as a deterrent. Plant theft is demoralizing to a garden's staff, but it is more noticeable to them than to the public, especially if the plants are quickly replaced. It's important to replant as soon as possible. Like graffiti removal, this seems to discourage repeats.

Other security issues you might consider are whether to light the space and what to do about locking up at night. The Conservatory Garden, for instance, has lights for night, but it is still locked half an hour before dusk. Each park or garden has different solutions for these problems, but in general, visiting parks at night should not be encouraged unless it is for a well-attended event.

The best security for parks is crime prevention. The visible security in Bryant Park countered predictions that it would remain unsafe. The New York Parks Department has a Park Enforcement Patrol (PEP) program: uniformed but unarmed PEP officers act as a deterrent and enforce rules. In the Conservatory Garden, for instance, PEP officers are bilingual so that they can communicate better with our Hispanic neighbors. Such security may be paid for by private funds or by parks organizations. Chicago has both its own park security and support from the Police Department. In Seattle, in the center of the city where security is more of a challenge, the Downtown Seattle Association, founded in 1958, has partnered with the Parks Department to create a park ranger program.

Will the Space Be Welcoming?

Generous paths, adequate seating, informative signage, plenty of trash cans—these amenities help make a space welcoming to visitors. If your budget allows, water fountains and restrooms are appreciated, but they require significant funds for installation and ongoing maintenance.

How wide should paths be? For public places, paths must be generous. In my experience, major paths must be at least eight feet wide in order to allow, say, a mother with a stroller and her companion to walk side by side and still leave room for others. The eight-foot paths in the Conservatory Garden easily accommodate lots of visitors, school groups, and tours. Paths that must accommodate maintenance or emergency vehicles may need to be wider still. The factor that most affects the size of the paths is the number of visitors who will be using them. Less important pathways can be six feet wide, but not much narrower if they are to feel comfortable to the public.

Where can people sit? Does your space need more benches and

seating areas? Scoffing at designers who did not consider the importance of seating space, Holly Whyte wrote that "the human backside . . .
is a dimension architects seem to have forgotten."[8] The presence of seating makes an important statement to visitors: "Come in, you are welcome here." If you offer no place to sit, you are in effect suggesting that
people not stay.

Options for seating include low walls, steps, and movable chairs, as
well as many kinds of benches. Most people like to sit in the shade in
summer, while in winter they enjoy the sun. Provide seating for both.
People like to see what everyone else is doing, so place seating where they
can—near athletic fields and views, on the edges of lawns, in playgrounds, and certainly in gardens.

One of Holly Whyte's most enduring legacies is the movable chairs
that he urged for Bryant Park. In his film and book of the same name,
The Social Life of Small Urban Spaces, Whyte illustrated how people like
to feel in control of their space by sometimes moving the chairs only a
few inches and then sitting down. Since Bryant Park's opening in 1992,
thousands of green metal chairs have been used and enjoyed by visitors
to the park. So popular has this idea become that movable chairs have
since been placed in many parks throughout the city. At first, everyone
predicted that the chairs would be stolen, and a few did disappear at
the very beginning, but they were immediately replaced. The only

Public places need wide paths to accommodate lots of visitors. Madison Square Park is busy
nearly every hour of the day.

People like to sit on low walls, like these at Columbia University's Avery Hall.

Good public places provide lots of seating. Bryant Park has benches and movable chairs. Photo by Joseph De Sciose.

problem over the years has been that the chairs wear out from so much use. People are always curious about why they are not stolen, but I have always thought that the public feels such a sense of ownership for the restored Bryant Park that if someone were seen to be carrying away one of those signature chairs, a passerby would say, "Hey, that chair belongs in my park!"

In 1990, when Gregory Long, the president of the New York Botanical Garden, hired architect Hugh Hardy and me to work on ways to persuade the public to return to the garden in the Bronx, we discovered there were only two or three benches in its 250 acres. NYBG has since installed hundreds of benches, and now thousands of visitors come and sit on them.

The little park at Park Avenue and 96th Street, where I designed the plantings, has two kinds of seating: raised walls in the shady upper section and many curved benches in the sunny area. The whole park is visible at once, and there are almost always visitors now, even on cold winter days.

Good signage is another important way to tell people that someone connected with the park cares about them and the place. Always communicate with your visitors about rules, events, construction, and closures. Use signs to explain why an area must be closed and for how long.

Central Park has welcoming signs listing activities that are permitted as well as those that aren't.

This attractive sign in a park in Battery Park City reminds visitors that feeding squirrels and pigeons also feeds rats.

Apparently pigeons don't read.

If you have new plantings, explain that they need protection. If your visitors understand what is going on and why, they will be much more willing to do what you ask. Using courteous, positive language conveys the message that visitors are part of the process and intelligent enough to understand the situation. They will feel complimented. Polite and respectful wording yields better results than long lists of prohibitions or blunt "Keep Out" or "No Trespassing" notices.

Control of animal pests also requires good communication with the public. Unfortunately, rats seem to be part of city life. An extermination program, combined with the presence of conveniently placed (and preferably covered) trash cans and regular garbage pickup, goes a long way to ameliorate, if not eliminate, this problem. Squirrels and pigeons become troublesome when visitors insist on feeding them. Try to anticipate this by posting signs. Remind visitors that feeding squirrels and pigeons also provides food for rats. Educate volunteers and any security presence in your park to politely discourage feeding the wildlife.

In a well-maintained public place, people will go to some trouble to dispose of their litter. Don't make them look too far. Provide as many trash cans as you can, especially where people sit to eat. City sanitation departments usually pick up the trash, though sometimes parks workers are responsible, and Business Improvement Districts may provide private garbage collectors. Remember that easy access to trash bins is important not only for visitors but also for those who collect the garbage.

For many years, a planting space in the 68th Street subway entrance in Manhattan was unbelievably ugly, filled with trash and old rags. After I was able to persuade Hunter College, which manages the space, to let me put in some soil and good plants, a trash can was essential. Despite mutterings that it wouldn't do any good and that someone would steal it, they finally did put one off to the side, chained to the railing. Everyone was astonished to discover that the public began using it right away, and that it is almost always full.

Among the many different designs for park litter receptacles, some are better looking and more effective than others. Consistency is the best solution, even if the containers are unattractive: people must be able to identify trash cans with ease. Black trash-can liners are preferable; clear plastic shows the trash inside. If you have planter boxes on the street, it is very important to have trash cans as well so people don't use the planters for their banana peels or coffee cups as they go by.

Will the Space Be Well Maintained?

Who is going to maintain the space and how will it be paid for? Is there a commitment to long-term maintenance? You must have a good idea of the answers to these questions before you proceed. Public landscapes cost money and must be maintained; without ongoing care, a new park will deteriorate and a restored one will revert to its previous condition, disappointing people and ultimately making them cynical about their city's commitment to their well-being. It is sometimes better not to take on a project that will not be maintained. Ideally, funding should come from public sources, though this seems to be rare today. Even if money is there for building the space, too often funds are not provided for ongoing maintenance, and private funding may have to come to the rescue. (See chapter 8 for more about private funding.)

The degree of horticultural maintenance depends on the kinds of plants you choose to use, the soil, and the availability of water. Volunteers can help, but a trained gardener is essential and should be paid accordingly. There is no formula for how many people are needed to take good care of a public park or garden. At a minimum, a hard-working, motivated, knowledgeable gardener with seasonal help can work miracles if he or she is well paid and feels appreciated. (For further discussion of these subjects, see chapters 5 through 8.)

Rats are attracted to a park full of litter, but people will avoid it. Photo courtesy of Central Park Conservancy.

Make trash cans readily available and people will use them. These trash cans in Central Park are designed for easy use and easy pick-up.

Will Horticulture Be Part of the Mix?

Public spaces landscaped with appropriate plants have a human scale and provide a connection with nature that people need and that will give them confidence to use the space. Few places are too small or unwieldy to accommodate intelligent landscaping. Even the simplest additions, such as sidewalk planter boxes and hanging baskets, have a softening effect on city streets.

Though landscape improvements are less expensive than capital projects, they are often harder to get approved and funded. Architects and landscape architects sometimes think of plantings as frills or last-minute additions to a project. Often, by the time plantings are ready to be considered, money has run short and they are eliminated. Some developers seem to think concrete and a little grass (and perhaps a tree if you are lucky) constitute a "landscape." They resist plantings as maintenance headaches, not a good attitude for success. Anyone who deals in real estate knows that houses with beautiful trees and plantings command higher selling prices than similar houses with less green around them, and well-designed landscaping is just as important in public spaces.

Year-round combinations of shrubs and perennials give visitors the pleasure of watching the seasons change. People love bright-colored annual displays, and these do give color and life to a public space. But annuals alone are not enough. In northern climates, after they are pulled for the winter, empty spaces are left in the beds. In my experience, well-chosen permanent plantings that develop through the seasons attract people like a magnet. The particular mix of shrubs, perennials, annuals, and bulbs may vary according to the needs of your particular site and climate, but the idea is to produce what Holly Whyte would have seen as horticultural triangulation, a reason for strangers to talk to one another in a place of enjoyment for urban dwellers all year long.

Well-chosen plantings are a magnet for visitors. Photo by Joseph De Sciose.

The Art of Garden Design

Mixed Plantings for Year-Round Interest

Horticulture is both an art and a science: the art of combining plants well and the science of growing them properly.   —Sarah Carter Roberts, former curator of herbaceous plants at the New York Botanical Garden

I have always believed that garden design for public spaces should be based on the same sound principles of art and science as design for private gardens, requiring both a keen eye for composition and a thorough knowledge of plants' growth habits and cultural needs.

Gardening as Art

Gardens are an art form, and designing gardens is the process of painting with plants. To do this, designers place them in relation to one another and to the garden as a whole, just as a painter blocks in sections of color or forms on a large canvas. Successful combinations please the eye and allow each plant to enhance the qualities of the others.

For many years before beginning work in public gardens, I was a painter making large abstract landscape collages. Like a collage, a garden is a collection of disparate elements brought together to form a composition. Whether you are restoring a formal garden or using great sweeps of plants in large open areas, always consider the overall composition. Louise Beebe Wilder, a fine American gardener and early-twentieth-century garden writer, wrote, "No occupation known to me is as absorbing as the distributing and arranging of flowers in the garden with a view to creating beautiful pictures."[1]

Public space should be as beautiful as a private garden. Visitors of all ages enjoy a stroll through the Conservatory Garden. Photo by Joseph De Sciose.

To my eye, the ideal composition is one that looks almost unplanned—but this actually requires careful planning and experience with plants. The great English gardener and writer Vita Sackville-West called this kind of gardening "a kind of haphazard luxuriance, which of course comes neither by hap nor hazard at all."[2] This type of planting may look as if some invisible hand had just dropped the plants here and there, but the effect actually takes considerable organization and definition.

Garden designers work with many of the same elements as artists: contrast, repetition, line, scale, form, texture, and color. A good garden, like a painting, needs order and hierarchy and variety among these elements. But plants, unlike paint, are a complex medium, contributing flowers, foliage, bark, and berries to the mix. The wonderful fact that plants are actually alive means that garden designers must deal with the effects of time and weather. A garden design is not fixed but always growing and changing. Creating that perfect composition or finding the perfect place for a plant to thrive is an ongoing and exciting process; Peter Del Tredici, senior research scientist at Boston's Arnold Arboretum of Harvard University, said, "Horticulture is the art of moving plants around," and anyone who gardens knows this is true.

My favorite plant palette consists of carefully chosen small ornamental trees, shrubs (both deciduous and evergreen), perennial plants that bloom at different times throughout the seasons, some annuals for all-summer color, and groups of bulbs for both early spring and summer interest—all in varying proportions depending on the type of landscape.

The artistry and effectiveness of this type of garden design applies as much to public space as to private. Resist the pressure to design "down" for the public. Municipal plantings with regimented rows of run-of-the-mill annuals are static and less satisfying than designs that provide vari-

Gardening is an art. Like a collage, a garden is a collection of disparate elements arranged to form a composition.

ety and change. Public plantings should be as varied and sophisticated as those in private gardens, because people will respond to them. Nature and innovative plant breeders and growers have created a huge, delicious plant palette for us to use. The City of Chicago uses thousands of different kinds of plants in its city plantings: they are anything but "municipal." The wide variety of plants in the Conservatory Garden and in other gardens around New York has inspired professional landscapers to try new plants in public places and homeowners to experiment in their own gardens. The smallest planting bed, next to a gas station or a playground or on a median strip, can and should be designed this way, using plants for four seasons that are appropriate to the site.

Many people told me that the Conservatory Garden's neighbors wouldn't appreciate complex plantings: "Just give them marigolds and red salvia. They will trash them anyway." But I was convinced that the Conservatory Garden and its neighbors deserved better, and the naysayers turned out to be wrong. The community of East Harlem noticed what we had done, and even presented me with a plaque that reads "In Grateful Appreciation for Improving the Quality of Life in 'El Barrio' through the Restoration of the Conservatory Garden." It is among my proudest possessions.

Gardening as a Science

In contrast to a painter, a gardener must consider two additional all-important elements: time and weather. How will the plants change over time and as a result of the particular climate or site? How will the soil—the canvas itself—change? To meet these challenges successfully, a garden designer must have knowledge of and respect for the science of horticulture. Plants are the tools of the landscape trade, like paints on a palette or notes on a scale, but uniquely, plants are constantly changing.

In many landscape architecture programs horticulture studies play a very small role in proportion to the whole curriculum, a shortcoming that colleges and universities should address in order to empower their students with an expanded knowledge of plants. Too often public landscape design consists of beautiful drawings and a lot of rhetoric that in the end lacks consideration for how the landscape will actually be used by people. "Greenery" is sometimes added as an afterthought, if at all, and then often only in the form of a lawn or a few trees. If a designer does not know enough about plants, the result can be cold and unwelcoming, with a disheartening array of straggly unhappy plants.

At Stony Brook University, a wide section of the main campus mall was planted with a grove of trees in the 1990s. The ground was covered with gravel—right up to the trunks of the trees—with stones so large the students could not walk on them. In summer, the stones absorbed so much heat that the trees baked and eventually died. With much of this thousand-acre campus consisting of concrete and stone, it's not surprising that Stony Brook had trouble attracting students. Our design team replaced this kind of landscaping with twelve acres of rich, varied plantings, as described in chapter 1.

Plants can enhance even the most modern, minimalist architectural setting if the designer understands how to use them to advantage. Great landscape architects do understand the importance of plants in their work. A designer of public space must not only consider how people will use the space but also specify the plants for all four seasons, taking into account what the plantings will look like in five years and what maintenance they will require—issues not usually covered in courses on public space design. An ideal public landscape design team should include a landscape architect, soil and irrigation experts, and a garden designer with horticultural training who will recommend the best plantings to enhance the design and take into consideration its development over time. Depending on the size of the project, an arborist may be added to the team, and in some cases an expert in engineering, lighting, or other specialties.

The Mixed Border for All Seasons

Experience has taught me the importance of using a variety of plants for all seasons. With adjustments for the needs of the particular climate and location, a good combination of mixed plantings (trees, shrubs, perennials, annuals, and bulbs) can be created for any garden, public or private. Displays of colorful annuals are exciting for a brief visit but often not sufficient reason for visitors to return again and again. Great sweeps of grasses and wildflowers are lovely when they are at their best, but in many areas of the country this may be for only a few months. Establishing a mix of plant types will greatly improve these types of plantings.

I first noticed mixed borders while visiting the beautiful English gardens at Hidcote, Sissinghurst, and Great Dixter in the late 1970s; because

I was a painter, I was fascinated by their artistic plant combinations. Returning to my own Connecticut garden, where I had designed a long yew hedge situated so that I had to look at it head-on twelve months of the year, I applied this mixed border technique in order to produce something satisfying to my eye no matter what the season. It took many years of weekend work—moving plants around, fixing obvious mistakes, and experimenting with different combinations and shapes—to find the solution: first, a backbone of various shrubs, some evergreen and some flowering, against the hedge, and a few large ornamental grasses as exclamation points. The shrubs and large grasses give structure and form to the border, particularly in the winter months, usually November through March in the northeastern United States. Then, for interest during the rest of the year, I added groups of perennials and pockets of bulbs and annuals.

This combination proved most effective in urban public gardens as well. The presence of plants that change from season to season connects the city dweller to the larger forces of nature. Human beings need respite from the exciting chaos of city life, and parks and plants provide that. In his book *Green Nature/Human Nature*, Charles A. Lewis writes about the importance of the physical planted environment and how it influences the way people feel about themselves and their city: "Plants take

I learned about mixed borders while working on my weekend garden in Connecticut. I was trying to produce something interesting to see in all four seasons.

away some of the anxiety and tension of the immediate Now by show-ing us that there are enduring patterns in life.... Plants signal the change of season with rhythms that were biologically set in their genes by the same forces that set human biological clocks. Plant rhythms differ from those of the built environment; their growth is steady and progressive."[3] Being in a garden surrounded by the variety and ebullience of plants— all within earshot of the honking cars and ambulance sirens—makes life sweeter for harried city dwellers.

In the North Garden at the Conservatory Garden, two large displays installed by the Parks Department—tulips in May and chrysanthemums in October—did not keep the garden from becoming the deserted place it was when I first visited it. Rather, it was the infusion of rich, varied four-season plantings in the South Garden that brought people back. As one group of fine plants finishes blooming, another begins, in a kaleido-scope of constantly changing colors. The unfolding of nature from sea-son to season is fascinating and comforting to city dwellers surrounded by buildings and sidewalks, traffic, and noise. Charles Lewis again: "In densely populated areas . . . green nature brings life to concrete, glass and asphalt."[4] A mixed border may take more planning, but your efforts will be noticed and enjoyed.

Winter in the Northeast

When designing year-round plantings for public spaces, I always begin by thinking of winter. The temptation for many beginning designers is to weigh down the garden with too many spring-blooming plants such as peonies and irises, which have a short bloom time and then take up valuable room in the border. I use these sparingly and have shifted the proportion of plants away from spring bloomers and toward the other three seasons, placing particular emphasis on fall and winter interest in order to give visitors reasons to return later in the year.

One of the great advantages of using this mixed palette of shrubs and perennials is that you *can* provide winter interest. If you know your plants well, you will have no reason to leave a park or garden devoid of plant pleasures in winter. Evergreen foliage, interesting bark, and color-ful berries are the joys of the season. "A garden that is not beautiful in winter is not a beautiful garden," said the Belgian Jacques Wirtz, a lead-ing landscape architect.[5] Winter in many parts of the United States occu-pies a substantial portion of the year, and being in a well-designed win-ter garden can be a great pleasure on a cold day in January. Some of my

Plantings in public places should be beautiful in all four seasons, including winter, as they are here in Madison Square Park. Photo by Joseph De Sciose.

The New York Botanical Garden's Perennial Garden is designed to give pleasure in winter to visitors, who can enjoy the ornamental grasses waving in the wind.

Evergreens are an essential ingredient of a winter mix in the Conservatory Garden.

favorite plant choices (discussed below) are those that enliven public spaces during this time of year.

The Plant Palette

The hardscape comprises the structural elements that attest to the permanence of a space. If you put into practice Whyte's observations about how public space works best, you will already have the underpinnings of good design: enclosures, openings, places to sit, perhaps water features, and paths that lead you and your eye around the space. The architectural elements are just the beginning, the form on which you will compose your garden using living plant materials: trees, shrubs, perennials, annuals, biennials, and bulbs.

Different proportions of plants can be adapted to many different kinds of sites. In large abstract plantings like those I designed at Stony Brook University, for example, for purposes of both design and maintenance the proportion of shrubs is much higher than it would be in a garden setting. The less formal a site, the higher should be the proportion of shrubs. Thus, if you are designing plantings for a median strip on a busy street, you will not use the same plants as you would for an enclosed garden. In a street mall, at the entrance to a playground, or alongside a building, use mostly shrubs, with perennials as ground covers under and around them.

The goal of a good planting design in a public or private space is to combine plants for all four seasons in such a way that each element enhances the others. Whether designing plantings for parks, at the intersections of streets, around schools and playgrounds, or in parking lots, you can create a garden for all seasons by choosing four to eight different plants attractive in each of the four seasons and combining them. The mixed border offers a constantly changing display, and the combinations—with varied textures, forms, and colors—hold the composition together through the year.

Since time and weather are the great challenges to garden design, consider their effects on your plant choices. Will a small tree or shrub eventually grow large and shade its neighbors? Will some plants, well behaved at first, grow fast and take over? How cold, how hot, how sunny, how shady, how rainy, how windy is the site? How will your plants look in spring, summer, fall, and especially winter?

Large groups of shrubs underplanted with perennials as ground covers are effective in a landscape like that of Stony Brook University. *Persicaria amplexicaulis* 'Firetail' is in bloom here.

The answers to these questions will help you narrow your choices. The United States Department of Agriculture produces and is currently updating a hardiness zone map for North America, and the American Horticultural Society has developed a heat zone map, both of which can be found on the AHS Web site, www.ahs.org. The AHS also publishes these maps in a very useful little book called *The AHS Great Plant Guide*, with pictures and descriptions of plants for every region and climate in the United States.

I have worked for more than thirty years with plants that do well in the Northeast, so I am able to choose plants that are hardy and noninvasive in my planting zone. The Plant Lists at the back of this book provide a guide to reliable plants for mixed plantings. Many of the plants I include do well in other parts of North America, but each region has different plants that can be counted on for public places. A number of regional organizations and resources are available to help you choose the best plants for your locale. For example, a wide variety of plants that do well in the Pacific Northwest are designated in "Great Plant Picks," available on the Internet (www.greatplantpicks.org).

Keep in mind that plants will perform differently in different parts of the country. For instance, certain ornamental grasses that are not invasive in one place may reseed prolifically in others. Always check to be sure that the plants you choose are not invasive and do not attract pests in your area. (See the Resource Directory at the back of this book for Web sites that can help you identify problem plants for your region.)

Plant Names

Common names for plants often vary from one place to another, from one city or region or country to another. For instance, a lovely blue-flowered perennial has a botanical name that is quite a mouthful: *Ceratostigma plumbaginoides*. Its common names, confusingly, are leadwort or plumbago, and *Plumbago* is also the botanical name of a blue tropical plant. But each plant has just one botanical name and can be recognized by that name—by anyone, anywhere. For this reason, if you are designing or working with public space, it is important to know and use the botanical names of plants.[6] I once took a group of Japanese gardeners on a tour of the Conservatory Garden, and although we couldn't communicate much, we all knew the botanical names of the plants and enjoyed our shared interest in them.

Magnolia x *soulangeana* is a fine tree to combine with shrubs and perennials. Some of the magnolias in Central Park's Conservatory Garden have been there for seventy years.

Acer palmatum 'Bloodgood' (Japanese maple) has rich red color all season, echoed by other red shrubs and pink roses in Wagner Park.

Trees and Shrubs

The "bones" of a garden are the trees and shrubs, woody plants that you see all year round. The Conservatory Garden, for instance, has "good bones": its trees and shrubs are handsome in winter. Consider these plants first—their sizes and shapes, from tall spires to large rounded shrubs or plants with outstretched branches.

For most urban garden sites, I recommend that you choose ornamental flowering trees that will grow no more than twenty or thirty feet tall. If they get too tall, they will shade your plantings too much. Trees that do well in the Northeast include *Prunus* (flowering cherries), *Cercis canadensis* (eastern redbud), various dogwoods such as *Cornus kousa* (kousa dogwood) or *Cornus florida* (flowering dogwood), and magnolias, such as *Magnolia* x *soulangeana* (saucer magnolia) or *Magnolia stellata* (star magnolia). *Malus* species (crabapples) also make good garden subjects, as you can plant right underneath them, but choose dwarf varieties that will stay a manageable size. *Lagerstroemia* (crape-myrtle) has both summer flowers and handsome winter bark; dwarf shrub selections are being developed, which makes them even more useful in urban gardens. They are used extensively in the South but can also be grown as far north as the New York City area.

Shrubs also provide garden structure and form through the year; place them next in your design after the trees. Mixed borders need a spine of shrubs, and some should be evergreens for winter interest. If a garden or bed will be viewed from both sides, place shrubs in the center along with large ornamental grasses, which read like shrubs. If the planting will be viewed predominantly or only from one side—if it is in front of a building or wall, for example—place most of the shrubs and grasses at the back of the bed. Stagger low shrubs along the front with the lower-growing perennials and annuals.

The more I design, the more importance I give to shrubs. If chosen properly so that they do not get too big over time, shrubs require much less maintenance than perennials, annuals, and bulbs, the other elements in the mixed border. In the Northeast, without shrubs there is little to see in winter after the perennials die back. This is not the case in warmer climates, of course, but shrubs always add structure to your composition, as do the many wonderful structural plants, such as aloes and agaves, that are perennial in warmer climates and look spectacular there in all seasons.

Evergreens are important elements of design, forming the backbone of good year-round plantings and providing structure and color in all seasons. Consider both needle-leaved and broad-leaved evergreens, such as *Ilex* (holly) in its many forms, shiny-leaved dark green *Prunus laurocerasus* 'Otto Luyken' (cherry laurel), *Skimmia japonica* (Japanese skimmia) with its red berries, and evergreen species of azaleas, such as *Rhododendron* 'Treasure' or *R.* 'Pleasant White'. The red bud set of *Pieris japonica* 'Dorothy Wyckoff' is at its best in winter and combines well with hollies or with the yellow foliage of *Chamaecyparis pisifera* 'Golden Mop' (false cypress). Camellias have lustrous green leaves all year and can be used as far north as the New York City area if sited in some shade to protect them from the winter sun. I especially like to use dark green evergreen verticals, such as *Thuja occidentalis* 'Smaragd' (emerald arborvitae), *Ilex crenata* 'Sky Pencil' (a small vertical Japanese holly), or *Taxus cuspidata* 'Capitata' (yew), kept tightly trimmed.

Consider using dwarf evergreens in your border along with some of the many slower-growing Japanese maples, both of which add form and interest to the garden in winter. But keep in mind that *dwarf* means "slower growing": dwarf plants do eventually get large.

Shrubs in the dogwood family are effective with evergreens during winter. To my eye, no four-season garden is complete without the variegated leaves and red stems of *Cornus alba* 'Elegantissima' (red-stemmed variegated dogwood) contributing to a mixed border all year long. The bright yellow stems of *Cornus sericea* 'Silver and Gold' and the red-orange

At Columbia University, red-dyed willow stems enhance the evergreens in winter.

Even though the foliage is yellow, the low-growing *Chamaecyparis pisifera* 'Golden Mop' is an evergreen and pairs well with *Juniperus squamata* 'Blue Star', which grows slowly at the front of borders. The red is *Imperata cylindrica* 'Rubra'.

The variegated leaves of *Cornus alba* 'Elegantissima' are combined with evergreen arborvitae and pink roses in Wagner Park. *Picea pungens* 'Montgomery' is in the foreground.

Many *Cornus* species are lovely all year, but they are especially useful in winter with their colorful stems. This is *Cornus sanguinea* 'Midwinter Fire' in front of *Juniperus virginiana* 'Burkii' in the Ladies' Border at the New York Botanical Garden.

Shrubs are very important elements in successful public plantings. At Columbia, several large *Prunus* x *cistena* are combined with evergreen *Prunus laurocerasus*, *Berberis thunbergii* 'Crimson Pygmy', and various hydrangeas.

stems of *C. sanguinea* 'Midwinter Fire' are striking accents in the winter garden. For additional color and contrast with evergreens and other shrubs in winter, buy bunches of long-stemmed five- or six-foot red-dyed branches from your local florist and push groups of them into the ground before it freezes. Add boughs of pine or spruce for a rich, colorful textural contrast that lasts until the beds are uncovered and prepared for spring.

I often use *Prunus* x *cistena* (purple-leaf sand cherry) for its dark red contrasting color, whether pruned as a shrub or left to grow as a small tree. *Berberis thunbergii* cultivars, such as *B. thunbergii* f. *atropurpurea* 'Rose Glow' and *B. thunbergii* 'Crimson Pygmy', have also been favorites of mine for years for their round form and their colorful presence in a mixed border. (In many areas, *Berberis* is considered invasive. My experience is that cultivars, like 'Crimson Pygmy', do not seed themselves invasively, particularly in the city, but I do not use the straight species.)

Spiraea (meadowsweet) species and cultivars are particularly useful in the mixed border because they don't grow too tall and out of proportion, making them very sustainable over time. *Spiraea thunbergii* 'Ogon' is a delicate yellow-green-leaved shrub that contrasts well with red foliage or bulbs. A number of other very good low-growing Japanese spiraeas (*Spiraea japonica*) are also available.

The genus *Hydrangea* includes many beautiful shrubs. Because of their large leaves and big flowers, they contrast well with *Spiraea* and small-leaved perennials, and public garden visitors love them. Many varieties and cultivars are available to the gardener, and they have become very popular in recent years. Hydrangeas thrive in many parts of North America, particularly in the South and at the seaside. *Hydrangea macrophylla* (bigleaf hydrangea), with its fat luscious blue or pink flowers and big shiny leaves, does well in shadier spots, although its blooms may be unreliable in colder parts of the Northeast. On the other hand, *Hydrangea quercifolia* (oakleaf hydrangea) really pays the rent all year long: interesting branch structure and peeling bark in winter, large white flowers in early summer, and rich purple leaves in fall.

People love roses, so I try to include them in my designs whenever possible. I was not a great fan of roses in the days when many of them had to be treated with chemicals to combat pests and diseases. Today, however, wonderful new roses are available, including fine shrub roses that are hardy, long-blooming, and disease resistant. When I first visited the Conservatory Garden, nothing was in bloom except some straggly pink roses by the south pool. These turned out to be a floribunda shrub rose, *Rosa* 'Betty Prior'. Old Betty, as I call her, is an indestructible, long-blooming shrub with clusters of bright shocking-pink flowers. She doesn't have to be sprayed, and she still blooms there from May to November.

Hydrangea macrophylla 'Glowing Embers' and *Hydrangea quercifolia* are combined with *Berberis* and grasses in the Cool Section at NYBG's Perennial Garden. The shrubs give solidity to large perennial displays. Photo by Joseph De Sciose.

Rosa 'Radrazz' Knock Out is planted with *Nepeta racemosa* 'Walker's Low' at 97th Street and Park Avenue; it blooms without care from May to November.

Roses should be incorporated into the plantings whenever possible. In Wagner Park, they go well with *Perovskia atriplicifolia* and *Verbena bonariensis*.

The old-fashioned shrub roses with romantic names are lovely, but many of them bloom only once, leaving nothing but green foliage for the rest of the season. David Austin, a breeder and grower of English Roses, has developed varieties with the forms and fragrances of old roses and the repeat flowering of modern roses. Most useful for gardens and landscapes is the Knock Out series of pink and red roses developed by the hybridizer William Radler. Other good long-blooming shrub roses are the Carefree series and Meidiland roses. Much research and breeding continues in the rose industry, and many more choices will undoubtedly become available.

Incorporating roses into the mixed border, as we did at Wagner Park, makes attractive gardens. Shrub roses can be combined effectively with many long-blooming perennials, such as *Nepeta* (catmint), *Geranium* (cranesbill), and *Alchemilla mollis* (lady's mantle). Many gray-leaved Mediterranean plants, such as *Santolina* (lavender cotton), *Lavandula angustifolia* (lavender), and *Salvia* (sages) also complement roses. The rose garden at the National Arboretum in Washington, D.C., is full of old and new roses interplanted and enhanced with herbs and perennials.

Perennials

Herbaceous perennial plants are the "flesh" on the "bones." Perennials are plants that live for more than two growing seasons. In temperate cli-

Late in autumn, when the foliage of oakleaf hydrangeas turns to wine colors and the grasses have plumes, many gardens are at their best. Photo by Joseph De Sciose.

At NYBG's Perennial Garden, people can learn about many different kinds of perennials to pair with shrubs and small trees. In the foreground are hostas and hydrangeas.

In the Conservatory Garden, the bluestone paving, which can become very hot, is a factor in choosing plants that will do well in the beds. *Echinacea purpurea* and *Phlox paniculata* 'Bright Eyes' can handle the heat easily.

mates, most die back in winter and appear again in spring (although some may be evergreen, retaining their leaves through winter); in warm climates they may grow continuously. Many excellent perennials are available, and more appear every year from nurseries large and small all over the country. One of the best ways to determine what grows well in your area is to visit local nurseries to see what they are offering. Get to know the people who work there and ask for advice. Plantspeople always like to share their expertise.

The best way to use perennials in a public space over a long season is first to consider the different shapes and colors of foliage in relation to one another and to the shrubs. Then the colors of the flowers can be worked into the picture. Though flowers are important and people love them, they are not the main event: they are the bonus with which nature rewards us.

Choose perennials also based on the timing of their flowers in order to extend bloom time through the growing year. Spring-blooming plants abound, so to enrich your garden integrate perennials that bloom in the height of summer and late into fall. Plants with the Latin prefix *helio*, which means "sun"—such as *Heliopsis* and *Helianthus*— can meet the challenges of summer's heat, humidity, and drought.

Euonymus fortunei 'Coloratus' is one of the most useful ground covers. It grows anywhere, in sun or shade, and works well here at Columbia University, paired with daffodils in spring and variegated yucca all year long.

Anemone x *hybrida* has attractive foliage and dresses up the garden in late summer and fall. It is paired with *Persicaria amplexicaulis* 'Firetail' at NYBG's Perennial Garden.

Alchemilla mollis is a great companion for all other plants in the mixed border.

Hellebores are almost perfect perennials: low-maintenance and beautiful for at least ten months a year.

Heuchera 'Plum Pudding' is a star all year, bringing rich color to the front of the border. When it is paired with *Brunnera macrophylla* 'Jack Frost', the similar-sized foliage and contrasting colors create a variation on a theme.

Anemone, *Sedum*, *Aconitum*, and *Aster* species and cultivars are effective perennials for fall display.

Underplanting shrubs is an effective use of perennials. *Geranium macrorrhizum* (cranesbill), an almost evergreen perennial in my part of the world, has very attractive leaves, nice pink or white flowers (that do not need to be deadheaded), and foliage that will cover an area so thickly that it prevents weeds. *Asarum europaeum* (European wild ginger) has shiny dark-green round leaves all winter, but it grows very slowly and is expensive for that reason. It divides easily, however, and will eventually fill in nicely. Perennials also make good ground covers. As an alternative to high-maintenance grass, try common *Vinca minor* (periwinkle or myrtle), *Liriope muscari* (lily turf), or *Euonymus fortunei* 'Coloratus' (purple wintercreeper euonymus).

For the mixed border, some of my favorite reliable perennials are various species and cultivars of *Helleborus*, *Alchemilla*, *Anemone*, *Geranium*, *Salvia*, *Sedum*, *Thalictrum*, *Hosta* and *Yucca*. Public gardeners from Toronto to Georgia attest to the usefulness of these perennials. (For other perennials, see the Plant Lists.)

Always make room for *Helleborus* × *hybridus* (Lenten rose), which contributes to the garden nearly twelve months of the year. Plant breed-

Yuccas are the stars of the winter landscape. Despite their tropical look, they are marvelous all year and especially in the snow, providing winter color for visitors to the little park on 97th Street.

ers and growers have produced hundreds of different selections, but I prefer the simpler form, with its shiny, evergreen, sharply toothed foliage and lovely pink-and-white flowers that bloom in very early spring and continue for many months. Its flowers are shy and bend down their heads until they are ready to go to seed. If you plant them in a raised bed or on a slope, as we do at the Conservatory Garden, then people can see the flowers better. Hellebores are also one of the least demanding, lowest-maintenance perennials, and I have found them in gardens in many regions of the country.

Any garden is improved by clumps of *Alchemilla mollis* (lady's mantle), with its yellow-green frothy flowers and felt leaves that hold raindrops like pearls. For fall bloom, choose any of the various cultivars of *Anemone* x *hybrida* (Japanese anemone). I particularly like the pink single-flowered *Anemone hybrida* 'Robustissima', as robust as its name. It often spreads, but slowly, and I find that a good thing. *Heuchera* 'Plum Pudding' is a fine plant on its own, but one of its best features is that it makes other plants look good next to its contrasting dark foliage. Perennial *Geranium* (not to be confused with the annual geraniums called *Pelargonium*) includes many fine species and cultivars with distinctive foliage and long-blooming flowers in a variety of colors. The hardy perennial sages (*Salvia*) include long-blooming choices, with new hybrids and cultivars introduced on the market each year. I am especially fond of *S.* x *sylvestris* 'Blauhügel' ('Blue Hill' sage), which has attractive green leaves and two seasons of bloom if you cut it back after its first flowering. The succulent foliage of *Sedum* (stonecrop) contrasts well with other plants, such as *Thalictrum* (meadow rue), with its elegant, delicate foliage. Many species and cultivars of *Hosta* have large sensuous leaves. I use *Hosta plantaginea* 'Aphrodite' most often; it holds up in the sun, has bright green leaves with beautiful ribs, and its white flower is sweetly scented in late summer. Variegated yuccas, deceptively tropical-looking plants, are actually native to North America and useful for many purposes, especially for winter plantings. *Yucca filamentosa* 'Color Guard' is one of the best.

For other favorite perennials for the Northeast and for different parts of the country, see the Resource Directory and the Recommended Reading section.

Grasses

Unless I am designing wide-open landscapes like those at Stony Brook University or Red Hook in Brooklyn, where I used grasses and shrubs in

At Stony Brook University, grasses are used effectively in great sweeps, along with many shrubs and perennial ground covers.

A gorgeous *Miscanthus sinensis* 'Gracillimus' explodes dramatically behind the charming statue in the Conservatory Garden.

Ageratum houstonianum 'Blue Horizon' is one of the best annuals in the Northeast, and it goes with everything.

great sweeps, I like to use large grasses as exclamation points in borders and as contrast to the plants around them. Of the many excellent large species and varieties, I love *Miscanthus sinensis* 'Gracillimus', *M. sinensis* 'Morning Light', and *M.* 'Purpurascens', which turns a rich dark yellow-orange in fall.

For small, front-of-the-border grasses, I am very fond of *Imperata cylindrica* 'Rubra' (Japanese blood grass), which does not seem to be invasive in the Northeast but is invasive in the South, so be cautious about using it. *Hakonechloa macra* 'Aureola' (golden Japanese forest grass) is very handsome in all seasons, in sun or shade, and is also not invasive in the Northeast. With its blue leaves, *Helictotrichon sempervirens* (blue oat grass) makes a fine specimen plant for the front of the border.

Whenever you can, try to place grasses where garden visitors can enjoy them backlit by the afternoon sun, blowing in the wind, or covered with a light dusting of snow.

Annuals

After the trees, shrubs, and perennials are in place in your design, choose the annuals, which complete their life cycle in a single season and are grown primarily for their flowers. They bloom profusely for a long period if they are deadheaded regularly (although some of the newer cultivars do not require this maintenance), and they die when the weather gets cold. Many annuals that slow down during the summer come back stronger when fall temperatures moderate. Plants that northeasterners consider annuals are often perennial in warmer parts of the country. In San Francisco and San Diego, street medians are filled with the handsome bold evergreen foliage of *Agapanthus* (lily of the Nile), a plant we treat as an annual in the Northeast because it is not fond of cold winters. *Lantana* (shrub verbena), which we also use as an annual in the Northeast, covers banks of highways year-round in warmer places and is hardy in Texas and in South Carolina along the coast.

The most useful annuals are those that require less deadheading and are particularly long-blooming, with lots of flower color and not too much green foliage showing. I do not use *Catharanthus roseus* (Madagascar periwinkle or vinca), for instance, because it has many more leaves than flowers. One of the best-performing annuals in my gardens is the blue *Ageratum houstonianum* 'Blue Horizon' (floss flower), which grows to about eighteen inches in height; it looks like a perennial and works in just about every situation. *A. h.* 'Blue Horizon' is vastly superior to its low-lying cousins—the small common *Ageratum* varieties sold in many garden centers that tend to burn out as soon as the weather gets hot. The taller variety's one fault is that it looks blue to the human eye but often photographs pinker than it is, because of the amount of infrared in its pigments. Take this oddity into account if you are designing with "hot" colors—reds and oranges—and don't want pink in your photographs, which is why I didn't use it in the "hot" gardens at NYBG and Wagner Park.

Almost any sage (*Salvia*) will provide long-lasting color, but I caution against the overworked *S. splendens*, whose harsh red flowers call too much attention to themselves and are difficult to integrate into a design. As noted above, there are also many lovely perennial salvias, but annual salvias come in more colors and larger sizes.

I also recommend many annual flowering tobaccos, especially *Nicotiana mutabilis*, with its pink and white flowers, and *N. langsdorffii*, with tiny green flowers that look like bells. Tobacco flowers can survive some frost, so they are often the last annuals still blooming in the garden.

Tropical plants, with their exotic flowers and dramatic foliage, are best used as accents. My favorite tropical annual is the sculptural, dark-red-leaved *Cordyline australis* 'Red Sensation' (tropical cordyline), which stands out in a border and enhances all its neighbors. Among the many fine nonflowering annuals, the innumerable cultivars of *Solenostemon*, commonly known as coleus, are grown for their excellent foliage in a rainbow of colors. They require little maintenance, but if you want them to be at their very best you should remove their small flowers; pinching them back periodically during the growing season is also helpful, as it promotes fuller, bushier growth. Although sometimes overused in municipal plantings, *Canna* cultivars, long-blooming tropicals with striking foliage, are very effective if used with restraint and combined well with other plants. I love to use *C.* 'Pretoria' sparingly as an accent; with its lovely green-and-white striped leaves and orange flowers, it provides contrast in form and color, as does *C.* 'Australia' with its shiny dark red foliage and bright red flowers.

Garden pansies (*Viola* hybrids and cultivars) are popular and much-loved spring additions to public gardens and often the only annuals in bloom in the Northeast in late winter. In some areas they can be perennial, but they do not like hot weather. If they are particularly choice, try moving them to a shady spot and adding some compost; sometimes they

Well-named *Salvia* 'Indigo Spires', in the foreground, with its Mexican cousin *S. leucantha*, gets quite big by the end of the season.

All gardens benefit from the striking foliage that coleus provides. This excellent cultivar, called 'Red Carpet', is combined with another good annual, *Melampodium*.

Dahlias bloom profusely until hard frost if deadheaded regularly, providing reliable color in the border. This one is *Dahlia* 'Gingeroo'.

will naturalize—survive and spread themselves around. If your winters are reliably mild, you can plant them in fall and they will bloom through the winter months.

Dahlias, which are treated as annuals in cold climates, provide excellent summer color. Many thousands of different hybrids and cultivars are available in a myriad of colors and sizes of blooms. You can order big bushy plants in gallon-sized pots that start to perform immediately, or you can plant tubers right in the ground but give them lots of room to grow. I prefer the smaller-flowered dahlias, such as *Dahlia* 'Crossfield Ebony', a pom pom dahlia, and in my own garden I store the tubers over winter and plant them again in the spring.

Biennials

Biennials are another tool in the designer's paint box. As the name suggests, these plants take two years to complete their life cycle. They are generally small in the first year, and they bloom the second year. You can move the small first-year plants around where you want them, an enjoyable springtime task. Many biennials, such as *Digitalis* (foxglove), *Alcea* (hollyhock), and *Eryngium* (sea holly), will seed themselves around if you are lucky.

Bulbs

The addition of carefully chosen bulbs lengthens any garden's flowering season. Everyone knows how much tulips and daffodils lift the spirits after a long winter, and they grow practically everywhere in the country. Many of the most attractive companions to these spring bulbs are blue, such as *Muscari armeniacum* (grape hyacinth); if you plant them under shrubs, you will not see their spent leaves once other perennials appear in spring, but watch out for their habit of showing new seaweed-like foliage in fall. *Anemone blanda* (windflower), a small bulb with blue daisylike flowers, also combines well with daffodils and tulips. Tulips will look bedraggled the second year if you leave them in the ground, so in public places you should lift them after they bloom, giving you the opportunity to try a different tulip for the next year.

One trick to get lots of spring blue is to mix together tiny *Scilla siberica* (blue squill) and *Chionodoxa luciliae* (glory of the snow) for a long spring bloom period. For a large garden planting, put them together in a wheelbarrow and stir them like a good minestrone. The *Scilla* blooms first and is darker blue; *Chionodoxa* blooms a little later in lighter blue

Hollyhocks are show-stopping biennials that will reseed if you are lucky, as they did here in Bryant Park. They are prone to an unattractive leaf rust; the affected leaves may simply be removed. Photo by Joseph De Sciose.

with a white center. Together they will brighten a garden in the Northeast for about five weeks.

Allium (ornamental onion), closely related to garlic, is a fabulous addition to any mixed planting, blooming in late spring or early summer. Many varieties have beautiful big heads made up of many tiny starlike flowers, fascinating to look at through a magnifying glass; some, like *A. cristophii*, have spheres reminiscent of Buckminster Fuller's geodesic domes. The big pinkish-purple blooms of *A.* 'Globemaster' are striking as a repeated pattern. The beautiful dried flower heads will go to seed and then show up next year in unexpected places. Their only fault is that the foliage can look tatty just when the flowers are at their best, so either cut it back or plant these with perennials like *Nepeta* (catmint) to hide the offending leaves.

Summer-blooming bulbs are a great joy. I like to use groups of species lilies, such as orange *Lilium henryi*, *L. canadense*, and yellow *L. citronella*. The elegant white *L. speciosum* var. *album* blooms late in the summer in the Northeast.

Native Plants

An increasing number of people feel very strongly about using only native plants. But how do we define a "native" plant? Are plants the English colonists brought with them "foreign exotics"? Are plants from a different area of the country "foreign" to other regions?

Grape hyacinths and tulips make a fine combination; the blue complements the colors of the tulips. To my eyes, strong blue in spring goes with everything. Photo by Catherine L. Redd.

Visitors enjoy *Allium* 'Gladiator', a decorative member of the onion family, in the mixed plantings at Madison Square Park.

Aster 'Little Carlow' and *Boltonia asteroides* are both excellent native plants for public gardens.

This native *Hibiscus* is a spectacular much-loved addition to any garden or landscape.

However defined, a native plant is not necessarily a good choice for a public park. Many—*Podophyllum peltatum* (mayapple) and *Mertensia virginica* (Virginia bluebell), for example—are wonderful but ephemeral; that is, they die back after a spring blooming, leaving an empty space for the other ten months. *Monarda* (bee balm) regularly gets powdery mildew and looks unsightly. On the other hand, there are many fine native plants that I use a great deal in public garden design, including *Veronicastrum virginicum* (Culver's root), *Heliopsis helianthoides* var. *scabra* 'Prairie Sunset' (false sunflower, a cultivar of a native), and *Eupatorium purpureum* (Joe Pye weed), an excellent native plant if you have sufficient room for it and you cut it back after it blooms so it won't seed itself everywhere. And I can't imagine any garden without *Hydrangea quercifolia* (oakleaf hydrangea).

For the purposes of most general-use public space, there is something rigid and confining about the attitude that a garden should contain only native plants. If I have two equally good plants that are appropriate and attractive for a certain spot and one of them is a native, I will choose the native with pleasure. But I believe in the many advantages of a diverse plant palette and continue to delight in the delicious variety of new plants that become available to us each year. We are going through a period of exciting plant exploration, with wonderful new plants being discovered

A great botanical garden like NYBG displays a wide variety of plants from many parts of the world.

and imported from all parts of the world. By knowing plants' origins and the conditions under which they thrive, and by carefully evaluating the issues of aggressiveness and potential invasiveness, we are more likely to be successful in acclimatizing these new plants to our gardens. Let's hear it for what writer Michael Pollan calls "multihorticulturalism"![7]

Invasive Plants

Whether native or exotic, some plants can be invasive, restricting the growth of other plants as they spread. Pulling up the non-native *Alliaria petiolata* (garlic mustard) is a year-round chore, as it is evergreen where I live. *Lythrum salicaria* (purple loosestrife) is a real problem in the Northeast, as is *Polygonum perfoliatum* (mile-a-minute vine), which resembles the dreaded kudzu of the South. But I have also seen our native *Clematis virginiana* (devil's darning needles) take over an enormous area in open woodland, requiring a great deal of hard work to control. Poison ivy (*Toxicodendron radicans*), also a native, is not only dangerous because of its toxins but also extremely invasive.

Invasiveness varies in different parts of the country. *Ampelopsis brevipedunculata* (porcelain berry), a deceptively attractive vine with pretty foliage and shiny blue and purple berries, is extremely invasive in parts of New England, where it covers trees along the highway as if throwing a tarp over them. It is regrettably still sold in some New England nurseries without warnings. But it is apparently grown without harm in other regions.

As responsible gardeners, we must stay informed about invasive plants in our areas and do everything we can to rid our gardens of them. In many cases, the only alternative to using chemicals is to recruit volunteers to help pull out these plants.

Just because a plant is widespread, however, does not necessarily mean it is invasive. For my part, until they are proven dangerous to the environment in the Northeast, I will continue to enjoy the lovely combination of white *Daucus carota* (Queen Anne's lace) and blue *Cichorium intybus* (chicory) in the summer months along our roads and parkways.

Design Elements

In order to combine plants effectively, you must consider the many elements of successful design, along with the habit of each of the plants you

The thin blue foliage of *Helictotrichon sempervirens* contrasts with *Tulipa* 'Ballerina', against a *Berberis thunbergii* 'Crimson Pygmy' hedge. This arrangement contrasts form as well as color.

Hakonechloa macra 'Aureola' has thin yellow-green strappy leaves that contrast with the large smooth blue leaves of a hosta.

Two handsome sculptural annuals, *Canna* 'Pretoria' and *Cordyline australis* 'Red Sensation', contrast in both form and color.

have chosen and the various ways the plants work together to form a year-round composition.

Foliage Contrast

Most of my favorite plant combinations are based on contrast. Plants that contrast strongly in form or texture enhance one another and please the eye. Create contrast by juxtaposing large full plants against tall thin ones, sharp against soft foliage, bold shapes against tiny leaves, swordlike foliage against creeping.

Big leaves make big statements and bold contrasts. They provide scale and drama and can be enjoyed from a distance. Many garden plants have wispy, thin foliage that does not stand out until paired with large-leaved plants such as *Hydrangea*, *Hosta*, *Rodgersia*, *Ligularia*, *Darmera*, or the annual *Colocasia*. Color contrast is discussed below.

Repetition

A successful mixed border repeats plant groupings in a variety of ways, often in an alternating or asymmetrical rhythm that carries the eye around a garden. Repetition lends continuity to the design and gives the seemingly random placement of plants a stable underpinning. Plants

Repeated clumps of blue *Nepeta racemosa* 'Walker's Low' carry the eye along the paths by the waterfront at Red Hook.

A visitor admires the *Colocasia* (often called elephant's ears) at the entrance to Madison Square Park. The big leaves enhance all the other plants in the display and pull the composition together, and they can be seen easily from the cars going by.

Grasses are repeated along this "stony brook" at Stony Brook University. The form of the grasses also repeats the form of the falling water.

Repeating large groups of important plants holds a design together. *Hemerocallis* 'Poinsettia' is the element repeated here in NYBG's Perennial Garden.

repeated loosely here and there, with a changing rhythm, tie the border together from one end to the other. To achieve this, repeat large specimen shrubs, grasses, or groupings of outstanding long-blooming perennials such as *Sedum*, *Phlox*, *Alchemilla*, and *Heuchera* at different intervals.

While symmetrical repetition in too much of the border can be static and boring, it is useful to mark entrances and exits or at the corners of beds. Repeat rounded shrubs or vertical evergreens—for example, dark green arborvitae on either side of a gate—to provide additional structure and formality to the design. In NYBG's Perennial Garden, I repeated box balls, blue cypresses, and green clipped hedges on either side of the paths to punctuate transitions to new areas.

Form

Because so many plants in the garden form round mounds, vertical elements provide important contrast in a well-designed border. Two garden designers from the Pacific Northwest, Glenn Withey and Charles Price, have a wonderful image for this: "domes and minarets." My favorite shrub minarets—harder to find for the garden than rounds—include *Juniperus communis* 'Compressa' (common juniper), *Juniperus scopulorum* 'Wichita Blue' (rocky mountain Juniper), *Ilex crenata* 'Sky

Late-blooming yellow *Salvia madrensis* is the spire against the round mound of *Miscanthus sinensis* 'Gracillimus' in fall.

Foxglove, *Persicaria bistorta* 'Superba', and alliums are the minarets against many mounded forms at NYBG's Perennial Garden. The permanent minaret is a white *tuteur*, a wooden support for plants.

Pencil' (columnar Japanese holly), and *Thuja occidentalis* 'Smaragd' (emerald arborvitae). If climate permits, use the elegant dark green spires of *Cupressus sempervirens* (cypress). *Digitalis* (foxglove), *Verbascum* (mullein), the gray spiky spires of *Onopordum* (Scotch thistle), and *Kniphofia* (red hot pokers) all can be used as herbaceous minarets. For more examples, see the Plant Lists at the back of this book.

Line

People are attracted to ebullient, varied, and constantly evolving plants in a city park or garden. Lush plantings bring softer natural elements into a place, making it more accessible to the human experience. But if you design rich plantings, as I urge you to do, it is essential to establish a sharp edge against which these plantings can play. Sydney Eddison, a Connecticut gardener and garden writer, calls this "romantic abundance with crisp discipline." The interplay between the straight line and the curved is important; the sight of plants spilling out on to the pavement creates a gentle rhythm against the hard edge. If hedges are part of the design, they must be trimmed regularly, not only to allow visibility but also for aesthetics: sheared hedges provide a geometric underpinning to the design and structure and backing for the voluptuous shapes of the shrubs and perennials in front.

Plants spilling over the edge break the hard line of the curbing, as here in Bryant Park's mixed borders in 1994.

In the Conservatory Garden, hedges create essential sight lines that contain the exuberant plantings.

Provide sight lines and focal points in your garden as well. Rows of hedges, allées, and pathways draw people into a space and direct attention to what you want them to see. A bench, a large pot or garden ornament, a statue, or a specimen tree or shrub—any of these can become an effective focal point at the end of a pathway or line of sight.

Scale

The eye first reads a garden or mixed planting composition from a distance, so large groups of the same plant are essential to an effective design. Treat groups of different kinds of perennials as individual units in relationship to one another and to the ensemble. Perennials are most effective in groups of at least seven to nine of a kind, or more if you can manage it (odd-numbered groups are more dynamic visually than even numbers). In a larger landscape, groups might include as many as fifty to a hundred plants. Take care that groupings do not all have the same bulk—add to some groups and subtract from others, creating a varied composition. Near traffic areas, use big groups of plants that can be enjoyed as viewers drive past; little dribs and drabs are never satisfying in any landscape composition and would certainly never be noticed from a car. Christopher Lloyd, the great English gardener and writer and influential garden designer, often witheringly referred to little groups of scattered plants as "incidents." When in doubt, use more rather than less; you will rarely go wrong with big sweeps.

A large fat pot is the focus at the end of a straight path.

Color

Most visitors to a garden look for flower color first. They often want to know when the entire garden will be in bloom, a question that makes designers and gardeners who plan for year-round effect roll their eyes in mild exasperation. As I can never say too often, a well-designed garden will have something of interest through the year. A satisfying garden never has only one climax but a series of exciting moments, even in winter.

If you design with the color of foliage before the color of flowers, you will have much for your visitors to enjoy all year. Flowers are wonderful indeed, but many perennials bloom for only a few weeks. Color contrast of leaves and bark—in addition to contrasts in form and texture—is far more satisfying and long lasting than the fleeting flowers. I once heard the great English gardener and writer Beth Chatto say, "Flowers come and go but foliage is always with us."

In the garden, green is a color with many variations. These combinations of shades and shapes in the New York Botanical Garden's Perennial Garden are just as satisfying as flower color when you learn to look for them.

This delicious purple smoke bush in NYBG's Perennial Garden highlights the pale blue of *Geranium* 'Brookside' and various alliums.

Rich reds, like those at Prospect House Garden at Princeton, create patterns that help lead the eye around the design.

Dark Red Foliage. Dark red foliage is very effective in nearly any garden. As a painter, I know that dark reds are complementary to greens, and each color makes the other richer to the eye. More and more beautiful plants with dark red foliage come on the market every year. To add excitement, I use *Cotinus coggygria* 'Royal Purple' (purple smoke bush) and *Prunus* × *cistena* (purple-leaf sand cherry) whenever I can. Various cultivars of purple-leaved *Heuchera* (coral bells), crimson-leaved annuals such as *Solenostemon* 'Red Carpet' (coleus), *Alternanthera dentata* 'Rubiginosa' (alternanthera), and the splendid shrublike annual *Euphorbia cotinifolia* (red spurge)—these dark reds help carry the eye around a planting bed or along the front of a border.

Gray and Silver Foliage. Many cities are dulled by the pervasive gray of sidewalks, streets, and buildings. If your garden is to be an urban oasis, minimize gray. If the site is framed with grass, gray- or silver-leaved plants such as *Santolina* (lavender cotton), *Lavandula* (lavender), and *Artemesia* (wormwood) are fine elements to repeat along the edge of a full-sun planting; they are prized for their foliage rather than for their insignificant flowers. The one silver-gray plant I recommend you *always* make room for is the low soft fuzzy *Stachys byzantina* (lamb's ears). It particularly appeals to children, who enjoy feeling it and guessing its name.

Blues. Looking at blue makes you feel cooler, making blue one of the best foliage and flower colors for cities with hot summers. Shades of blue go with everything in the garden and enhance many other colors. By using lots of blue—with foliage or flowers—you can keep strong, vivid colors, such as bright reds and oranges, from being discordant.

Stachys byzantina, called "lamb's ears" for its irresistible soft leaves, appeals to the child in all of us.

Picea pungens 'Montgomery', a spiky dwarf blue spruce, contrasts with the soft yellow-green of *Amsonia hubrichtii* and the small red annual *Gomphrena* 'Strawberry Fields' at the New York Botanical Garden.

An excellent blue perennial is *Salvia* × *sylvestris* 'Blauhügel'. At Columbia University, it makes a striking contrast to the large blue leaves of *Hosta sieboldiana* and the delicate yellow foliage of *Spiraea thunbergii* 'Ogon'.

Shrubs and perennials with blue-green or blue-gray foliage, such as *Picea pungens* 'Glauca Globosa' (dwarf blue spruce), bring out the best in other plants in the border, especially when combined with dark red plants. The blue flowers of *Vitex agnus-castus* (chastetree) are showstoppers each year in the summer border. The shrub *Hibiscus syriacus* (rose-of-Sharon) can grow almost as large as a tree, and the beautiful form called BLUE BIRD is especially lovely; *H. s.* 'Blue Satin' is reputed to be an even finer form. *Hydrangea macrophylla* 'Nikko Blue' (bigleaf hydrangea), with its luscious fat flowers, adds summer blue to the garden.

Perennials such as *Platycodon* (balloon flower), *Adenophora* (ladybells), *Campanula* (bellflowers), and *Nepeta* (catmint) all provide lovely shades of blue. *Baptisia* (perennial wild indigo) has small blue flowers in spring and, more important, blue-green foliage through the growing season. For blue annuals, use tall *Ageratum houstonianum* 'Blue Horizon', the sun-loving *Browallia americana* (Jamaican forget-me-not), and blue sages such as *Salvia guaranitica*, *S.* 'Indigo Spires', and *S. guaranitica* 'Black and Blue'.

As I mentioned earlier, small blue bulbs—*Muscari armeniacum* (grape hyacinths), *Scilla siberica* (blue squill), *Chionodoxa luciliae* (glory of the snow), or *Anemone blanda* 'Blue Star' (windflower)—enhance tulips and daffodils.

Yellows. In my compositions, yellow (whether from flowers or foliage) sings a minor note to the major notes of both hot-color and cool-color designs, and I prefer pale yellow hues. For yellow blooms, use the lemon-yellow flowering shrub *Corylopsis pauciflora* (buttercup winterhazel), pale yellow perennial *Heliopsis helianthoides* var. *scabra* 'Prairie Sunset' (false sunflower) with its dark-red center, *Rudbeckia maxima* (great coneflower) with its huge gray leaves, *Hemerocallis* 'Happy Returns' (daylily), *Coreopsis verticillata* 'Moonbeam' (threadleaf coreopsis) if your soil is not too rich, and the annual *Nicotiana langsdorffii* (flowering tobacco). Particular favorites for yellow foliage are *Chamaecyparis pisifera* 'Golden Mop' (false cypress), *Spiraea thunbergii* 'Ogon' (meadowsweet), and the many yellow-leaved varieties of *Spiraea japonica* (Japanese spiraea), such as *S. j.* 'White Gold' and *S. j.* 'Golden Elf'. And I can't imagine a situation that is not improved by the wonderful structure and color of *Yucca filamentosa* 'Color Guard' or *Y. flaccida* 'Golden Sword' (variegated yucca) through the year.

A river of dark blue violas shows off this spectacular tulip display, designed by Sarah Carter Roberts for the New York Botanical Garden.

The yellow foliage of *Berberis thunbergii* 'Aurea' contrasts with the elegant blue of *Helictotrichon sempervirens* and a rich red coleus.

Yucca filamentosa 'Color Guard' adds excitement to this composition at Stony Brook University, with *Juniperus squamata* 'Blue Star' and *Pennisetum alopecuroides*.

Blues and oranges go together. Blue-gray *Perovskia atriplicifolia* shows off the spectacular hot colors of *Kniphofia*, *Helenium autumnale* 'Autumn Brilliant', and *Canna* 'Pretoria'. Photo by Joseph De Sciose.

The Hot Section in NYBG's Perennial Garden displays many different oranges, reds, and yellows, such as the aptly named *Croscosmia* 'Lucifer', whose delicate red flowers contrast with the coarser flat-topped flowers of *Achillea* 'Coronation Gold'.

The annual *Tithonia rotundifolia* 'Torch' is well named; here it holds its flame colors above other shrubs and perennials at Wagner Park.

Reds and Oranges. Over the years, I have come to love hot colors like reds and oranges in the garden, especially when combined with blue and dark red. Blues that work well for contrast include the perennial *Salvia* × *sylvestris* 'Blauhügel' ('Blue Hill' sage), *Nepeta* (catmint), and *Perovskia atriplicifolia* (Russian sage).

When you combine red flowers with other hot colors, choose "fire engine" or "pure" reds that have no blue cast. The bluer reds look better with pastel colors. *Crocosmia* × *latifolia* 'Lucifer' has exciting pure red flowers, as does *Lychnis chalcedonica* (Maltese cross). Among the many wonderful orange plants are the tall annual *Tithonia rotundifolia* 'Torch' (Mexican sunflower) or the short, almost-evergreen *Geum chiloense* cultivars (avens), with charming flowers in spring and attractive bright green foliage all year. I am enormously fond of various orange or red *Kniphofia* species (red hot pokers).

Pinks and Pastels. Generally, I use pastels as a separate palette and don't combine them in the same beds with hot colors. I especially like them with pink-flowering ornamental trees, such as crabapples and magnolias. Among the most versatile pinks are *Anemone tomentosa* 'Robustissima', *Geranium macrorrhizum*, *Helleborus* × *hybridus*, and *Nicotiana alata* 'Daylight Sensation'; deeper pinks for bolder effects include *Allium cristophii*, *Gomphrena* 'Lavender Lady', *Hibiscus moscheutos* 'Lady Baltimore', and *Persicaria bistorta* 'Superba'. See the Plant Lists for a more extensive list of pinks.

Plant Placement

Planting plans provide a guide to placement when it comes time to install the garden. But never hesitate to deviate from the plan as you lay out the design and see the plants before you; better and more exciting associations often arise on the spot.

Separating Annuals and Bulbs

For the future of the overall border design, it is important to plant bulbs and annuals separate from the perennials and shrubs; if they mingle too closely and in large numbers, the annuals and bulbs will eventually crowd out the perennials. (This arrangement is also easier to maintain.) In woodland or more naturalistic designs, scatter bulbs and leave them in place to spread themselves around.

In the Conservatory Garden, the annuals and bulbs are displayed in different beds than the perennials, with only a few choice ones tucked into the big mixed borders. Another approach is to make a formal arc of

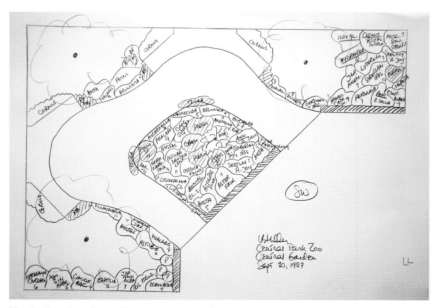

My planting plan shows the general layout of one of the quadrants of the garden at the Central Park Zoo.

In the Conservatory Garden, the annuals and bulbs in the foreground are in separate beds from the mixed borders in the background.
Photo by Joseph De Sciose.

Avoid planting annuals and bulbs in static rows; mix them to show off their many different qualities, as in the Conservatory Garden. *Artemisia* 'Powis Castle' (not a perennial in New York) is combined with the red-leaved annual grass *Pennisetum setaceum* 'Rubrum'.

evergreen *Liriope muscari* 'Big Blue' (lily turf) in the front of a bed and reserve it for the seasonal annuals and bulbs, as I did with the large mixed borders at the New York Public Library from 1992 to 2002. You could also use a low-growing boxwood, such as *Buxus* 'Green Velvet', for this purpose, and keep it sheared.

Lush Plantings

To give people pleasure and restore their faith in a once dangerous or neglected place, you must supply instant gratification. When plantings are sparse, people may walk on them by mistake. Get the best and biggest plants you can afford and plant them close together and in large groups to achieve an instant full effect. Chicago's magnificent gardens are planted with closely set annuals. Adam Schwerner, director of the Department of Natural Resources for the Chicago Park District, told

Chicago has gorgeous display gardens everywhere; the closely placed annuals are a delight for visitors.

me, "Plant them close and they will stretch up." He should know; he is responsible for many spectacular public garden displays around that beautiful city.

In public places, it's often best to ignore directions about leaving required distances between plants, at least in the beginning; plant with very little soil showing. (Generally, plant bulbs and small annuals six to eight inches apart and medium-sized perennials on nine- to twelve-inch centers, farther apart if the plants are larger. Shrubs need room, however, and they should be planted three to six feet on center, depending on how big they will ultimately get.) In the end, it is more cost-effective to make the garden look good right away so that people will visit and respect it. You can always remove extra plants in the future and use them elsewhere in your park or donate them to another public space.

Defensive Horticulture

When spectacular plants bloom, some people feel that they just have to step into the beds to get that perfect picture of the plant or put their relatives in among the plants for that perfect memento of the day. Hard-working gardeners frown upon such intrusions. In my experience, the plants most likely to attract this kind of attention are the lavish blooms of *Paeonia suffruticosa* (tree peony) in spring and the equally lavish summer blooms of our native perennial *Hibiscus moscheutos* (hardy hibiscus). As a preventive measure, position a bench or an extremely prickly plant, such as a shrub rose or a *Berberis thunbergii* 'Crimson Pygmy' (barberry), in front of places where visitors may want to step. In Battery Park City, *Rosa rugosa* keeps people from walking too close to the water's edge.

᪐

Train your eye for design by reading about plants and gardens and visiting as many gardens as you can. The Garden Conservancy, a national nonprofit organization, makes hundreds of private gardens all over the country accessible to the public almost every weekend from spring through fall (annual schedules are available at www.gardenconservancy.org/opendays). Visit botanical gardens as well, and tour public gardens with those who look after them. Take notes on what you like and what you don't.

Plants and gardens are always changing. Stand back regularly and evaluate the design, just as painters evaluate their work: does it remain effective, or does something need to be moved or removed? The poet Alexander Pope, who was a gardener as well, wrote to a friend in 1736, "My garden, like my life, seems to me every year to want correction and require alteration."[8] Plants will continually surprise you. A plant you were sure would be a success decides not to play with the team. Or perhaps a group of plants gets too big and must have its enthusiasm curbed.

Gertrude Jekyll, the influential English garden designer and writer, said, "It seems to me that the duty we owe to our gardens . . . [is] to use the plants that they shall form beautiful pictures; and that, while delighting our eyes, they should be always training those eyes to a more exalted criticism; to a state of mind and artistic conscience that will not tolerate bad or careless combination or any sort of misuse of plants, but in which it becomes a point of honour to be always striving for the best."[9]

4

Soil

Before you can feed the soul, you have to fix the soil.
—Monte Powell, Seattle gardener and developer

Shortly before Christmas in 1990, when I was trying to choose the best soil for the beds in Bryant Park, I received a small brown package in the mail. I decided it was undoubtedly a present from a relative and put it under the tree without opening it. On Christmas morning I opened it to find several samples of dark rich soil from the soil contractor for Bryant Park, who had sent them for my consideration. I imagine I was the only woman in New York that Christmas morning who was delighted to find a package of dirt under her tree.

Nothing is more important to the success of any garden, public or private, than the soil. Without good healthy soil, no garden will ever thrive. It might limp along, but it won't thrive. Echoing a campaign slogan of the past, a sign over my desk declares, "It's the Soil, Stupid."

The importance of good soil has been understood for many thousands of years. In his *Natural History*, published in 77 AD, Pliny the Elder wrote, "It pays to choose soil of the highest quality."[1] The soil is the first thing to evaluate when beginning work on a public park or garden. To start, pick up a handful, squeeze it, and smell it. Ideally it should be dark brown and smell fresh, and it should make a ball in your hand when you squeeze it. If the soil is in good condition, your hands will hold millions of invisible useful microorganisms, more than there are people on the face of the planet. Most urban soils are a far cry from this ideal.

The most visible organisms in good soil are worms, so greet them warmly. Worms thrive in healthy soil, and their travels through the soil

Just above the Conservatory Garden is Central Park's area for producing compost and mulch to use all over the park. Gardeners call this beautiful soil "black gold."

The soil in every public space I have worked on has called for immediate and serious attention. Before restoration in 2000, the soil in Madison Square Park looked like gray face powder, and there was little growing there.

It was hard work making holes for plants in Madison Square Park's compacted soil.

After the planting was complete, the whole park was mulched with compost.

help to break it up and keep it aerated. They also provide entertainment for city children.

In every public space I have renovated, the soil has needed immediate and serious attention. At Columbia University we discarded two feet of what could only generously be called "dirt"—it was light brown and full of pieces of metal, concrete, and plastic, the result of years of neglect. At the Broadway Malls, the soil was so compacted that only rats could live there; when it rained, water would either puddle or run off into the street.

The soil at Madison Square Park was even worse, so depleted of organic matter that it looked like gray face powder and so compacted by the feet of generations of city dwellers, pigeons, and squirrels that there was not enough pore space for oxygen, water circulation, or root expansion. Virtually nothing was growing there but a few fine old trees whose roots presumably reached deep enough to find some nourishment. Because I was called in late in the process to landscape the park, there was not enough time between the end of construction and the scheduled opening to address the soil conditions. The twenty thousand shrubs and perennials I ordered began to arrive and had to be planted as soon as possible. The ground was so hard that the landscape contractor's strong men used pickaxes to make holes for the plants. To compensate, we put compost, an organic fertilizer, and a root enhancer in each planting hole, and after we had finished the installation we spread two to three inches of compost as a mulch over the entire park. Adding compost this way remedied the terrible soil conditions, and a year later the soil was like butter.

The most common problems with urban soil are compaction, lack of organic matter, poor drainage, and lack of nutrients. To correct these problems, analyze the quality of the soil and make adjustments. The first step is to examine the soil by hand; the second is to have it tested. Although it takes effort and a small expense, this is an important step in ensuring the long-term success of your efforts. Each state has an extension service that will explain the procedure for taking samples and provide a detailed analysis of soil quality; private companies also perform this service. Read the test results carefully. They often look quite complicated, but some test centers will assist you in interpreting them. The most important things you will learn are the amount of organic matter present in the soil and its pH (that is, whether it is acid or alkaline). The report also gives the nutrient content of the soil and may provide addi-

Bagged soil samples from the Conservatory Garden are ready to go to the lab for testing.

tional information as well. The results will help you determine which plants will do well in the existing soil conditions and what is needed to amend the soil for optimum conditions for your plants.

Everything is connected. If the soil is compacted, lacks organic matter, and drains poorly, it will seriously narrow your plant choices. When you are choosing plants, consider where the plant originated in nature for clues to its soil requirements. For example, many gray-leaved plants, such as *Santolina* (lavender cotton) and *Artemesia* (wormwood), which hail from the Mediterranean, grow naturally in hot, dry, sandy soil among rocks, sometimes along the sea. It was no surprise that they did not like the rich, composted soil at the Conservatory Garden; they soon deteriorated and within about a year had disappeared completely. If your site has naturally damp soil, choose plants that will tolerate such moist soils, such as willows, hydrangeas, dogwood shrubs, and hostas. (See the Recommended Reading section at the back of this book for books that provide information on plant origins.) While you certainly can (and should) amend soil in order to improve it, it is almost always easier, more cost effective, and more environmentally sound to adjust your plant palette to the soil than to try to change the soil substantially.

Depending on the results of the soil test and the plants you have chosen for your site, you may amend the soil in any number of ways to relieve compaction, poor drainage, or nutrient deficiencies. In my experience, the addition of compost has always been the most beneficial course of action to address any of these issues.

Farmers have been adding organic matter to their fields for millennia by spreading manure; Pliny mentions it in his *Natural History*. Elizabeth von Arnim, author of *Elizabeth and Her German Garden* (one of my favorite books, first published anonymously in 1898), wrote, "The longer I live the greater is my respect and affection for manure in all its forms."[2] If she had known the word *compost* she would have used it. Compost can be made in many different ways. Different types of organic plant matter are blended, brought up to about a 50 percent moisture level, and infused with air to begin the composting process, which is the decomposition of the organic matter by microbes such as bacteria and fungi.

Adjust the mix of organic matter to match the needs of the plants being grown. A more fungal compost is good for trees and shrubs; a compost with more bacterial content is good for perennials, annuals, and bulbs. Generally speaking, compost made from fallen leaves will add more fungi to the soil; compost made from the foliage of perennials, grass clippings (in moderation), and other garden waste will encourage bacteria. Incorporate compost into the existing soil before planting or, if this is not possible, spread it as a mulch after planting is complete as we did in Madison Square Park.

My motto: *When in doubt, throw compost at it.*

As I mentioned in chapter 1, before Betsy Rogers founded the Central Park Conservancy, the leaves from 26,000 trees were being removed from the park every fall at considerable cost to New Yorkers—just because it had always been done that way. One of the first things the Conservancy did was to set aside an area of the park where fall leaves could be left to break down into the fine composted leaf mold that is now used all over the park for planting and mulching. By great good fortune, that operation is right above the Conservatory Garden, so we have always had access to this wonderful stuff. What goes on there is huge and exciting: workers shred bark and leaves and turn the mammoth piles with an excavator every two months. One positive development in public parks and gardens is that more and more municipalities are making compost for their parks and for local citizens, especially as they come to understand its benefits.

So no matter how large or small your project, don't rake up all the leaves and take them away. The best thing you can do for the future of your garden is to designate a nearby area to make a compost pile. If you encounter opposition (some people believe, wrongly, that compost attracts rats), post an informative sign to help educate the public. What belongs in your compost pile is shredded leaves, a few grass clippings (not too many or the compost will smell), and the cleanup debris from nonwoody plants throughout the season. Keep your pile aerated by turning it over every few weeks or whenever you can; this helps to speed the composting process. You can learn more about making compost from botanical gardens, community gardens, and master gardener programs. Many other resources, both on the Internet and in print, give detailed instructions and explanations of the science behind this gardening miracle. (See the Resource Directory and the Recommended Reading section.)

The soil you need may be beneath your feet. When excavating under the two-acre lawn area of Bryant Park to create stack space for the New York Public Library, restoration crews dug a very big hole—thirty-two feet deep. When soil experts from the Central Park Conser-

Set aside a place in your garden or park to make compost. You will need bins for turning and aerating, like those shown here at the New York Botanical Garden.

vancy came to look at it, they ran their fingers through the rich dark stuff in wonderment, thinking it was the very best soil they had ever seen. Over the years, the decomposing of millions of leaves that had dropped from Bryant Park's tall, arching plane trees had vastly enriched the soil. But the construction team did not recognize its value, and it was trucked out of the park and never seen again. Some years later, when I was creating the two 300-foot borders that flank the great lawn, it cost $80,000 to buy 750 cubic yards of specially made soil with lots of organic matter to fill the beds. Fortunately, the new soil was excellent and the plants have thrived.

Because the excellent soil in Bryant Park was discarded during construction, we had to order specially made soil to suit the plants.

The soil for Wagner Park in Battery Park City was ordered to the same specifications as that used successfully in Bryant Park, yet after a week or so, the healthy plants began to turn alarmingly yellow. It turned out that the supplier had followed the wrong soil specifications; the soil contained very little organic matter and a lot of sand, and it had a low pH. It was not appropriate for the shrubs and perennials we were growing. The Battery Park City Conservancy, which manages the landscape there, treated the soil with horticultural lime and compost, and mercifully the plants revived in time for the opening that fall.

The foundation for the projects at Stony Brook University required two types of soil for two different kinds of plants. "Soil A," with 6–8 percent organic matter, was ordered for the lawns, and "Soil B," with a higher organic content of 12–15 percent, for the mixed planted areas. The two formulas have proven very effective and are now being used in many projects in the New York area.

Monitor soil sources carefully. Suppliers may call something "compost," but what do they mean by that? Beware of those who propose bringing in "topsoil." This is a loose term that can mean just about anything from anywhere. It could be wonderful rich stuff, or it could come from a construction site, a landfill, or just the side of a road somewhere. When ordering soil for a job, use a reputable contractor, always check the source, and carefully detail specifications for the pH and amount of organic matter.

If you buy a large amount of soil, make sure you get what you ordered. The soil should be inspected before it leaves the site of origin and again when it arrives to confirm that the good stuff wasn't dropped off somewhere else and inferior topsoil substituted. Have samples sent to you and have them tested. At the very least, examine the soil to get a feel for what it looks like, or test the pH with a kit you can purchase. If you

Nothing is more important to the success of any garden, public or private, than the soil. Good soil, as used here in NYBG's Perennial Garden, produces good healthy plants.

order compost, the same rules apply: purchase it from a reputable source and be sure you know its content and pH. The best way to ensure the quality of compost is to make your own.

Soil science is developing rapidly, with new information available nearly every day. Designers of public spaces need to know as much about soil as they can. For instance, the latest research seems to suggest that the benefits of adding compost and increasing the number of beneficial microorganisms in the soil make it inadvisable to rototill regularly or unnecessarily disturb the soil once you have improved it. (See the Resource Directory for information on the soil food web.) This is great news for those of us who were told for many years that we should do the hard work of digging and "stirring" soil as much as possible. "Compost tea" is also gaining popularity in public horticulture. Many organizations in New York, including the Central Park Conservancy, the New York Botanical Garden, and Battery Park City, are experimenting with this liquid biological soil amendment brewed from good compost in an aerated tank of water with the addition of microbial foods. The process produces a "tea" full of beneficial organisms that improve the biology of the soil. Some people swear by it; others are still waiting to see the long-term results.

You can learn more about soil, its properties, and ways of amending it from many different organizations and resources. Contact your state or county cooperative extension service, easily found via an Internet search, or take a course at your local botanical garden. Visit the USDA's Web site for its Natural Resources Conservation Service, at www.nrcs.usda.gov, for a treatment of this topic. (See the Resource Directory for details.)

The most important ingredients in a successful garden—public or private—are an effective design implemented with the best soil and plants you can afford. Now you must take care of what you have created.

Maintenance

It is not graceful and it makes one hot, but it is a blessed sort of work, and if Eve had had a spade in Paradise and had known what to do with it, we should not have had all that sad business of the apple.

—*Elizabeth von Arnim*, Elizabeth and Her German Garden

A successful public garden is one that is well maintained. Developing the design, preparing the soil, and installing the best plants for the site are the first steps in a long-term process. The most vital thing I have learned in my years of restoring and designing public places is that if you make it beautiful, they will come. But you must also keep it that way. If you don't, all the benefits gained will soon be lost.

Clients often assume that the job is finished once the garden has been installed. When the borders in Bryant Park were finished, I urged the Bryant Park Restoration Corporation to hire an accomplished gardener to work with me to maintain them. Because the garden was something of an afterthought in the long evolution of the park's restoration, the budget did not provide for garden maintenance. The BPRC thought that gardeners wouldn't be necessary; I could just "come down every once in a while and take care of the garden." Fortunately, from the funds raised to install the garden I had set aside enough to hire a gardener for the first season. After that, the park's budget for horticulture grew steadily, and it now supports the work of five gardeners who care for nearby Herald Square and Greeley Square as well.

At the end of the day, a landscape, garden, or park is only as good as the maintenance it gets. To thrive in the city, it must survive insult and injury: pigeons, squirrels, rats, pollution, wind, salted snow, dogs,

Keeping gardens beautiful attracts visitors, who will in turn help keep them safe.

drought, blowing trash, and many footsteps. This is a lot to ask. But if the plants are well cared for, people will respect the plantings; they won't step on them and will even offer to help with maintenance chores. On the other hand, an uncared-for public space will quickly become unkempt and overgrown, leading to the social problems that so often beset public parks and gardens.

Preserving the Spirit of the Design

Experience has taught me the importance of establishing long-term relationships with clients in order to oversee maintenance after a project is installed. I advise designers not to take on a project of any kind—especially a public project—unless the client makes a commitment for maintenance. Ask for a contract or find a relationship that will allow your continued involvement for at least two years after installation, with services that include visiting frequently, keeping in touch with the staff, supporting and training the gardener(s), helping to order new plants, and ensuring that the goal of the original design endures.

The Importance of a Good Gardener

An essential element of garden maintenance is hiring a first-rate gardener, one with enthusiasm, energy, and a knowledge and love of plants. How does a gardener walk and move? A quick, determined step is a positive sign. Knowledge is important, but enthusiasm can be more so. Individuals who love plants and nature can learn more about the plants they will care for. Many people pursue horticulture as a second career, as I did, and this can be a major asset. Not only are these people more mature, but they also bring expertise from other areas. Many of the best gardeners I know have had some artistic training. In the best of all possible worlds, a gardener should have experience both with plants and with design.

Urban gardeners need considerable determination to persevere. I once visited a valiant New York Parks Department gardener who cared for a twenty-five-acre park in a poor area with only two water sources and one rather unstable fellow employee. When I asked him how he could succeed under these conditions, he replied cheerfully that he had

Every public garden needs an accomplished, knowledgeable, and energetic horticulturist. Diane Schaub has been curator of the Conservatory Garden for many years. Photo by Sara Cedar Miller.

been in the Peace Corps. I understood perfectly. That experience and a love of plants seem to be great qualifications for an urban gardener. Some courageous gardeners, also Peace Corps veterans, are doing amazing work with the New York Horticultural Society teaching horticulture to prisoners at Rikers Island, a large detention center in New York City.

Finding well-trained gardeners to maintain public spaces is not easy. The public sector has a great need for more experienced hands and for more horticultural training programs like Longwood Garden's Graduate Program in Public Horticulture (offered with the University of Delaware) and the New York Botanical Garden's School of Professional Horticulture.

A good gardener is someone to be respected and compensated generously. One of the reasons it can be difficult to find gardeners for public places is that they are often not paid enough. Knowing how to grow and maintain plants is a skill, and living and working in a city is expensive, so treasure and reward those who work to beautify our public parks and gardens. Pay your gardener a fair wage.

Gardeners interact with the public daily, and they represent the group or institution who hired them. Provide them with some kind of identifying uniform, even if it is only a T-shirt with the name of the garden on it. Identification is especially important if you are restoring a public garden that needs to regain the public's trust.

Uniforms encourage visitors to ask questions and to tell the gardeners how much they appreciate their hard work. Photo by Sara Cedar Miller.

Horticultural techniques are constantly evolving, so it pays to offer your staff ongoing opportunities to improve their skills and knowledge. Local universities, botanical gardens, and agricultural extension programs are all good sources for training. The New York City Parks Department sends its gardeners to master gardening classes at the Brooklyn Botanic Garden and to forestry training at the New York Botanical Garden. Gardeners who work at NYBG are allowed ten field-trip days a year to visit other gardens and parks, to educate their eyes and learn new plants and techniques. The Central Park Conservancy provides courses for its staff on many facets of horticulture. The Conservancy also collaborates with Cornell University to offer an urban ecology and horticulture training program for parks professionals and volunteers. I encourage the gardeners I work with to meet often with one another to exchange ideas and plants, which is also great fun. (See the Resource Directory to find a master gardener program in your region.)

If the maintenance of your park is provided by an outside contractor, as is often the case at universities and in cities, work closely with them and encourage best maintenance practices (described below). Many landscape crews include very experienced planters and caretakers who will respond positively to your emphasis on quality horticulture. After talking with civic and parks groups around the country, I learned that some of the cities with the greatest success in beautifying their public parks, streets, and gardens outsource growing, planting, and in some cases maintaining their parks and plantings. The outside source is usually a landscape contractor, who has to submit a bid and conform to high standards to win the contract. This approach can save money and, if standards are kept high, deliver quality results.

Effective Management

A traditional approach to maintaining parks is with roving crews that travel to various parks within a city system, visiting each section only occasionally. This system does not allow individual gardeners to bond with a place or its visitors or to feel directly responsible for the condition of a particular park. No matter how big or small a public space, it benefits from having dedicated personnel who remain there, in uniform and recognizable to the public.

The Central Park Conservancy has developed an innovative system for maintaining the park's 843 acres. It has divided the park into 49 different zones, each maintained by at least one "zone gardener," trained in horticulture and responsible for the management and maintenance of his or her zone. Thus, the gardeners know many of the people who visit their areas and, equally important, the visitors know them. Parkwide crews assist the zone gardeners in many aspects of park maintenance, including tree, bench, and playground care, graffiti removal, monument conservation, soil conservation, and water management. The zone gardeners also supervise a group of regular volunteers. In this system, the individual gardener matters: each has direct accountability and enjoys pride of ownership. This zone system is much more effective than roving crews. Buffalo, New York, has implemented this system in its parks, as has Golden Gate National Park in San Francisco, and it is now being applied to the management of many other public parks around the country.

Another growing trend for parks is consolidating horticultural maintenance into an independent department, separate from other forms of maintenance such as sanitation and caring for the general grounds. This arrangement improves morale by allowing skilled horticulturists to focus their efforts on the work for which they are trained.

Plant Selection

Another essential element of garden maintenance is selecting appropriate plants for your site. Plant selection affects the degree of maintenance a garden will need, but no matter what nursery catalogs may say, there is no such thing as a maintenance-free garden. Some plants, however, are lower maintenance than others. You should design for the most practical degree of maintenance possible, depending on the site, the budget, and the available labor.

Maintenance should never be the only criterion for selecting plants. Public gardens are for sharing the beauties of nature with visitors, so always use the best-quality plants. Landscapes endure when the right plant is in the right place. The term *sustainable* is used a great deal these days to cover a multitude of important issues, but sustainability in a public garden can mean choosing the best plants to survive and thrive under the conditions of the site, without undue use of chemicals or fertilizers, and with the level of maintenance available. For urban landscapes in particular, the right plant is one that is beautiful in at least three seasons—if not all four—with dependable color, texture, or form. Choosing the right plants for a particular urban situation takes trial and error, experience, and an open mind for new ideas.

The following are tried and true plants that I use not only for their contribution to good design but also for their low maintenance demands.

Helleborus x *hybridus* (Lenten rose) is one of the best plants for gardens throughout most of the United States, and I use it in nearly all my designs. It can be left to go to seed; additional hellebores spreading through the garden are always a bonus. The flowers come early and the foliage remains attractive until the end of winter. The plant's only requirement is that you cut off the damaged leaves early in spring so the emerging flowers can be seen and enjoyed; in New York this happens in late February. New shiny foliage soon appears. Although it is often said that hellebores belong in the shade, I have found that they can survive in partial sun as well. Hellebores make excellent choices for sites that need early-blooming plants, such as schools and universities.

This garden visitor is getting right down to admire the hellebores in the Conservatory Garden.

Variegated yuccas, such as *Yucca filamentosa* 'Color Guard', are handsome low-maintenance plants all year.

Dryopteris erythrosora is a good ground cover, reddish in spring and virtually evergreen in winter.

Hakonechloa macra 'Aureola', shown in a large planting in Battery Park City, is a splendid yellow-leaved grass for sun or shade, as a specimen or a groundcover.

Another extremely low-maintenance plant that I love to use in my designs is the variegated *Yucca flaccida* 'Golden Sword', or *Y. filamentosa* 'Color Guard', which is more upright. (I am not a fan of the straight species, the plain bluish *Y. filamentosa*, which gets very large and can be difficult to remove.) These tough plants look handsome all year and are happy anywhere they get enough sun. Though yuccas appear to be tropical, they are actually at their most spectacular and useful during the winter months. They need very little attention, although I sometimes cut off the ungainly white flowers, which seem to weaken the plant. Yuccas and their relatives grow well in much of the United States.

Most sedums and daylilies are low-maintenance perennials, as are ferns. *Dryopteris erythrosora* (autumn fern), named for its reddish spring growth, is lush, full, and green for most of the year. I recommended it for the sculpture garden at the Museum of Modern Art, where it adds color in winter. As long as the soil is good, it requires little care. The beautiful *Hakonechloa macra* 'Aureola' (golden Japanese forest grass) and the shiny evergreen *Euphorbia amygdaloides* var. *robbiae* (Robb's euphorbia) are also attractive all year long.

For a perennial that provides dark red accents, I love to use *Heuchera* 'Plum Pudding' (coral bells). Its foliage does not turn orange in the summer sun, and it usually retains its leaves all winter. Its flowers are incon-

Two undemanding stalwarts are *Hosta plantaginea* and *Heuchera* 'Plum Pudding'. They can be used effectively in sun or in shade for contrast of color and texture.

spicuous. It pairs well with hostas, and both require little maintenance. Hundreds of other *Heuchera* cultivars in many foliage colors are available today.

For shady spots *Polygonatum odoratum* var. *pluriflorum* 'Variegatum' (variegated Solomon's seal), with its tiny white bells and green and white leaves, is attractive in any design and needs little care to look its best. Its leaves turn a lovely honey color in fall. Though slow to establish, it is worth the wait.

Around the building that houses the café at the New York Botanical Garden, the palette consists mostly of shrubs, particularly evergreens, for the winter months, including green and variegated hollies, *Skimmia japonica* (Japanese skimmia), *Hydrangea quercifolia* (oakleaf hydrangea), the red winter buds of *Pieris japonica* 'Dorothy Wyckoff' (Japanese pieris), and the choice low-growing *Rhododendron* 'Boule de Neige' and *R.* 'Dora Amateis'. Perennials provide ground cover, with only a few white annuals by the entrance (the white shows up well for visitors at evening events). After more than a dozen years, this garden remains a very easy landscape to maintain, requiring just a little pruning and mulching and the yearly addition of a few carefully chosen bulbs and annuals.

The little city park at 97th Street and Park Avenue receives virtually no maintenance, so I had to choose especially tough plants. Faithful performers include *Yucca filamentosa* 'Color Guard' (variegated yucca), which stands cheerfully tall with its sharp yellow and green leaves through the year, and a low hedge of *Buxus* 'Green Velvet' covering the base of an ugly concrete seating wall. The shiny evergreen foliage of *Prunus laurocerasus* 'Otto Luyken' (cherry laurel) contrasts with the yellow thin-leaved *Spiraea thunbergii* 'Ogon' (meadowsweet). The fat green leaves and blue and pink flowers of *Hydrangea macrophylla* 'Endless Summer' (bigleaf hydrangea) and the white flowers and oak-shaped leaves of my beloved *Hydrangea quercifolia* (oakleaf hydrangea) are planted in both sun and shade; the latter's dark red leaves looking splendid in fall with the sturdy, handsome *Hosta plantaginea* (plantain lily). For plants with effective foliage and flowers, I chose *Nepeta racemosa* 'Walker's Low' (catmint) and the very resilient *Geranium macrorrhizum* (a cranesbill collected on the slopes of Mount Olympus) for the sunny areas. The dark red *Heuchera* 'Plum Pudding' (coral bells) provides color even in winter. For the park's opening, we added *Rosa* Knock Out 'Radrazz' with *Cornus alba* 'Elegantissima' (red-stemmed variegated dogwood), and the roses bloomed with no care until cut down by a hard

Polygonatum odoratum var. *pluriforum* 'Variegatum' is elegant in three seasons in shady spots, and it needs no care. It combines well with *Hakonechloa*, *Hosta*, and *Yucca*.

This planting around the café at the New York Botanical Garden is mostly evergreen and has proved to require very little maintenance.

The plants at 97th Street and Park Avenue had to be as low-maintenance as they come, because they get little care. Some of the tough plants next to a low box hedge are *Heuchera* 'Plum Pudding', *Hydrangea quercifolia* 'Snow Queen', *Spiraea thunbergii* 'Ogon', and *Hydrangea macrophylla* 'Endless Summer'.

Geranium macrorrhizum has wonderful evergreen foliage and pink or white flowers. It will control weeds by covering the ground entirely.

frost in late November. No annuals are used in this park, but daffodil bulbs send up flowers through the always reliable perennial ground cover *Euonymus fortunei* 'Coloratus' (purple wintercreeper euonymus). The park is mulched in spring with several truckloads of compost to feed the soil and retain moisture.

Year-Round Maintenance

Gardening is as much about process as product. Plants grow and change; taking good care of a garden requires constant vigilance. I have never stood back and said, "That's it," and walked away. When I have felt that things looked just right at a given moment, I have often said to the plants, "Okay now, stop growing and stay that way," but they don't listen. No garden is ever truly finished.

The typical maintenance routine of a good gardener—aided by seasonal help and volunteers—includes some tasks that must be done at a specific point in the growing season and others that are ongoing or performed at regular intervals. The list of topics I discuss in the following sections can be modified to address the complexity of the plantings, and choosing the right plants for the right place can reduce or eliminate some of these tasks, but most of them are necessary to some degree to adequately maintain an urban public space.

Spring Cleanup

In spring, the garden needs to be rid of the ravages of winter. Wait until the soil has warmed a bit before you step into the beds to work; cold wet soil compacts easily underfoot, diminishing essential pore space. If it is absolutely necessary to work in the garden early, put down wooden boards and step on them rather than stepping onto cold soil; they will protect the soil from compaction by distributing your weight over a wider area.

Most perennials left standing over the winter for their attractive foliage, such as sedums or ornamental grasses, should be cut to the ground in spring. Add these cuttings to your compost heap. This is also the time of year to thin out the brown stems of the lovely, very useful *Cornus alba* 'Elegantissima' (red-stemmed variegated dogwood); cut these to the ground and the plant will replace the brown with new bright red.

The gardener at NYBG's Perennial Garden is taking out the old brown stems of *Cornus alba* 'Elegantissima' in early spring to encourage new red growth. He is protecting the spring soil by kneeling on a board.

When ornamental grasses first became popular in this country, they were marketed as maintenance-free. This is false advertising. Most ornamental grasses need to be cut back in early spring—or sooner if snow has caused them to collapse—and cutting them down can be a major undertaking, especially if you have a great number of large grasses. To lighten the load, two people should do the job—one to hold the grasses in a clump and one to cut them. Know what type of grass you have, as the timing and technique for cutting back varies according to whether the grass is "cool-season," "warm-season," or evergreen. For example, cutting *Helictotrichon sempervirens*, the lovely blue oat grass, will usually kill it in climates where it is evergreen. Instead, in spring just run your fingers through the blue foliage as though you were combing its hair; the dead brown leaves will come away and it will grow and fill out as the weather warms up.

As you cut back grasses, you may need to spade around the edges of the area to keep them from spreading beyond their bounds. Unfortunately, grass clumps will eventually die out in the middle, requiring division. For large grasses, it may be necessary to dig them out using a pick-ax or mattock, and cut through their dense root balls with a chainsaw. Some ornamental grasses, like *Miscanthus sinensis* (maiden grass), can

Ornamental grasses are not maintenance-free, as they may need staking and dividing. Cut them down when they collapse in winter.

Beautiful *Helictotrichon sempervirens*, seen here with the annual *Gomphrena* 'Strawberry Fields', should never be cut back—just comb out its dead blades with your fingers in the spring.

also be invasive in certain parts of the country. As I have said before, know your local environment. Use grasses that are appropriate for your space and for the labor you have at hand.

A word of caution: While you are spring cleaning, mark the location of perennials that will emerge later in spring, such as *Platycodon grandiflorus* (balloon flower) and *Anemone* x *hybrida* (Japanese anemone), and avoid stepping on their delicate new shoots. If you mark the locations with a label or a stick when you cut them back in fall, you will be able to spot them easily.

Planting and Replanting

After the initial garden installation is complete, planting will continue in each season as you add new selections or replace those that die, are stolen, or must be removed for some reason. Try not to leave holes for the public to see and seize as opportunities to step into the beds. Replace plants as soon as possible or tidy the space and encourage foliage to fill the hole so that the empty spot looks intentional.

Many shrubs and perennials will get established better if you plant them in early spring, before heat, humidity, and possibly drought set in. Plants that are flowering during this time are exceptions to the rule, as it is often best to avoid transplanting when a plant is focusing its energy on flowering. Generally, though, container plants can be planted at any time, as long as you improve the soil first and then water them well. I always think of the great English garden writer Christopher Lloyd saying that the best time to do these things is when you can do them best.

If plants are in containers, water them before planting, but allow them to drain; they should be moist, not wet, when planted. Carefully cut open congested root balls with hand pruners and loosen or "tease" the roots so they can grow out into the soil. I usually knock off some of the potting soil before I plant perennials, which helps the plant adapt to its new soil surroundings more quickly. Generally, the planting depth should be the same as it was in the container; there are exceptions, however, and you should learn your plants' needs in advance. Before watering in a plant, press the soil down firmly to eliminate air pockets and help the roots establish contact with the soil.

Plant Protection

Although fencing is often necessary around new plantings to keep people from stepping on them before they get established, there are few things uglier in a public park (or anywhere) than the familiar orange plastic mesh, wooden snow fencing, or chain link fencing, all unsightly and unfriendly. Don't use them.

Black wire mesh fencing is more attractive and useful. Basically chicken wire coated with black vinyl or PVC, it comes in a number of different gauges and heights. It appears throughout Central Park, usually in 21-gauge thickness, and has been used effectively at both Columbia and Stony Brook universities. Because passersby can see through it, it allows you to share improvements with the public while politely keeping them at a distance to spare the plants. Unobtrusive yet neat, it can be attached to any existing pipe-rail fencing, which stabilizes it and eliminates the need for extra posts. Another option is hoop fencing, an elegant way to protect established plantings in gardenlike settings.

Snow removal is often a problem in northern cities and may necessitate winter protection for garden beds. A good snow cover actually insulates your plantings, but heavy snow can bend branches and crush smaller plants, and the salt used to clear streets and sidewalks stresses and eventually kills most plants. Most municipalities use some kind of salt on their streets, although some of the newer snow- and ice-removal products are less corrosive and more environmentally friendly. In city parks, snow and ice must be removed immediately for public safety on slippery walkways; if the crews are not gardeners, they will often apply salt to the paths and then plow the salt-saturated snow into the garden beds. If they cannot be persuaded to change this practice, install burlap fencing between the snow blower and the plants to protect the garden or choose relatively salt-tolerant plants, such as *Hosta*, *Geranium*, *Helleborus orientalis*, or *Sedum spectabile* autumn joy, for the front of the beds.

Pruning

Since shrubs and small ornamental trees are the backbone of a good design, maintain their form and structure by pruning them when necessary. Many of these woody plants will need a "haircut" each year—some more than once.

For many shrubs and trees, late winter or early spring is a good time to prune; many plants are dormant during this time, and you can easily see the shape of the plant before it leaves out. But plants that form their flower buds in the previous growing season (those that bloom on "old wood")—*Corylopsis* (winter hazels), *Hamamelis* (witch hazels),

Unobtrusive black mesh fencing protects the plantings of *Hakonechloa macra* 'Aureola' in Madison Square Park and still allows the public to see and enjoy them.

Public plantings may need protection from salt in winter, especially on campuses. Stony Brook University uses low burlap effectively for this purpose, and it looks more attractive than other barrier materials.

Shear *Thuja occidentalis* 'Smaragd' in spring to keep a good tight vertical, so important to the garden's design in Wagner Park.

Lagerstroemia is a beautiful long-flowering summer shrub or small tree.

Never chop *Lagerstroemia* back to eye level. This unsightly practice is referred to by gardeners as "Crape Murder."

Hydrangea quercifolia (oakleaf hydrangea), or summer-blooming *Hydrangea macrophylla* cultivars (bigleaf hydrangeas), for example—should be pruned immediately after flowering. Other factors, such as susceptibility to insects and disease, may play a role in determining the best time to prune certain plants, so time spent researching your plants is time well spent.

To give geometric solidity and contrast to your plantings, prune structural plants so that some have clearly defined round shapes and others are vertical. Some evergreen rounds, such as boxwood balls, need to be kept sharply clipped. Vertical evergreens like *Thuja occidentalis* 'Smaragd' (emerald arborvitae) should be sheared to keep them tight; otherwise they may splay out from the weight of winter snow. (In warmer parts of the country this may not be necessary, of course.) You can also maintain the shape of vertical shrubs by tying branches together using biodegradable string; do not use wire, which will cut into the stems.

For shrubs that are not part of the structural backbone of the design, prune with an eye to their natural shapes and habits. *Lagerstroemia* species and hybrids (crape-myrtle), for example, are fabulous large shrubs or small trees with beautiful winter bark. They have a lovely graceful shape and should be pruned of only a few stems.

Dividing and Regrouping

Dividing large clumps of existing perennials is a good way to increase the number and size of plants in your garden. Do this in early spring as soon as you can see where everything is growing. Inevitably some perennials die out in the middle, so clumps may need to be dug up, the dead part eliminated, and the remaining pieces replanted.

Despite the advice given in some English gardening books, in this country you need not completely redo perennial borders on a regular basis. Some perennials, such as *Baptisia* or *Platycodon,* resent being disturbed. In the Conservatory Garden, many of the perennials and shrubs planted in 1983 are still in place. I have clumps of *Phlox paniculata* 'Bright Eyes' (garden phlox) in my own garden that have been in the same place for thirty years, slowly increasing their size. I wouldn't dream of touching them. Experience is the best judge of which plants in your garden should be left alone.

Some perennials tend to seed themselves around, "wandering" away from their original groupings. Wanderers can dilute the effectiveness of your composition. Every garden has its own wanderers, but I have noticed that *Pulmonaria* cultivars (lungwort), *Brunnera macrophylla* (Siberian bugloss), and *Alchemilla mollis* (lady's mantle) are especially peripatetic in gardens in the Northeast. Reuniting wandering perennials with their pals and reorganizing the borders is a joyful thing to do on a fine spring day. At that fresh green time of year, anything seems possible—even a perfect garden.

Soil Improvement

After you provide the appropriate soil for your design at installation, you must continue to feed the soil as necessary. If you move a plant to a new location with different soil properties or introduce plants with special drainage needs, be sure to adjust the soil accordingly. For example, *Dianthus* (pinks), *Sedum* (stonecrop), and other succulents originating in hot dry climates will appreciate the addition of so-called turkey grit (small stone chips) to the soil for better drainage. The most important general rule, however, is to add compost to your soil annually, whether you incorporate it into the soil, apply a layer of it on top, or add it to each planting hole. Its beneficial properties will feed the soil, which in turn will feed your plants.

Mulching

The best time to mulch garden beds is after you have completed all your spring chores, such as clean-up, planting, transplanting, and division. Mulching helps to protect plants, discourage weeds, and retain moisture in the soil, and it gives a garden a tidy, finished look.

Garden centers stock many different kinds of mulch, both in bags and in bulk. Choose a mulch that is a rich dark brown—raw wood chips look awful, and *nothing* justifies the use of dyed mulch, which is not only harsh in appearance but also adds unwanted elements to the soil. Better choices are small, fine- to medium-grade dark wood chips (not large pieces) or ground bark products. Buckwheat hulls are attractive but often too expensive for large public projects. Shredded leaves or compost, used as mulch in Madison Square Park, can be more cost-effective. Any good-quality mulch will continue to decompose, further enriching the soil and plants.

As a rule of thumb, apply mulch two to three inches thick, but do not let the mulch cover the crowns of perennials or rest against the stems of shrubs and trees; when the mulch gets wet, it can rot the plants.

Mulching helps to control weeds and retain moisture after all planting is complete. Wet mulch can rot plants, so make sure it does not touch their crowns.

In the Conservatory Garden, with crabapples blooming, a *Spiraea thunbergii* hedge is loosely pruned and an *Ilex crenata* hedge is tightly pruned for contrast. There is also color contrast between the yellow-green and the dark green. Photo by Joseph De Sciose.

Hedging

Tightly clipped hedges establish contrasting geometry while creating a sense of enclosure. They make your garden space feel special and serve as a backdrop for colorful plantings. As mentioned previously, hedges grown in public places should never be so high that people cannot see easily into and around the space; generally, four feet is the maximum height.

Yew hedges should be trimmed once in midsummer after their growth spurt. Other hedges, like *Ilex crenata* (Japanese holly) and *Euonymus kiautschovicus* 'Manhattan' (evergreen euonymus), must be clipped repeatedly, so I don't use them often, although I incorporated a number of handsome existing ones into the design for the Conservatory Garden. Various *Buxus* species (boxwood) make attractive hedges and need less trimming than the others, at least in the Northeast, so I use box whenever possible to cut down on maintenance. (And while this is not usually a problem in urban areas, it is worth noting that deer do not eat boxwood.)

Hedge pruning requires practice (beginners tend to turn every shrub into a meatball) and the right tools. Use good sharp hedge shears for trimming. Gas or electric hedging tools may be necessary for longer hedges. For hard-to-reach spots, try a power tool with a wand and hedg-

Gardeners use long-handled power hedgers and hedge shears to trim the boxwood at the New York Botanical Garden.

ing blade that can be articulated or adjusted to provide the right angle for the job.

Edging

Maintaining clean edges around planting beds goes a long way toward helping a public garden look well cared for and helps preserve the integrity of the original design. Like well-cut hedges, a sharp bed edge also enhances the fullness of the plantings, even in their most overblown midsummer extravagance. Use a sharp spade or a trimmer if the garden beds have lawn surrounding them. Consider installing any one of a variety of edging materials, such as brick, stone, metal, or granite, to help reduce the frequency of this maintenance chore.

This bed in Madison Square Park looks better because of the sharp edge around it. Keeping edges sharp is good housekeeping and makes a big difference in the appearance of the plantings.

Weeding

It is often said that one person's weed is another's most cherished plant. *Never* pull what you think is a weed in a garden that is not your own. (In the Conservatory Garden, I once found someone pulling a *Clematis montana* out of an old magnolia where I had trained it to climb. "I thought it was a weed," she said.) Some desirable plants like *Digitalis purpurea* (foxglove) will behave like weeds, seeding themselves around, and this can be a bonus. A good gardener learns to recognize the desirable seedlings.

A bed that is thickly planted, as discussed in chapter 3, gives weeds less chance to thrive. But it is still a good idea to rid the garden early of obvious and invasive weeds—such as *Alliaria petiolata* (garlic mustard) and the orange-flowered *Impatiens capensis* (jewel-weed or touch-me-not), both of which we battle in the Northeast—and then mulch to prevent new weeds from getting established. "Weeds" are defined differently in different parts of the country and in different individual gardens, so you must decide which seedlings to keep and which to remove. Learn when each weed goes to seed in your garden and try to remove it before that time.

This experienced gardener at NYBG's Perennial Garden knows which plants to weed and which to spare.

Instead of a hoe, try the weeding tool known as a swoe: it reaches weeds with less disruption of the soil, and you can use it without stepping into the beds, compacting the soil, or exhausting your back. It is best not to disturb the soil unless you are moving or dividing a plant, lest you interrupt beneficial soil activity, as discussed in the chapter on soil. And weeds proliferate in disturbed soil.

At the end of day, the most effective way to weed is good old-fashioned bending over and pulling. A gardener friend once joked, "The only

Many people find weeding easier with this tool, called a swoe, which has a sharp angled blade.

Staking is sometimes necessary, but it should never show. A better idea is to choose plants that don't need staking.

Thalictrum rochebruneanum 'Lavender Mist' has delicious blue-green foliage and tall stems with small lavender flowers. If it grows in the sun, it usually doesn't need staking. Photo by Diane Schaub.

This grass in front of a *Hydrangea macrophylla* was cut down and is now being staked with a peony hoop for the coming season.

true low-maintenance plants are weeds that have grown so tall you can pull them without bending over." I do not recommend that approach.

Staking

Staking is the art of providing support for herbaceous plants. Shrubs have woody stems and do not usually need support. Perennials and annuals that rapidly grow very tall, like *Rudbeckia laciniata* 'Herbstsonne' (autumn sun coneflower) and *Thalictrum speciosissimum* (meadow rue), or those that tend to fall over in a windy thunderstorm, like *Lilium henryi*, *L. speciosum* var. *album*, or *L. speciosum* var. *rubrum* (summer lilies), often benefit from staking.

To my eye, stakes in a garden are more unsightly than plants falling over. But if you must stake a plant, do it as unobtrusively as possible. Push multibranched dead twigs (the English call them "pea-stakes") into the ground around the plant in spring. Crabapple twigs are useful, as are dead branches of butterfly bush, which you can collect when you cut it back after the winter. Pea-stakes should be installed in early spring, after the first flush of growth, so that the plant's foliage will eventually cover them.

More permanent staking tools, often referred to by gardeners as peony hoops, can help support peonies, grasses, and other plants that flop. They are attractive enough to be left in the border all winter, ready to be useful early in the season. Alternatively, set two bamboo canes in front of perennials in an X shape in order to support the stems; let plants fall over the stakes to hide them. *Nepeta* and low-growing *Salvia* can be staked this way if you don't want them to spill out over a path.

Better yet, choose plants that do not need staking, such as *Thalictrum rochebruneanum* 'Lavender Mist' (meadow rue), a lovely perennial with elegant foliage and tall spires of tiny lavender flowers. If you grow it in the sun, it will support itself.

Some large ornamental grasses, such as *Miscanthus sinensis* 'Gracillimus' (maiden grass), must be staked or they may collapse in heavy rain or from their own weight. But their arching forms add so much grace to a garden that they are worth the trouble. Use a large peony hoop or a very large grid hoop, or place a group of sturdy stakes around the plant with string twined around them; these supports will not be seen as the plant grows.

Deadheading

Removing spent blossoms, called deadheading, fools plants (particularly long-blooming annuals) into thinking that they have not yet bloomed and prevents the energy-consuming formation of seed, leaving the plants enough energy to bloom again. Like most aspects of gardening, good deadheading is an art. It requires attention to detail, a close eye, and sharp hand pruners. The results should not be obvious; nothing is uglier than a plant with visible, blunt cut stems. Remove the blooms just above a significant leaf, taking care not to remove other buds growing along in the process. If done well, deadheading enhances the overall appearance of a garden. (A skilled volunteer at NYBG's Perennial Garden refers to herself as "The Grateful Deadheader.")

Deadheading most annuals will keep them blooming constantly all summer (although in the South some annuals will stop blooming until cooler weather). But deadheading annuals is very time-consuming. Despite their contributions of summer color, annuals cost money to buy, install, and grow, and they require lots of maintenance and water. In cold climates, you throw them away at the end of the growing season. For these reasons, I discourage institutions with limited budgets and maintenance staff from using too many annuals. There are other opinions on this, however; the gardeners at Wagner Park think that although they may cost more each year, well-chosen annuals actually require less maintenance over the long term than many perennials and they keep the garden colorful between the flowering of perennials.

Deadheading perennials after they bloom is a good way to tidy their appearance so their foliage can continue to contribute to the garden during the rest of the season. It does not usually encourage new blooms—most perennials will bloom only once. An exception to this rule is the gorgeous native perennial *Hibiscus moscheutos* (hardy hibiscus), with its huge flowers, which can be persuaded to keep blooming by

Deadheading, or removing spent flowers, fools a plant into thinking it hasn't bloomed yet. When done correctly, deadheading is not noticeable.

Echinacea has tiny new flower buds tucked into the leaf stalks. Watch for them and be sure not to cut them off.

At the New York Botanical Garden, workers use a long-handled tree-pruning tool to deadhead individual tulips in a large planting. This innovative method prevents a gardener from having to step into the beds and could be adapted to large annual plantings as well.

Hemerocallis 'Happy Returns' is a lovely pale yellow, long-blooming daylily that benefits from deadheading to tidy its display. It is thriving in Red Hook.

deadheading. *Echinacea purpurea* (purple cone flower), another native perennial, will also bloom for a long time if deadheaded.

Some perennials, like *Nepeta* (catmint), will bloom again sporadically if cut back in late spring after their major show, but be sure to watch for new growth at the base before you cut them. In the Conservatory Garden, the native *Vernonia noveboracensis* (New York ironweed) and *Salvia* x *sylvestris* 'Blauhügel' ('Blue Hill' sage) will continue blooming for a long time if properly deadheaded. Most *Hemerocallis* (daylilies) will not bloom longer if deadheaded, but removing spent blooms tidies their appearance and encourages more flowers for the next year. Use your fingers to gently snap off the spent blooms before they form seeds.

To reduce maintenance, avoid perennials that require too much deadheading. I stopped planting *Aster* x *frikartii* (Frikart's aster) for this reason, despite its pretty blue flowers.

Fall Cleanup

After the first hard frost of fall, remove annuals and add them to the compost pile. If the design has enough shrubs to carry interest in the garden all winter, you can also start cutting back some of the perennials as foliage and stems die back, adding these to the compost pile as well, but culling out large woody stems that break down too slowly. My rule of thumb about cutting perennials is "As long as it looks good, keep it up." This is obviously a matter of personal taste, but I love the russet seed heads of *Sedum* and the honey color of *Hosta* leaves, *Polygonatum*, and *Platycodon* after the first frost. In early spring, clean up and rake away all remaining dead foliage. Then the whole process begins again.

Watering

One of the most challenging and most important maintenance issues for any garden, particularly a public garden, is watering. As our world gets warmer, plants need more water, and water is increasingly scarce. Now more than ever we must find ways to irrigate properly in order to promote deep root growth so that ultimately the plants can survive on less water.

Learn as much as possible about your plants' native habitats to help determine their water requirements. Group plants with similar irrigation needs together and water accordingly. Overwatering can be just as destructive as underwatering. Use a rain gauge to track how much rain has fallen each week; one inch of water a week is thought to be optimal for most plantings. Teach crews to water long and deeply: let the water puddle up, move to another area, and then return when the first pass has soaked in.

A good irrigation system should be part of the planning of a new site. The choice depends on the types of plants used, the budget, and the staff. This is a highly complicated subject; systems range from hand operated to automated, from surface to underground placement. You can research the relative merits of various systems on the Internet, but talking to an irrigation specialist (not a salesperson for one particular product) about your particular situation is best. The system need not be expensive if kept simple, but even with an automated system it is essential to have well-spaced water valves throughout the landscape for hand-watering when needed.

All irrigation systems have some drawback for urban gardeners. Sprinklers are popular, but some of the water is wasted through evaporation, and individual sprinklers need to be moved and adjusted constantly. Soaker hoses, surface systems that are laid on top of the soil, can be attractive to squirrels and their less popular rodent relatives, who frequently bite through the hoses looking for water. Drip hoses placed underground or covered with mulch can malfunction, and gardeners must take extra care when digging not to break into the buried lines. Too often they are inadvertently left running for long periods of time, doing injury to plants and wasting water. An automated system has the advantage of not requiring a gardener to spend hours each summer day dragging around hoses and causing tripping hazards, but these too can malfunction or break. I prefer pop-up systems—black plastic sprinklers of varying heights that literally pop up out of an underground water system, spray water, and retract when done. They are operated by a gardener, the heads are visible, and the height and radius can be adjusted as needed. They are a good option for large expanses of lawn, and Columbia University uses them for the plantings there as well.

Very few parks or public gardens requiring restoration have watering systems other than outlets for setting up sprinklers. Obviously it is easier to lay out a system before planting a new bed than to retrofit one into an established planting. New systems are really designed to be installed before the plants.

As an example of retrofitting on a large scale, in 2006 a donor funded an irrigation system for the whole Conservatory Garden (six acres). After much thought and research by the curator, Diane Schaub, and the Central Park Conservancy, the half-acre lawn now has a programmable

An automated irrigation system can help you avoid the chore of dragging hoses around.

At the end of the day, no automated watering system is as good as a thoughtful, knowledgeable gardener.

pop-up system. In the mixed borders, a programmable system beneath the surface conserves water by sending it directly into the root zone. In the large display beds in the North Garden and in the woodland areas that require less frequent watering, the staff manually hooks up and monitors above-ground impulse sprinklers.

At the end of the day, a good gardener who knows the plants' requirements and the staff's capabilities is the best irrigation system. T. H. Everett, in his comprehensive ten-volume encyclopedia of horticulture, writes: "Watering remains an art dependent for its successful practice on close observation and human judgment."[1] Diane Schaub of the Conservatory Garden agrees. Even with an automated irrigation system, she is on the alert at all times, preferring to water in the mornings rather than at night both for improved water pressure and for the ability to readily spot a problem—water pooling on the surface, for instance—that might indicate a break in the irrigation line.

A completely automated system that turns on and off regularly but operates without human oversight could be watering your plants while it rains for a week. An example of what can happen when no one is watching occurred at a university campus a few years ago. A large, beautiful red-leaved *Fagus sylvatica* 'Riversii' (Rivers purple beech) began to die. When the tree finally had to be removed, the irrigation system was found to have been left on twenty-four hours a day for months. The tree had simply drowned. Think of the waste of water and energy!

Whatever system you choose, it should help you to use water wisely, only where and when it is needed. In gardening, as in life, nothing is perfect. One comforting thought: if you use shrubs and perennials that grow well in your area, combined with good soil and sufficient water in the plants' first year, the plants will establish themselves within a year or two and then will not need much watering or a fancy irrigation system to continue to thrive.

Managing Pests and Diseases

Whenever possible, I avoid using chemicals in my gardens. Chemical pesticides, herbicides, and fertilizers are incompatible with safe public spaces. They have long-term detrimental effects on plants and the environment, and they harm the soil and its complex web of life.

Because stressed plants are more prone to attack, sound horticultural practices such as choosing appropriate plants, maintaining healthy soil, and watering deeply, especially during drought, will help establish a resilient garden. Avoid using plants that require chemicals in order to grow well, or those that are especially susceptible to pests or disease in your area. If a plant develops continued problems that cannot be solved without chemicals, remove it, add it to the compost pile, and replace it with something else. (If the plant has a disease, like Verticillium wilt, discard it but do not compost it.)

For example, I do not use bee balm (*Monarda didyma*) because, as I mentioned earlier, in the Northeast it consistently succumbs to powdery mildew, becoming very unsightly. Some of our native *Phlox paniculata* (garden phlox) are susceptible to mildew as well, so I usually use the white cultivar 'David', which is quite mildew-resistant. On the other hand, I love hostas and refuse to knuckle under to the slugs who love them as much as I do and eat holes in their leaves. Jeff Lowenfels, a soil expert, suggests using coffee grounds around the plants and spraying the leaves with coffee, and I plan to give it a try.

Many common pests, such as aphids, can be dealt with by hand. Place your thumb over the nozzle of a hose and knock the bugs off with a hard jet of water. You may have to do this a number of times, but it is preferable to using chemicals. Knocking Japanese beetles off into a cup of bleach or soapy water takes care of them, although it is time-consuming. Do not under any circumstances use the bags that are sold for the purpose of ridding you of these nuisances; they only attract additional beetles to your garden.

Many gardeners use organic insecticidal soaps or horticultural oils, which work by suffocating or dehydrating the insect pests. The Conservatory Garden uses horticultural oil in early spring as a preventive measure against scale, an insect that sometimes attaches itself to the leaves of shrub hedges like *Euonymus kiautschovicus* 'Manhattan' and *Ilex crenata*. Affected leaves can be sheared off at the end of winter.

An increasingly popular approach to many pest problems is to use beneficial insects such as lady beetles and parasitic wasps. New York's Museum of Modern Art used to have to cover the sculptures in their Sculpture Garden with plastic when anything in the garden was sprayed with chemicals, and the garden had to be closed to the public for safety. But in the summer of 2007 a mite infestation in the birch trees prompted a new solution. Instead of spraying chemicals, MoMA had the trees washed with insecticidal soap. Soil experts injected a highly concentrated compost extract solution into the soil and brought in locally cultured beneficial mites. These tiny deputies apparently can survive the New

York winter, and they helped solve the problem. This biological control approach requires knowledge of plants and pests and their interrelationships, but it is much friendlier to both the environment and people.

The Battery Park City Conservancy uses chemical-free sustainable maintenance practices on a very large scale: managing nearly thirty-six acres of parks along the Hudson River. Their methods include using compost, compost tea, nontoxic pest and disease controls such as beneficial insects, and careful plant selection to reduce problems in their landscapes. They mow their lawns at three inches and use different kinds of irrigation to promote deep root growth and conserve water. They do a superb job of taking care of Wagner Park, and I have been working with them and learning from them since the park opened in 1996. (To read about their practices, visit their Web site at www.bpcparks.org and click on Operations.)

For other strategies, seek reliable print and Internet sources, send plant samples to your local cooperative extension service for analysis, or consult with an Integrated Pest Management (IPM) specialist. A consultant can provide you with many methods currently in use to protect plants in a natural way. More and more people are using compost tea to prevent pests and disease in addition to feeding the soil. The Resource Directory and the Recommended Reading section cite a number of Web and print resources for pest and disease management, including the United States Environmental Protection Agency site for information about using intelligent biological and cultural controls instead of traditional chemical pesticides.

Fertilizing

One summer early in my gardening life when I was eager to get my own garden going, I applied a lot of fertilizer to the plants in my border. What happened was quite extraordinary: they produced masses of foliage and then basically collapsed in a heap. I never did that again. Likewise, in public gardens I use organic fertilizers very sparingly. As always, if your soil is good and you add compost regularly, your plants will be healthy and fertilizers will be unnecessary for established shrubs and perennials. When in doubt, always strive to feed the soil, not the plants.

Lawn Maintenance

Grass used as lawn is one of the highest-maintenance features of a landscape. Trying to wean clients off grass, I often quote writer Michael Pollan, a knowledgeable gardener, who in his book *Second Nature* writes, "A lawn is nature under totalitarian rule."[2] Indeed, the poor little green blades just get going, doing what you ask of them, and then you come along and cut them off.

And yet, people—and especially city people—love to sit on lawns, and they are an important public amenity. Given the built-in conflict between people and beautiful lawns, a full battery of maintenance is required to keep lawns in good shape: aeration, reseeding, fertilization, pest and disease control, and constant irrigation.

In my opinion, some lawns are only worth the trouble if they create a frame for the garden, like the beautiful half-acre lawn in the Conservatory Garden, a wonderful big horizontal in a vertical city. Only couples having their wedding pictures taken are permitted to walk on this lawn. Otherwise it would soon be lost to picnickers and soccer games. An expanse of lawn is available for recreational use right outside the Conservatory Garden gates in Central Park.

Central Park closes its lawns on a regular rotating basis and fences off playing fields in winter or after a heavy rain. Some people complain, but this rotation ensures that the lawns can be heavily used and still remain the beautiful green oases everyone loves. Unfortunately, some parks departments have been replacing hard-to-maintain lawns and

Madison Square Park on a pleasant day demonstrates that city dwellers like to sit on lawns. The lawn is closed at certain times to protect the grass.

playing fields with synthetic turf made from various products such as polypropylene, polyethylene, or nylon. Many of these "carpets" are made with ground-up or shredded rubber tires or a combination of sand and rubber. They look very green, and I can understand the pressure to use synthetic turf for recreation. But since synthetics get hot underfoot in summer and the jury is still out on the environmental health risks from the fumes of these products, I do not recommend synthetic turf, especially for more passive use and certainly not until we know more about the risks.

If you must have a lawn, don't mow the grass too short; three inches is the length often suggested. Mowing a large rectangular lawn on the diagonal looks particularly fine, and changes in the cut direction benefit the lawn. In the Conservatory Garden, the mowing pattern is rotated each time to allow the grass to grow in different directions and assure that wheel marks are in different places. It is also good practice to leave the grass clippings in place to decompose and improve the soil. In fall, instead of raking the leaves and taking them away, mowers can shred fallen leaves for use as compost.

Path Maintenance

When people are determined to cut across a lawn to go somewhere, the worn path that results is called a "desire line." It is not easy or popular to try to stop people from going where they want to go in a public space; they are telling you what they need. Wherever possible, if you can't beat 'em, join 'em and put paths there. At Stony Brook University, a desire line developed after one of the landscape projects was completed; we simply made a nice stone path out of it, and it actually establishes a very attractive diagonal in the design.

A desire line is a path worn where people want to walk. At Stony Brook University, we made a desire line into a pathway that enhances the overall design.

Try to find room for a protected holding area for plants in your public space.

Tools and Equipment

Every gardener has a battery of favorite tools, and the number, type, and complexity of these will vary according to the plantings and budget for each project. If you can, include in your project a secure, conveniently placed shed to store tools, mulch, and plants.

Garden staff understandably love to use labor-saving devices such as leaf blowers, but many of these make a great deal of noise and create an enormous amount of air pollution when used throughout a large park.

In Central Park, the noise level of this equipment was the number-one complaint from the public. Responding to this and to environmental concerns, the Central Park Conservancy discontinued the use of large backpack and handheld blowers, but gardeners in most areas of the park can still use rolling blowers on large lawn areas. String trimmers, also called weed whackers, are useful for many gardening chores, such as edging planting beds and removing weeds between the cracks in bluestone paving, but they should always be used with appropriate safety gear and with caution around visitors, as they can easily throw pebbles that might injure workers or passersby.

If your park's staff uses noisy and potentially dangerous machinery, establish the rules early on and train them well in safety precautions. In a public place, it's good practice to limit the use of this equipment to large projects and to operate machinery as early in the morning as possible to spare visitors a noisy intrusion on their enjoyment of the space.

Learning While You Work

As you continue to work on a garden, you will learn how your plantings change and develop over time. This experience-based knowledge is the foundation of any intelligent maintenance program. Plants will constantly surprise you. Just when you think you know for sure one thing about a plant, it does something else. Stand back and look at the garden objectively and often, and it will tell you what maintenance it needs.

Ideally, the gardening staff and the designer should work together, walking around the garden to assess its condition and to consider how the intent of the original design can be enriched. If a plant has become too big, too tall, or too floppy, you can decide together whether to remove it, prune it, or let it be.

While there is no substitute for hands-on experience, you can learn strategies for reducing maintenance. Every gardener should read *The Well-Tended Perennial Garden* by Tracy Disabato-Aust. I always give it to the gardeners I work with. It provides detailed information on how to maintain individual plants—including how to pinch or cut perennials in half in the late spring to minimize maintenance later in the season.

One of the most important tools for garden maintenance is not to be found in a shed maintenance building, but should always be with you: your garden notebook. Keep records of the plants, their behavior

The designer and those who care for the space should work together, constantly reevaluating the needs of the plants and the public. Photo by Ronda M. Brands.

Nurturing a garden also nurtures the gardener.

and their needs, growing conditions, seasons of bloom, exciting plant combinations, and new ideas. Carry a digital camera to document what you see.

❧

A garden is like a child; it needs to be fed and cared for. In *Green Nature/Human Nature,* Charles Lewis writes: "From a human perspective, the strength of gardening lies in nurturing. Caring for another living entity is a basic quality of being human. Plants are alive and dependent on the gardener for care if they are to survive."[3]

Maintenance is essential to the survival of your public space. Volunteers can help.

6

Volunteers

Volunteers are not paid—not because they are worthless but because they are priceless.
—*Anonymous*

In the best of all possible worlds, every public space with plantings would have trained, well-paid horticulturists in charge and plenty of extra hands during the growing season. This is not always possible, so in many cases it is helpful, even essential, to have volunteers to supplement the professionals. Volunteers also serve as ambassadors for your garden, spreading the word among their friends and bringing in new visitors.

Recruiting

If you renovate or design a public space—even a small triangle between streets—the place itself will usually attract people offering to help. They wander in and start talking with whoever is working there. If you already have a few volunteers, identify them by T-shirts, caps, or badges—a good way of recruiting others. Visitors who see volunteers working in a garden may ask how they too can get involved: welcome them. Keep on hand a supply of leaflets with your contact information and details about your garden's needs.

   Begin by looking for garden volunteers among your own friends and colleagues. Experience shows that word of mouth is most effective; if you are interested in and involved with public space, chances are you know others who are too. To reach new people, post a sign in your park or garden or on bulletin boards at places where gardeners tend to go,

Volunteers supplement professional staff and can act as ambassadors for your project—the raindrop on the lens shows how determined this group was to help.

Many volunteers are delighted to get outdoors and work in a city garden or park.

such as botanical gardens and nurseries; include information about your project, your organization, and your volunteer needs. Set up a booth at a popular local fair with a sign-up sheet for volunteers, or place appeals on college Web sites and in local papers. A number of Web sites facilitate volunteer recruitment as well, such as www.volunteermatch.org.

Garden clubs and park "Friends" groups are obvious sources of volunteers. Consider collaborating with a church, scout troop, PTA, community organization, or local school. Umbrella organizations and city agencies can sometimes help you recruit volunteers. The New York City Parks Department's Partnership for Parks program successfully connects interested individuals, businesses, and organizations to city parks on a large scale: their twice-yearly It's My Park! Day attracts more than twelve thousand people to help plant and clean up 150 parks in all five of the city's boroughs; some of these people then become regular volunteers for those parks.

The Central Park Conservancy has a volunteer force of about 350 people who work in the park's landscape throughout the year. They must carry ID tags and wear Conservancy T-shirts in summer and sweatshirts in winter to identify themselves to the public. On Saturdays, a regular Green Team of fifty people does large-scale planting and horticultural maintenance projects. Other volunteers serve as greeters and tour guides.

The New York Botanical Garden has a docent program that prepares large numbers of volunteers to lead tours of the 250-acre garden; it requires forty-five hours of training in basic botany, horticulture, and landscape design. A smaller number of trained volunteers work in the gardens; three of them regularly assist the gardener in the Perennial Garden.

Neighboring businesses or civic groups may offer to send large groups of volunteers for a few hours on a given day. If they are untrained in horticulture, they are most useful for tasks such as planting bulbs or ground covers or spreading mulch. Too many volunteers at any one time, however, can be hard to manage; you can't teach horticulture to a large group on a lunch hour. In general, try to limit groups to no more than thirty people at a time.

Because Madison Square Park is surrounded by many banks and businesses that have supported the park's restoration and like to offer park work to their employees, the gardener began a program of Twilight Volunteer Events. Employees come from these businesses in groups of ten at a time after work, between four and six in the afternoon, several times a year. If you organize such events, alert local neighborhood organizations so that they can join in, too. This works both ways: the community feels recognized by the businesses and the businesses can brag about their contributions to the community. Working with local businesses can also be an opportunity to raise funds for the future maintenance of the park.

During the Conservatory Garden's heyday in the 1940s and 1950s, its staff included fourteen professional gardeners. When park funding was cut in the 1960s and 1970s, garden staff were let go and the landscape deteriorated without them. As I helped rebuild the garden, we also had to rebuild its complement of caretakers. In 1983, there were only two of us; the Conservancy had hired a young seasonal worker with the money I had raised, but there was more to be done than we could possibly handle. That first spring, I persuaded some enthusiastic and accomplished gardener friends to help. They were happy to get out of their apartments and put their hands into the soil after a long winter.

Ever since that first spring, the Conservatory Garden has had about two dozen volunteers each year, a very diverse group from all parts of the city. They wear identifiable T-shirts so that the public doesn't think just anyone can come into the garden and start working there. Many of these volunteers have been coming regularly for years, and many friendships have been cultivated along with the plants. When one of them moves away or retires, another miraculously appears to fill the gap.

It's a good idea to give volunteers T-shirts to identify them, and many organizations require it.

Conservatory Garden volunteers help with many tasks, large and small—here they are planting twenty thousand tulip bulbs in the North Garden. Photo by Joseph De Sciose.

Volunteers work from mid-March through late November, assisting with everything from spring cleanup and reviving the beds, dividing perennials, and weeding and deadheading throughout the season, to fall cleanup and planting of the last of the bulbs in early winter. They are not permitted to use power tools such as lawn mowers or hedge pruners, and the staff prefers to do the heavy jobs and those that require special skills, like pruning and hedging.

Big jobs—like bulb and annual plantings—would be unthinkable without loyal helpers working under the direction of the staff. Every May, about a hundred different varieties of annuals grown especially for the Conservatory Garden arrive from a local nursery. The volunteers and the staff work together to plant three thousand annuals in the South Garden in one hectic and exciting morning. In June, also in a single day, they help replace the tulips in the North Garden with two thousand Korean chrysanthemums that will bloom from late October until mid-November. In late November, at the end of our gardening year, they pitch in to remove the chrysanthemums and plant about 20,000 bulbs in the North Garden beds and around 25,000 in other places.

The volunteers are essential; it would be impossible to do all of this without their help. But we also have fun! We laugh and say we are only looking for perfection, and their work gets us pretty close.

Nancy Berner, a garden writer and editor, has been a Conservatory Garden volunteer for more than ten years. She believes that volunteers develop a very personal relationship to the welfare of the garden and also to one another. She says, "It is so easy to feel quite isolated in the city, but then, when you find a place where you can come together and connect with other people—no matter how different they are from you—it changes the city for you and you realize how lucky you are to have found common ground. And in the case of the Conservatory Garden, it is such beautiful common ground."

Volunteers sometimes come to us when they are thinking of a career change into horticulture. Kristi Stromberg Wright, a former dancer who was working in a restaurant, began as a volunteer, became an intern, and then worked with me for five years as my assistant before moving on to start her own business. Nancy Berner and Susan Lowry, who met as volunteers in the garden, went on to write an excellent book together about a hundred gardens to visit in all five boroughs of New York (see the Recommended Reading section).

Diane Schaub has many wonderful stories to tell about the Conservatory Garden's volunteers. Here is one of my favorites, in Diane's words:

> On a rainy Tuesday morning in mid-October 2004, the Conservatory Garden volunteers and staff were working in the South Garden. Among our diverse accomplished volunteer gardeners, there are a few published authors, an editor, a landscape architect, a former ballerina, a retiree from the Broadway stage, a former school headmaster, several arts professionals, a banker, a political activist, etc.—in short, the typically delicious "stew" of New Yorkers who make time to volunteer in Central Park. This was a somewhat sad occasion as we were pulling out all of the annual plants, many of which remained in glorious bloom, to make room for the 25,000 spring bulbs that would cheer our souls in the South Garden the following spring.
>
> About halfway through the morning, a large tour group of senior citizens came into the garden and walked around, rather quietly I noticed. Eventually a woman approached me and asked, "Are you in charge here?" I replied that I was. She leaned in a little closer and inquired, "Do you have any help?" Completely baffled, I turned and gestured to our soiled and toiling volunteers and said, "Well, yes!" But my inquisitor was just working up to her point. Coming closer still, she whispered, "Are they inmates?" I stared at her, dumbstruck. "That's what we do in my home town," she explained with no small hint of satisfaction, if not triumph.
>
> As soon as the tour left, I ran around and told all the volunteers what she'd said. They were delighted, and the incident spawned an obvious and endless supply of terrible jokes. From that day on, the Conservatory Garden Volunteers officially became the Conservatory Garden Inmates, and I, naturally, their Warden. Many of them appear to be serving life sentences; others, when summering away, are said to be enjoying the "work release" program.

On a more serious note, many municipalities *do* use supervised prisoners for state park clean-ups and environmental restoration projects. In Boston, incarcerated men from a minimum security facility are escorted to work in its Olmsted-designed Emerald Necklace park system. Many people sentenced to perform community service elect to serve in city and state park systems around the country, but they are unlikely to be doing horticultural work. As I mentioned in the previous chapter, the New York Horticultural Society has a much-admired program for prisoners at the Rikers Island facility. The inmates learn horticulture in greenhouses and gardens at the jail. If they show promise and commitment, they can continue learning through paid internships after they are released, and some then go on to work in parks. (See Recommended Reading for a fine book, *Doing Time in the Garden*, about this program.)

Management, Training, and Supervision

A successful volunteer program always depends on a positive relationship between volunteers and the staff, and since horticulture is a special skill, volunteers require oversight. Not every gardener is comfortable working with volunteers. If you know you are going to have to depend on volunteers, determine whether your gardening staff are willing and able to deal well with this, and provide supervisory training for them if necessary.

To make the most of your volunteers, you must manage them effectively. One way to maximize their talents and your resources is to choose a convenient, specified day of the week for all gardening projects conducted with volunteers. The garden staff will know when to expect the volunteers and can prepare tasks for them ahead of time. My first spring in the Conservatory Garden I chose Tuesday mornings, so that anything that might have occurred over the weekend could be dealt with first by

Fall clean-up in the Conservatory Garden in November is a big job, requiring many volunteers.

the staff on Monday. Tuesdays have remained Volunteer Day in the Conservatory Garden ever since. (A few special volunteers come in with the permission of the staff to work on other days throughout the year; your staff can decide whether this is acceptable or not.)

Volunteer gardeners can accomplish many tasks, large and small, depending on their level of horticultural skill; the experience required will depend on the type and diversity of the garden's plantings. In the Conservatory Garden, volunteers must be knowledgeable gardeners, not just gardening enthusiasts. But the best volunteers for any project are those who believe in the mission, take instruction well, and are flexible and personable. People who have free time to work in the garden, such as retirees, make excellent volunteers, though sometimes they can't do all the physical work required. I have found that dancers make good garden volunteers; they are often free during the day, they don't mind hard physical garden work, and they have a highly developed sense of visual space. Many potential urban volunteers with green thumbs have settled for potted plants on a windowsill—give them the opportunity to tend a real garden.

Before accepting volunteers, interview them. If they do not have enough experience, suggest they take courses at a local botanical garden. Verify your volunteers' experience before they start, and until you're sure they know what they're doing, keep them under the supervision of a staff member or a more experienced volunteer. Although it is impossible to watch every volunteer at every moment, someone on the staff should try to monitor what everyone is doing.

You may be surprised by what can happen if you don't interview your garden volunteers and watch their work: One fall Tuesday, a woman came into the Conservatory Garden and said she wanted to work with us. I thought she had been vetted by the staff, so I asked her what she knew about annuals and perennials. "Oh, I know everything about plants," she announced. (That should have warned me. I have been working with plants for forty years, and I know that no one can ever know *everything* about plants, even in a lifetime.) Foolishly I said to her, "Okay, would you please deadhead the white cosmos?" (I'd planted *Cosmos bipinnatus*, an attractive white annual, in the center beds.) When I checked on our new volunteer, I found her nowhere near the cosmos; instead she had cut down the very choice perennial *Anemone* x *hybrida* 'Honorine Jobert' (a white Japanese anemone) that was just beginning to bloom.

Curator Diane Schaub is also a great cook; she makes hot apple pies for the volunteers when they are finished planting bulbs in the Conservatory Garden.

As volunteer programs get bigger, they require more careful oversight to prevent injuries to people and to sites. Central Park Conservancy volunteers must apply formally, provide references, attend an interview, and sign an extensive volunteer agreement. The Parks Department requires a formal permit application cosigned by a Parks employee. Both organizations give their volunteers a comprehensive handbook clearly describing the policies, procedures, and safety regulations that all must follow. Because Central Park receives twenty-five million visitors a year, volunteers must also be taught how to interact with the public. All volunteer work is supervised by trained staff. (See the Resource Directory for relevant sources of volunteer handbook information.)

Appreciating Volunteers

Just as they nurture the garden, volunteers also need to feel nurtured. You should express your gratitude to the people who are donating their time to your project, While working with plants in a lovely garden is a satisfying experience, volunteers will especially enjoy coming as often as they can if they feel welcomed and appreciated. (I myself have tried to go to the Conservatory Garden every Tuesday since that first spring to work with the volunteers, no matter what other projects I am working on.)

It is worth spending time and energy to convey to volunteers that they are valued. During the winter months, the Conservatory Garden provides horticultural lectures, informal get-togethers, and potluck lunches for its volunteers, whose steady presence contributes so much to the garden's success. Many organizations hold recognition events to honor their volunteers and offer special courses to them along with the staff.

❧

Parks and gardens are vastly enriched by volunteer help, just as working in those places enriches the lives of the volunteers. But trained staff, dedicated volunteers, and the ongoing garden maintenance they provide must be supported by funding for salaries, tools, plants, and other necessities. Next we will consider ways to pay for all of this.

7

Advocacy

I have to be conservative because I want to conserve my neighborhood, liberal to keep my mind open and radical to carry a picket sign.

—Anne Devenney, Bronx community activist

Nearly every city has a determined individual, a natural advocate with contagious enthusiasm for civic improvement and an impressive ability to influence others and make things happen. The efforts of these individuals to beautify their cities and improve lives should inspire us to fight for the public spaces we care about in our own cities. As city parks, botanical gardens, and public gardens around the country receive less and less support from public funds, it becomes more and more important to advocate for them—in good economic times and bad.

Among the many such parks advocates I have met are Jean Woodhull, Louise Godwin, and Cindy Mitchell. For more than forty years, Jean Woodhull has been working with unfailing energy to improve the parks and streets of her native city of Dayton, Ohio. A knowledgeable gardener, she helped create the Cox Arboretum in the Five Rivers MetroParks system. She spearheaded a downtown revitalization effort called Riverscape along the Miami River. She organizes groups and events, talks to city officials, and raises money to get things done. Woodhull has always believed that beautification brings economic revitalization; characteristically, she thinks that much still needs to be done in Dayton. In gratitude for her lifelong commitment, the city named a lovely restored prairie for her.

Louise Godwin of Tupelo, Mississippi, is another longtime advocate and activist for beautiful plantings. She began in the 1960s, when she

An oasis in the city is worth advocating for.

founded an organization called Tupelo Clean and Beautiful, which planted street trees and filled urns with flowers in the downtown area. Under her guidance, magnolias were planted at all the entrances to Mississippi. Lady Bird Johnson recognized a kindred spirit, and in 1985 she invited Godwin to visit the Johnson ranch in Texas. Not having the right long dress for the occasion, Godwin bought some sheets decorated with wildflowers and made a skirt. Mrs. Johnson was enchanted. Louise Godwin has inspired three generations of Tupelo citizens to recognize the importance of city beautification.

Cindy Mitchell has been involved with parks issues and preservation since she moved to Chicago in 1968. A deeply committed citizen, she worked tirelessly and enthusiastically, both in and out of government, to help make Chicago the beautiful city it is today. She is the cofounder of Chicago's Friends of the Parks and, as president of the nonprofit Parkways Foundation, she—along with others—was respon-

sible for restoring the once dilapidated Garfield Park Conservatory and
creating its Children's Garden. The gorgeous glass palm house designed
by the great Jens Jensen in 1906 has been restored and is now a destination point for people from all over Chicago. The previously neglected
park, now an anchor of the community, has a significant effect on the
local economy and the pride of local residents. Mitchell sits on numerous boards, and in 2002 she was appointed a commissioner of the
Chicago Park District.

Funding Issues

Parks and beautiful places, lots of trees, and attractive year-round plantings raise public morale by making people feel that their city cares about
them. In turn, business improves. As we know, parks and plants need to
be maintained, and qualified gardeners are essential. Like the need for
maintenance funds, the need for gardeners can be a blind spot for city
funders. In 2005, New York City, with its huge population and 29,000
acres of parks, had only twenty-eight gardeners (the number has
increased since that time); on the other hand, Chicago, with 7,500 acres
of parks, has more than seven hundred gardeners working in their parks
each summer, and the results are traffic-stopping.

This is what happens to city parks—this one
is in New York City—without adequate maintenance. Tax-paying citizens deserve good
parks, but city budgets often skimp on parks
funding. Photo by Laura Napier.

When New York City ran into fiscal difficulties in the 1970s and
1980s, one of the first budget items slashed was parks funding and maintenance. When the city began to recover, parks were among the last to
have their funds increased. After more than a quarter of a century of
working in and for parks and seeing the benefits of beautiful well-maintained parks all around the country, I can say unequivocally that public
funding for parks and their care should be among the *last* items cut—
not the first, as is so often the case. Elected officials need to know that
parks are important to their constituents. Get to know your public officials and contact them not only when you see a problem but also when
you see improvements.

Even if a garden or park is well established, you will encounter situations that require advocacy. In 1985, when I heard that developers were
lobbying for a zoning variance that would allow them to build twenty-
five-story buildings overshadowing the Conservatory Garden, I took
action to help ward off this threat. The existing five-story buildings let
plenty of light and air into the Garden, but the shade cast by tall build-

Let public officials know that good parks are
important to their constituents. This rally for
parks improvement was held in Union Square
Park two days before 9/11.

ings would have spoiled this oasis and required us to completely rethink the plantings along Fifth Avenue.

Joining with members of the East Harlem Community Board and other city activists, I went to City Hall to testify against the proposal at a public zoning hearing. Since showing what might happen is often more effective than just talking about it, I brought large prints of wedding photographs taken on the Conservatory Garden's central lawn and showed the officials the visible sky behind the existing buildings on Fifth Avenue. Then I used black paper to cover the sky—the view if the proposed buildings were built. It got people's attention. Thanks to this and other testimony and community effort that day, the Board of Estimate rejected the zoning variance, and the garden and other parts of the neighborhood were protected. Joining forces with like-minded preservationists and park advocates brought a successful outcome.

In order to advocate for parks support, you need to know how public parks are funded. Usually, two different public revenue streams pay for parks and gardens—capital funds and operating funds—and it is essential to understand the differences between them. Capital funds are used for major park restorations, construction of new facilities, and similar improvements. Operating funds, on the other hand, are annual allocations for parks from the overall city budget, and these are the funds that keep parks alive and functioning. They pay for gardeners, tree pruning, sanitation, and other maintenance essentials. City parks compete for operating funds with all of the city's other important services, such as fire, police, education, and transportation; budgets are almost always slim and many politicians believe that if they cut parks funding, no one will complain. Vigorous advocacy is needed to change that attitude.

In New York, a city councilperson or other local representative may allocate capital funds to create or improve a park for his or her political advantage: the politician gets attention from the press and credit from his or her constituency. But without day-to-day maintenance drawn from operating funds, the new park will deteriorate, perhaps for years, until another politician comes along with the next infusion of capital funds. Capital funding also allows city officials to paint a rosy picture of park funding. Beware when politicians tell you that the budget includes lots of money for parks; they may be referring only to capital funds. Each time a park is restored or created, adequate operating funds should be allocated to it at the outset so that gardeners, arborists, plumbers, and other maintenance workers can sustain it and the public will not be let down.

This park in Brooklyn needs capital funds for restoration and operating funds for plantings and maintenance. The boarded-up building has grass growing out of the roof.

Lack of city funding has inspired the creation of public-private partnerships in many places around the country. In New York, these partnerships are responsible for bringing some of the city's highest-profile parks—Central Park, Prospect Park, Bryant Park, and Madison Square Park—back to conditions that allow everyone to enjoy them. Ideally, private funds should supplement city dollars, not supplant them, and the accomplishments of public-private partnerships should not become an excuse for a city to let private money do ever more to restore and maintain parks. But because private funds have become increasingly necessary, I will show you how to encourage and obtain them in chapter 8.

Cities Making a Difference

Many cities are working to beautify their parks and streets. Detroit, Michigan (population 951, 270, according to the 2000 census), has been called America's most dangerous city.[1] On December 29, 2007, the *New York Times* reported that the City of Detroit was considering selling its small parks; it was not clear to whom. A Detroit city councilwoman, JoAnn Watson, said, "They call some of these parks 'surplus' but I don't know what the heck that means because there is no such thing as a surplus of something that is necessary for the good and welfare of the community."[2] Recently, civic leaders began the process of improving open space to revitalize their community. A small part of the downtown area has already been successfully restored, and many private citizens of all socioeconomic levels are marshalling forces to save and renew Belle Isle, a large island park originally designed by Frederick Law Olmsted that has long been a popular part of the city. One of the leaders is Sarah Earley, who founded the Belle Isle Women's Committee and has assembled many prominent women to raise the money needed to make these improvements.

In Portland, Oregon (population 529,121), city parks have been well supported with operating funds for many years (8.1 percent of the city's budget in 2008), and Portland's 181 parks look great. Even so, the city's parks department regularly uses volunteers to help the thirteen staff horticulturists at their public gardens. The budget for 2008 indicates that Portland intends to raise capital funds for repairs and will not reduce the operating funds for the parks, which is enlightened thinking.

Minneapolis, Minnesota (population 382,618), has a nationally recognized parks system with an independently elected, semi-autonomous

Vancouver, British Columbia, is a beautiful city, in part because it spends 10 percent of its annual budget on its parks and horticultural staff.

Richmond, Virginia, is working on a new downtown master plan that emphasizes the importance of well-designed parks and green spaces.

board responsible for the maintenance and development of over 170 park properties and 49 year-round neighborhood-based recreation centers. Des Moines, Iowa (population 198,682), spends $16 million from its operating budget for parks, almost as much as it does from its capital budget ($18 million), with good results.

Vancouver, British Columbia (population 611,869),[3] is a city with the right priorities, and it shows. The city spends slightly over 10 percent of its budget on its 200 parks and recreation facilities and has about 150 staff working on street trees, horticulture, and park maintenance. It is no wonder that Vancouver is such a beautiful, flourishing city, popular with tourists and businesses alike.

Other cities are tackling the wider issues of city planning, green space, and city beautification. Richmond, Virginia (population 197,790), is working on an exciting new master plan for its downtown, emphasizing making the city more livable by creating additional parks, increasing public access to the riverfront, planting trees, and restricting the number of large developments. Community development director Rachel Flynn says, "You can increase the value of real estate by providing green space and open space,"[4] citing the example of what New York's Central Park has done for the value of nearby real estate. With support from both the public and private sectors, including the Lewis Ginter Botanical Garden, civic and business leaders are working together to preserve, develop, and beautify Richmond's public landscape, including restricting development along the James River. (For more information, see the Resource Directory.)

Tupelo, Mississippi, is a progressive city of 35,000 with a long history of enlightened civic leaders who have worked to improve their community. In May 2008 Tupelo's City Council approved a new program—the brainchild of civic activist and at-large councilwoman Doyce Deas—to enhance the quality of life. The Tupelo Water & Light company's twenty thousand residential and commercial customers have begun to contribute voluntarily to beautification by "rounding up" their monthly bills to the next dollar; enrollment in the program is automatic, but customers can opt out if they wish. Since the average contribution is about fifty cents per month per customer, and only 9 percent have opted out, the city is gaining thousands of additional dollars to spend on beautification. The president of the Tupelo city council, Dick Hill, said that the money raised will also help them to "seek grants, come up with new ideas, review projects that other cities are doing and actually implement them."[5]

Chicago is one of America's most beautiful and livable cities thanks to the leadership of Mayor Richard M. Daley. This is just one of hundreds of spectacular public plantings that enhance the lives of the city's residents.

The city everyone should be learning from is Chicago (population 2,896,016), which has made parks and gardens a public priority under the dedicated leadership of longtime mayor Richard M. Daley, who believes strongly in the power of beautiful, well-maintained public spaces. He has put those beliefs into action, cultivating and improving every possible inch of his city with spectacular plantings, transforming it into a state-of-the-art garden city.

Since the nineteenth century, Chicago's civic leaders have believed in the importance of parks as cultural as well as recreational spots, and many open-space areas were saved over the years by leading industrialists.[6] Chicago has 570 parks, about a third as many as New York, but its operating budget is much larger than New York's, and the Chicago Park District employs two hundred full-time and five hundred seasonal workers. Chicago takes its horticultural transformation very seriously; the city's motto is *Urbs in Hortu* (City in a Garden).

Each year, the Chicago Park District designs, plants, and maintains eighty individual gardens with five hundred different plant species and cultivars and half a million annuals. (Additional plantings are created throughout the city under the management of other agencies as well.) Half a million new trees have been planted since Mayor Daley came into office in 1989, and a hundred miles of median strips have been planted with trees, shrubs, perennials, and annuals.

Every development in Chicago, from office buildings to parking lots, must install and maintain landscaping. The city's *Guide to the Chicago Landscape Ordinance*, the intent of which is to "make Chicago healthier and more beautiful," specifies the requirements. It sets uncommonly high standards for publicly funded landscape contractors and requires the collaboration of many different city agencies under the oversight of the mayor's office. The Landscape Advisory Task Force, made up of professionals and prominent citizens, reviews all plans for public projects, and the Department of Transportation evaluates trees, shrubs, perennials, and vines for survival rates and aesthetic qualities. Mayor Daley allocates city resources for these tasks because he and his administration understand the far-reaching consequences of beautifying public space: attractive streets, lower crime, cleaner air, higher property values, increased tourism, and the ability of all Chicagoans to take pride in their community. In a speech in 2001, Daley said: "Trees, flowers, parks, attractive open spaces—these things are contagious. When people experience them, they want more of them. And they are willing to pay for them because they know they are getting something for their money"[7] (see Resource Directory).

Starting an Advocacy Organization

Advocacy organizations come in all sorts of shapes and sizes, but you need not reinvent the wheel when forming a new group; rather, look to established groups for models. The Delaware Center for Horticulture and the Tennessee State Parks, for example, have produced a number of helpful documents on how to establish a "Friends" group and what such a group can accomplish (see the Resource Directory). When these groups were getting started, they were able to draw on information from existing organizations in Utah, Wisconsin, Florida, and California. "Friends" groups (or Citizen Support Organizations, as they are called in Tennessee) are eligible for designation as tax-exempt public charities by the IRS, opening doors to a variety of corporate and government grants, among other financial and organizational benefits.

In New York, the advocacy organization New Yorkers for Parks (NY4P, formerly called the Parks Council) has been supporting parks for more than a hundred years and is the only independent watchdog for all New York City parks, beaches, and playgrounds. NY4P works to ensure greener, safer, cleaner parks for all New Yorkers. Its constituents include over a thousand greening and civic organizations representing more than a million New Yorkers across all five boroughs, from small "friends of parks" groups to organizations representing the big parks. By reaching out to community groups who have a stake in the welfare of local public places, NY4P has created a strong and vocal political constituency that can more effectively lobby city officials for adequate park-funding allocations.

The executive director of NY4P, Christian DiPalermo, has said, "Successful parks require four things: a long-term strategic vision, effective ongoing management, significant community involvement and local advocates."[8] NY4P works to effect change on a citywide level with policies, partnerships, and planning to promote a higher level of park service in every New York City community.

NY4P researches each council district and creates individual district profiles to show officials what is and isn't being done in each district, publishes facts about the benefits of good parks on surrounding neighborhoods, and produces yearly report cards on New York City parks that document both good and bad conditions. The staff attends many community meetings and hearings at the City Council. They also organize an annual Advocacy Day, during which individuals, joining a coalition of community groups, participate in press conferences at City Hall and visit their city councilpersons to request more operating funds for parks; this approach lets people get to know their public officials and show them that their constituents care about parks. All of these efforts together have succeeded in increasing the operating funds for the seventeen hundred parks in New York. While there is still a long way to go before funding is adequate for all parks—in 2007, the city of New York was still spending less than one percent of its annual $56 billion budget on its 29,000 acres of parks—some improvement has been made. NY4P has an active Web site (www.ny4p.org) that lists the community groups affiliated with it, provides information about parks issues, and suggests ways to get involved.

A number of national nonprofit advocacy organizations also assist cities in improving parks and open spaces. Project for Public Spaces was founded in 1975 to further the insights of William H. Whyte; the organization strives to connect people on a global scale with "ideas, expertise, and partners who share a passion for creating vital places."[9] You can read more about their community-building work at www.pps.org. City Parks Alliance is a coalition of city parks leaders working together to strengthen America's urban parks; it sponsors international conferences on the subject and maintains an Internet list of national job openings in city parks across the nation. Its members include representatives from public agencies and park departments from around the country. For more information, consult the CPA's Web site at www.cityparksalliance.org. The Trust for Public Land is another national organization working to protect the American landscape. Its Parks for People initiative organizes efforts in cities and suburbs across the country to ensure that everyone can enjoy access to a nearby park, playground, or natural area. In New York City, the Trust was a major player in saving many community gardens in the 1990s. You can contact them through their Web site at www.tpl.org.

Finding Advocates in Your Community

Dedicated people with a commitment to the public good can be found in every community large or small; your job is to find them, persuade them of the importance of public space for quality of life, and invite them to join your efforts. Spread the word among your friends and colleagues. Assemble some prominent people from your community who

The Delaware Center for Horticulture works with city and community groups in Wilmington to sponsor and organize street plantings. Photo by Gary Schwetz. Courtesy Delaware Center for Horticulture.

are interested in improving public space, research the issues, and show your elected officials that their constituents are concerned. Aim to mobilize community leaders behind parks issues. Important businesspeople, politicians, clergy, educators, CEOs, newspaper editors, and labor leaders can make a big difference when they advocate for parks with city officials. Because parks issues are nonpartisan and should remain so, civic leaders of any party can become parks advocates. Be sure that you keep them well briefed; when the opportunity arises, they should already know just what funds to seek.

Wilmington's mayor, James Baker, is also a believer in the value of beautification. His message welcomes you when you enter the city. Photo by Gary Schwetz. Courtesy Delaware Center for Horticulture.

The support of well-known people—even celebrities—can sometimes produce amazing results. In 1995 Bette Midler, "The Divine Miss M," appalled by the conditions of some of the parks in the Harlem area and parts of the Bronx, started the nonprofit organization New York Restoration Project to "restore, develop, and revitalize underserved parks, community gardens, and open space."[10] Since then, NYRP has restored many of the parks in northern Manhattan, created new green spaces, saved numerous community gardens, and made an impressive commitment to ongoing maintenance. Beyond a doubt, Bette Midler's high profile and passion for the cause have helped to bring attention to the issue of underserved parks in poor areas.

In Wilmington, Delaware (population 72,664), the mayor, Jim Baker, is also committed to this cause. In 2004, he and the city council formed the Wilmington Beautification Commission, asking city employees, businesses, and citizens to join a citywide campaign whose slogan was "Think Green for a Change." The commission is a coalition of prominent local institutions, such as Winterthur and the Delaware Center for Horticulture, along with city agencies and community activists, working together with the mayor to enhance city parks and public spaces. The focus is on maintenance, and Mayor Baker has also allocated generous funds for improvement of plantings. The Delaware Center for Horticulture, with its long history of working with community groups to transform city spaces, is taking the lead in this effort. (For more information about this campaign, see the Resource Directory.)

Getting Out the Word

As a parks advocate, one of your most important functions is keeping people informed. Observe and document the actual conditions of as many parks and public gardens as possible, whether they are large or small, especially those in less affluent neighborhoods. Note broken glass, damaged play equipment and benches, trees in need of pruning, neglected plantings, water fountains that don't work, and locked or unusable bathrooms. Pay special attention to the effects of budget cuts or reductions. Then circulate your findings to the press and city officials, highlighting the challenges while recommending solutions.

NY4P releases an annual report card on New York's parks to the media and city government. Funded by a number of foundations that believe in the importance of parks, the report card is a park-to-park survey of conditions in two hundred neighborhood parks of between one and twenty acres all around the city. In 2007, nearly a third of them received failing grades. This information made advocacy easier. By bringing to light specific problems in these parks, the report card program has encouraged the Parks Department to make a number of improvements in trash pickup, bench repair, and the state of bathrooms and water fountains. NY4P also published fifty-one district profiles—one for each city council district—with maps and little-known statistics about each park. Subsequent profiles will show whether the parks have improved or deteriorated.

However you decide to make your voice heard, make sure your ideas also reach the general public through the press. Large events like concerts, picnics, and races make good stories; you might consider organizing a citywide bicycle race for parks support, for example. And always look for photo opportunities—such as rally participants carrying signs from their neighborhood parks. NY4P's workbook *Climbing the Advocacy Tree* offers excellent suggestions about how to conduct a meeting with city officials, how to write an Op-Ed piece, tips on call-in radio shows, and more. You can request a copy via their Web site at www.ny4p.org.

Help your local real estate companies and developers understand that good parks and beautification projects in all neighborhoods are in their best business interests, and that supporting parks is good for their image as well as their bottom line. Well-maintained parks stabilize communities, and in turn, property values increase. In Chicago, the opening of huge Millennium Park in 2005 caused the value of nearby real estate units to increase dramatically. In 1999, NY4P worked with the accounting firm of Ernst and Young on a report titled "How Smart Parks Investment Pays Its Way," which details the dramatic positive effects of parks such as Bryant Park on the economy of the surrounding community.

This workbook from New Yorkers for Parks has many detailed tips on becoming an effective advocate for parks.

During the period from Bryant Park's opening in 1992 to 1999, nearby real estate values rose as much as 225 percent. Since real estate developers and companies are private businesses, the next chapter will address their role in greater detail.

Successful Advocacy

Organizations working together can successfully tackle parks issues. In 2004, in response to conditions documented by the NY4P's report card, that organization joined with the Central Park Conservancy, the City Parks Foundation (another private-public organization), and the NYC Parks Department to start the Neighborhood Parks Initiative. The program's goal was to remedy the discrepancy in the number of gardeners for the poorer parks. Bringing this about took several years of meetings with public officials and conversations with private donors. The private groups raised funds to initiate the program, and these funds were then matched by city funds on a 2-to-1 basis, providing capital dollars as well as three years of maintenance funding from a combination of public and private sources. The success of this program was due in large part to parks commissioner Adrian Benepe and his unwavering commitment to the role of horticulture in New York City parks.

The Central Park Conservancy then trained thirty gardeners to work as seasonal staff in the thirty small parks identified by NY4P as being most in need of help. The Parks Department subsequently hired many of these trainees for full-time positions as assistant gardeners. Advocacy and cooperation with the city were the keys to success. By 2007 the number of city gardeners had increased—a step in the right direction. I hope this initiative will serve as a precedent and be replicated many times over.

In 2001, timed to an upcoming mayoral and city council election, the Parks Council (the forerunner of NY4P) created a campaign to bring the parks issue to the attention of those running for public office. The council distributed leaflets, buttonholed the candidates, and held well-attended forums on the issue of the underfunding of parks. On Sunday, September 9, 2001, it held a big rally in Union Square Park, where hundreds of people from all five boroughs gathered with placards to represent their parks. The mayoral candidates and other city officials came, saw their constituents campaigning for parks, and signed a pledge to work to bring the funding of parks up to one percent of the city budget.

This 2001 advocacy campaign brought parks issues to the attention of elected officials in New York City.

Since the World Trade Center attack occurred just two days later, it's hard to evaluate the effectiveness of this effort. But for the first time in many years, the press covered the issue of parks, public officials responded, and hundreds of people were energized. NY4P intends to conduct a similar campaign in 2009, when the mayor and much of the city council are again up for reelection.

In an ideal world, every city would wholeheartedly support its parks. No matter what the state of the economy, people need parks, *and this is especially so in bad times*. Movements in support of urban green spaces are active around the country, and the subject has been addressed in national symposia as well as a number of books and articles. If public funding in our cities were raised to sufficient levels to provide good day-to-day maintenance by trained gardeners, private funding could be used to provide the extras, such as cultural events, food concessions, and artworks. Nearby businesses could help pay for additional gardening tools or special plantings, thereby improving their images with their customers and the community.

Now we need to learn how to raise those private funds and how best to use them.

Private Funding and Benefits for Business

The role of beautiful public spaces, and visual appeal in general, in the social and economic enhancement of communities these days is well documented. They produce safer, more attractive places for people to live and work in an era in which the look, feel and quality of life of a city are critical to attracting residents and businesses. . . . Community appearance and ambiance are critical to community health and prosperity, now more than ever. —Lloyd Gray, Northeast Mississippi Daily Journal, *February 24, 2008*

A successful park is often the best advertisement, and success is contagious. By 1985, the Harlem Meer, a Dutch-named body of water in northern Central Park between 106th and 110th streets, had become unsightly, dangerous, and completely unusable. The muddy water was full of old tires and trash and surrounded by ugly fencing and broken asphalt paths. A graffiti-covered burned-out restaurant stood on its northern perimeter.

The restoration of the Conservatory Garden next door showed previously skeptical donors that private money could be well spent in the Park's neglected northern end. With this stunning example, the Central Park Conservancy was able to raise $6 million from private sources to completely renovate the Harlem Meer. The Meer is now clean and stocked with fish and water plants. Ducks, geese, swans, cormorants, and herons are regular visitors. A child-sized sand beach and a handsome center for park education, community meetings, and exhibitions are among the amenities. Best of all, the Meer's Harlem neighbors are proud that their area of the park is as beautiful as the southern end. The benefits of the restored area have spread. People are renovating their buildings, adding sidewalk plantings, and opening

Private funding is often necessary to create and sustain beautiful public places for people to enjoy.

The Harlem Meer, with its burned-out boathouse, discouraged visitors from coming to the northern end of Central Park. Photo by Sara Cedar Miller.

new stores and restaurants along the northern border of Central Park.

Making a garden or park costs money, and so does maintaining it. Fund-raising for public space requires creativity, persistence, and resourcefulness. Research as many different types of funding sources as you can. The two general types of funds for parks and gardens are public (city, state, or federal) and private (individual donors, public-private organizations, foundations, and businesses). As noted throughout this book, public funding for many urban parks is on the decline; often there is not enough money to improve parks, especially in poorer areas. Individuals and businesses have devised innovative solutions, including different forms of public-private partnerships such as conservancies and Business Improvement Districts.

The successful restoration of the nearby Conservatory Garden gave skeptical donors the assurance that private money could be well spent, and $6 million was raised to restore this lovely body of water. Photo by Sara Cedar Miller.

Public-Private Partnerships

A growing trend in parks support is the public-private partnership. Because they are not restricted by the red tape of bureaucracy, these partnerships are able to avoid many of the roadblocks to neighborhood improvement and beautification and produce faster and better results.

The usual type of organization established to receive private contributions and disburse those funds for public projects is a charitable corporation that qualifies under section 501(c)(3) of the Internal Revenue Code; most experienced accountants and lawyers are familiar with requirements and can guide you through the process. (You might consider asking such individuals to donate their services to help you establish this type of corporation.) Public-private partnerships between these charitable corporations and the city's Parks Department have improved some of New York's most high-profile parks, and similar entities exist all across the country.

The Central Park Conservancy, a 501(c)(3) corporation formed in 1980, is one such example. Since its founding, the Conservancy has overseen the investment of $500 million in Central Park, of which $390 million was raised from private sources—individuals, corporations, and foundations—and $110 million was contributed by the City of New York. In recognition of all the Conservancy has done and continues to do for Central Park, the city granted the Conservancy a park management contract, which includes additional financial support to further help ensure the continuing restoration, maintenance, and programming of the park. The Conservancy receives an annual fee for its services, the amount determined by a formula that requires the Conservancy to raise and spend a specified minimum amount of private funds in the park on an annual basis. The Conservancy has an astonishing twenty thousand donors each year—from $35 annual members to seven-figure contributors—and its annual budget is $27 million.

The Conservancy has become a model for such organizations; similar groups now help support Buffalo's Olmsted-designed park and pathway system, San Francisco's Golden Gate National Park, and Boston's Rose Fitzgerald Kennedy Greenway. Civic leaders in Los Angeles are considering the idea. Chicago's Parkways Foundation is a similar successful nonprofit support group for parks.

Innovative Approaches

In 1984, Grand Army Plaza, at the southern end of Central Park, was an eyesore, marred by empty flower beds, a broken fountain, and abundant trash. The relatively new Central Park Conservancy determined that the poor condition of this entrance to the park was adversely affecting both tourism and local use. The city was still recovering from the financial crisis of the 1970s and needed a new approach to funding. The Conservancy approached businesses with offices in the General Motors Building and the other buildings that overlooked the plaza at 59th Street and Fifth Avenue, pointing out that this tawdry public space in such a prominent spot was bad for business. Together they came up with a plan to fund the Plaza's restoration by asking anyone with a view of the plaza to pay a voluntary "window tax." The idea appealed to a number of real estate owners, among them the Estee Lauder Companies and Donald Trump, who at that time owned the Plaza Hotel, which also overlooks the site. The Conservancy was able to raise $3 million to restore the pavement, the fountain, and the lovely statue of Pomona, and to add trees, seasonal bulbs, and annual plantings.

Now Grand Army Plaza, run by the Conservancy, is enjoyed by millions of office workers, shoppers, and visitors, and its renovation has demonstrated to businesses and property owners that beautifying pub-

In 1984, the Central Park Conservancy had an innovative idea to restore Grand Army Plaza: they raised a voluntary window tax from businesses owning property overlooking the plaza.

lic space improves property values, retail income, and the well-being of everyone in the area. This imaginative funding approach could be duplicated elsewhere around a main square or along an important downtown street that is home to many businesses.

Business Improvement Districts

Another means of generating business support for parks is to create a Business Improvement District (BID), a state-regulated area within which property owners pay a tax or assessment calculated on the basis of square footage. A BID's purpose is to underwrite quality-of-life improvements in its area that are not being provided by the city government. A simple majority of district property owners must approve the creation of these districts before a BID is established. The first BID in North America was formed in Toronto in 1965; there are now more than twelve hundred BIDs of various sizes in many cities, including Philadelphia and Los Angeles. By 2007, fifty-six BIDs had been established in New York City, of which twelve are directly concerned with parks and landscape improvements. They include more than seventy thousand businesses, and contribute nearly $80 million in services to the city.

The BID for Bryant Park, called the Bryant Park Management Cor-

Bryant Park is supported by a Business Improvement District, a state-regulated way for neighborhood owners to fund services that are not being provided by city government.

poration, was one of the first specifically created to support a public park. It funds the park's maintenance, sanitation, and security and oversees two restaurants as well as many events, which in turn bring in additional revenue and make it possible to sustain Bryant Park's high level of service to its community. The 34th Street Partnership, another BID, has restored two triangular pocket parks on Broadway near Macy's flagship store. These parks have done much to revive the area economically; tables and chairs and lavish plantings attract people, providing many more customers for the local businesses.

Business Improvement Districts do have limitations. Since they are usually supported by neighboring businesses and tenants, less affluent neighborhoods with fewer successful businesses mean less private funding potential for public space. The BID on 125th Street in Harlem, for example, languished for years for lack of funds until the recent real estate boom began; with the improvement of Harlem's business economy, prospects for public-private activity for its parks have improved.

Private Funding from Individuals

Increasingly, much of the support for city beautification must come from generous individuals or local foundations committed to the betterment of the community. At an early fund-raising lunch for Central Park in 1985, Betsy Rogers, then administrator of the park and head of the Central Park Conservancy, led donors from their comfortable seats at the lavish Tavern on the Green (a private restaurant within the park) to a bus that took them on a tour of the park's northern acres, then largely neglected. When they reached the Conservatory Garden, Betsy ordered everyone off the bus and asked me to show them around. At first many of the donors looked apprehensive—these were the days when people were worried about going to the upper end of Central Park—but soon the garden began to work its magic and everyone relaxed. During the tour I mentioned that the steps to the wisteria pergola badly needed repair, and afterward we received a much-needed donation for that purpose from some people who had been on the tour.

That was my introduction to Joan and Bob Arnow and Alan and Elaine Weiler, members of a successful commercial real estate family. These generous, thoughtful, and modest people cared deeply about the importance of the garden's location and the impact of its beauty on its

Private donors can make a big difference. The Weiler-Arnow family generously endowed the maintenance of the Conservatory Garden in 1987 and underwrote the gardens in Bryant Park in 1992. *Left to right:* Bob and Joan Arnow, Lynden Miller, Alan and Elaine Weiler.
Photo by Sara Cedar Miller.

The annual Frederick Law Olmsted lunch in the Conservatory Garden is very popular, and it raises more than $2 million each year for Central Park. The guests like to wear festive hats.

neighbors. One spring a few years later, Joan Arnow called to tell me that the family wanted to make a special donation to Central Park in honor of their parents' sixtieth wedding anniversary. She asked if I had any ideas for a suitable project. I suggested an endowment for the maintenance of the Conservatory Garden so that it would never again become the neglected place it had been before it was restored. To my great joy, the entire four-generation Weiler and Arnow family gave the Central Park Conservancy a $1.5 million endowment for just that purpose. At that time, in 1987, it was the largest private donation to a public park in the country, and of course it was a fantastic gift to the city. When it came time to fund the gardens I was designing for Bryant Park, they again stepped up to the plate.

Generous people in many cities care about public spaces and the quality of life, and there are many ways to reach out to them: meetings, mailings, Web sites, newsletters, plant giveaways, and special donor events. Some gardens and parks also host gala fund-raisers each year. The Central Park Conservancy holds many fund-raising events; the most publicized is the fashionable Frederick Law Olmsted Luncheon held each May in the Conservatory Garden. Sometimes referred to as "America's Ascot," it has become one of the biggest social events of the New York year. Twenty thousand tulips are in bloom, and the pink crabapple allées are flowering. Twelve hundred guests fill several hundred tables set up on the half-acre main lawn under a mammoth tent. Every year, the luncheon is sold out, with a waiting list, and the $2 million in proceeds go to support the park's operating budget.

This model has been successfully copied in other cities. Chicago's Parkways Foundation hosts a similar very popular fund-raising lunch, and in Boston, eight hundred guests attend the lunch held by the Emerald Necklace Conservancy for the benefit of the city's eleven-hundred-acre chain of Olmsted-designed parks.

Because it can take years to develop a dedicated group of major donors, private-public organizations usually hire development staff. A long-term plan can inspire a faithful group of donors, particularly those who can be brought to understand that improvement of parks for the rich and the poor is essential to everyone's quality of urban life. Clergy, garden clubs, hospital boards, schoolteachers, environmentalists, real-estate entrepreneurs, enlightened politicians. and many other professionals can, over time, become leading donors to your cause.

Private Funding at Work

Seattle (population 2,414,616), often called the Emerald City, has the support of many generous private citizens for its extensive parkland, and the city spends proportionately more on its parks than most. But the Seattle Parks Foundation, an independent not-for-profit organization founded in 2001, wants to do even more. "People do value their parks here," Karen Daubert, the executive director, told me, "but the Seattle Parks Foundation wants to go above and beyond what the city is doing." Since 2001, the Seattle Parks Foundation has raised over $28 million and completed more than two dozen park projects. The dedicated civic lead-

Lake Union Park opened in 2008 in Seattle, Washington. It was financed and built by the Seattle Parks Foundation with $20 million in private funds. Photo by City Investors, courtesy of Seattle Parks Foundation.

ers on its board work hard to introduce new friends to the cause through meetings and fund-raising events, often sponsoring speakers from other places to inspire them. With private funds they have built a twelve-acre waterfront park called Lake Union Park, a $20 million project. (For more details see their Web site at www.seattleparksfoundation.org.)

In York, Pennsylvania (population 40,000), a private nonprofit organization, the York County Community Foundation, has been working since 2003 to supplement public funds by raising private money for beautification. Their initiative, called Beautiful York, is based on a simple idea: "The way a city looks . . . has a great impact on whether a city succeeds."[1] Among other things, the plan calls for reclaiming York's central square, recapturing its riverfront, and beautifying the cityscape with plants and landscaping. The foundation has developed the Beautiful York Action Plan, as well as a survey that solicits comments on the plan. The efforts of the foundation are impressive, and their work should inspire other cities. (See the Resource Directory for a link to the action plan, which offers many specific ideas and action steps.)

In Charleston, South Carolina (population 96,650), Darla Moore, a successful businesswoman, became concerned about the lack of resources allocated to the city's parks. Familiar with the Central Park Conservancy, she contributed $10 million in 2007 to form the Charleston Parks Conservancy, with the mission of enhancing and improving the city's parks. This public-private partnership is working with city government, local neighborhood organizations, and the Charleston Horticultural Society on the design phases of several important parks and is also planning a volunteer program to organize advocacy for Charleston's parks. One of their first joint endeavors was a mall beautification project. You can read about these initiatives at www.charlestonparksconservancy.org.

A Cautionary Note. Be on the lookout for two unfortunate side effects of the reliance on private funds and public-private partnerships. First, the two-tiered system: more affluent neighborhoods can afford to contribute enough private funds to support beautiful, safe, well-maintained parks, while parks in poorer neighborhoods remain in varying stages of decay. All city dwellers in every neighborhood love and deserve decent parks. The stark difference is sometimes visible even in the same park: good conditions exist where the park abuts the more affluent neighborhoods, but the poorer end of the park is noticeably shabbier and therefore sometimes more dangerous. A second danger of heavy reliance on private funding is that a city may be tempted to reduce or eliminate allocations for public parks.

Attracting Private Funding

Once you have determined your potential funding sources, you have to get their attention. The best way to raise money for a public garden or park project is to appeal to the imagination. In *The Wizard of Oz*, when Dorothy leaves Kansas and lands in Oz the film changes from black and white to color. In a way, that transition represents what happened to New York City when Central Park's restoration began. Central Park is now an inspiring sight, and it has led to many other beautification efforts around the city.

Potential donors are persuaded by pictures of success: document "before" with snapshots of existing conditions such as graffiti, broken bottles, overgrown plantings, trash, and empty space, and contrast that with "after": images of what you have done in other places or hope to do. If you don't have a success story yet, show parks you admire as models. Many organizations bring in outside speakers to inspire their donors; advocates from the local community can then provide specifics about

One way to raise private donors' awareness is to show them examples of other projects "before" and "after." Before: Small Verdi Square on Broadway looked like a tag sale of unwanted plants.

After: This dramatic but simple intervention with thousands of *Euonymus fortunei* 'Coloratus' groundcover and daffodils shows what can be done with plants to improve a city space.

budgets, matching funds, and the like. Often the crucial step in convincing donors to support a park is to bring them in for a visit once you have some results to show. This is why it is important with a new public space project to begin with a small area and make it the best you can with new plantings. Start with the best soil and buy the biggest and best plants available; do not skimp on materials. Quality may increase initial costs, but it actually saves money in the long run and provides better results to show the public and your donors. By starting on a small scale you are more likely to succeed, and by demonstrating what you have already done, you will give your audience confidence in the project and funds will be easier to come by. Show naysayers that you can use private money in a poor section of the city and that people will love and respect the place you have created for them. Take people on tours of your park in progress, and let them see for themselves what needs to be fixed: a pergola dropping pieces of iron, broken steps, leaky staff headquarters.

Fund-raisers know it is important to be specific in order to help people visualize where their money might go. The Broadway Mall Association offers potential donors a detailed list of practical items for funding: in 2007 a donation of $50 funded the purchase and planting of a shrub, $250 a small tree, $500 the planting and maintenance of one flower bed with annuals, and $5,000 the planting, cleaning, and maintenance of one median mall for one year. This approach can be applied equally well to a new project or a restoration.

Make lists of special gardening projects or improvements and present them as fund-raising opportunities. When we realized that the Conservatory Garden had no formal entrance at the northern end, the Conservancy designed wrought-iron gates that were then donated by a doctor in memory of his wife. Many people enjoy giving money for specific projects that capture their imaginations. For a number of years, the twenty thousand tulips that bloom each spring in the north section of the Conservatory Garden were underwritten by a mother in memory of her daughter.

Naming Opportunities

People love to put their names on things. Plaques are popular fund-raising tools, and for gardens and parks, plaques on benches—symbols of welcome—can be especially meaningful for donors. As the *New York Times* reported in 2007, two strangers who met sitting on a bench at Broadway and 80th Street fell into conversation and ended up sharing

The Lewis Ginter Botanical Garden in Richmond, Virginia, had an imaginative fundraising idea: donors to their Children's Garden are recognized by hands with names on a fence.

the $2,500 donation for new benches for the spot. They even had a bench-warming party in the middle of Broadway for their friends.[2] The Broadway Malls Association reports that their bench program is a very successful way to raise funds.

Many places engrave paving stones with donors' names. The hexagonal paving stones along the stately elm-lined Mall in Central Park bear the names of donors to the park's Tree Trust program. The Seattle Parks Foundation is installing a wall with donor names at the entrance to their Lake Union Park project. As mentioned in chapter 1, the brick pavers in Tribute Park in Rockaway, Queens, have the names of all the donors who gave money in memory of their neighbors who died on 9/11.

When determining the price of these naming opportunities, be sure to add enough to the cost of the materials, installation, and overhead for the item itself so that you will be left with a sufficient donation or perhaps enough to fund a longer-term endowment. For instance, if a bench costs $500, an organization might request a much larger sum, with the dollar amount of the donation itself clearly communicated to donors.

Events

Public events build awareness of your park and help nurture a sense of ownership. A successful event will bring you many new friends and put money in your park's pockets. Each year from 1985 to 1995, Central Park hosted an innovative one-day fund-raising event called "You Gotta Have Parks" to help fund general maintenance. All over the park on these days, volunteers manned tables asking everyone entering the park to donate one dollar. This was a great way to give everyone, not just major donors, a chance to support the park. Corporate sponsors donated T-shirts and buttons, and volunteers convened for a massive clean-up effort.

On a much smaller scale, the lovely one-and-a-half-acre Abkhazi Garden in Victoria, British Columbia, once a private home, also hosts many fund-raising and awareness-building events each year. Director Valerie Murray, three staff members, and eighty volunteers run antique shows, lectures, concerts, cooking demonstrations, auctions, local wine tastings, cocktail parties, and a special Dog Days of Summer event, when the garden allows dogs on leashes and even sponsors dog singing and dog trick contests.

Events also attract new visitors who may become donors in the future. An imaginative and well-publicized event can improve the image of a park. Don't forget to invite the local press to your events; a newspaper story or televised clip will bring more attention to your cause. Event donations can be especially useful for underwriting "extra" visitor services, such as free concerts, information brochures, walking guides, and public education programs. Every garden or park has different needs and constraints and different opportunities for creative fund-raising.

Special events for select audiences and donors also can help provide crucial support to public spaces. But think carefully when major donors ask to use your space for a private event. On one hand, of course, their support is necessary and should be appreciated; on the other, frequent large events cause undue wear and tear on a park. Places that were oases when first restored may lose their magic if taken over too often by fund-raising events. Different parks have developed different strategies to respond to these requests, but it is important that people are not excluded from a public space any more than absolutely necessary or it breeds resentment. Write strict guidelines for the private use of public space—you can always make exceptions if necessary.

Determining Costs and Budgets

Potential donors will want to know quite specifically what a park will cost to build or renovate and what you anticipate the annual budget will be. A park's or garden's initial cost and its ongoing annual budget will vary widely based on its size, design, and location. Other variables are the types and complexities of plantings, the proportion of hardscaping to plantings, the number of maintenance staff needed, the willingness of local governments to participate, and the likelihood of private funding. Know your facts and figures before you begin to talk with potential donors.

The six-acre Conservatory Garden, privately funded through contributions to the Central Park Conservancy, had an operating budget of $400,000 in 2007 to cover the costs of five full-time staff members, a part-time security guard, seasonal help, plants, supplies, equipment, and a newsletter. A portion of the garden's annual income comes from its endowment. Beyond this specific budget, the Conservatory Garden receives parkwide services from the Conservancy, such as tree care, bench repair, sculpture conservation, and comfort station maintenance.

The original capital cost for the restoration of Bryant Park was $9 million in federal, state, city, and private funds. Its annual operating budget of over $6 million covers the many things it takes to run the park, including horticulture. Dan Biederman, founder of the Bryant Park Restoration Corporation and director of the park, has a long-term com-

Lake People Park, a one-and-a-half-acre park given to the city by a developer, cost little to build. Neighbors have come together to maintain the park's simple native plantings.

The park at 97th Street and Park Avenue, built with New York City capital funds, needs little maintenance apart from occasional trash pick-up and watering. It has had a positive impact on its neighborhood.

mitment to the role of public horticulture in the city. For Bryant Park, which is about the same size as the Conservatory Garden, the horticultural portion of the operating budget was more than $400,000 in 2007.

The Portland Classical Chinese Garden in downtown Portland, Oregon, was constructed in 2000; it was designed and built using authentic traditional methods by a landscape architect and craftsmen from Suzhou, China, with support from American architects and contractors. This small garden (about 40,000 square feet, the size of a large city block) cost $12.8 million to build, and it was paid for in equal portions by a combination of private citizens, corporations and foundations, and funds for urban renewal from the City of Portland. A public garden operated by a private nonprofit to be self-sustaining, it has an annual budget of $1.5 million that funds two to three gardeners and one maintenance person for the hardscape.

These examples are high-end, high-maintenance projects with a correspondingly high impact on their surrounding neighborhoods. But less expensive parks can also be oases for city dwellers. Lake People Park is a small, privately funded neighborhood park in Seattle, built in 2005 on land donated to the community by a generous developer. About one and a half acres in size and filled with native plants, it cost about $100,000 to build and has an annual maintenance budget of $20,000. The little New York City park at 97th Street and Park Avenue was constructed in 2006 for $900,000 in city capital funds allocated by the local councilman. Operating costs are minimal; the city provides little maintenance beyond occasional watering and cleanup. The park is successful because the basic design is attractive, with lots of seating, decent-looking trash cans (and people do use them!), and signs prohibiting dogs and pigeon feeding. The plants calm this otherwise chaotic spot in the middle of the street and contribute enjoyment twelve months a year. These smaller parks too have a positive impact on their neighborhoods.

Demonstrating That Parks Are Good for Business

The benefits that well-maintained parks bring to surrounding neighborhoods and their cities show that beautiful parks are not frills, they are good for business. Frederick Law Olmsted was aware of the part Central Park would play in increasing the value of real estate on its perimeter and began tracking those values more than one hundred years ago: "Olmsted proposed that the tremendous increase in property value, and tax revenue, was a direct result of Central Park."[3] In 1903, his stepson

The Classical Chinese Garden created in the heart of downtown Portland, Oregon, has transformed the neighborhood and created business opportunities. Photo courtesy Portland Classical Chinese Garden.

John Charles Olmsted drew a similar conclusion when he predicted what the presence of parks would do for the city of Portland: "All agree that parks not only add to the beauty of a city and to the pleasure of living in it, but are exceedingly important factors in developing the healthfulness and business prosperity of its residents."[4] Presenting to potential donors the facts that support this argument can be one of the most effective ways to persuade them to make investments in their cities' parks and gardens.

The Portland Classical Chinese Garden, described in the previous section, is an example of how a public garden can bring economic growth and benefits to business. The architecture and the plantings are superb in every detail, but particularly exciting is that this traditional scholar's Chinese garden exists in the midst of the modern city. The garden is in the middle of historic Old Town/Chinatown, a nationally registered historic district with cast-iron buildings and red Chinese lamp-posts. Skyscrapers rise above it in the distance. The funding to sustain the garden is private: donations, entrance fees, foundations, membership, programs, and after-hours garden rentals for events.

The mission of the Classical Chinese Garden is "to cultivate an oasis of tranquil beauty and harmony to inspire, engage, and educate our global community in the appreciation of a richly authentic Chinese culture."[5] The hope of those who built this garden was that it would serve as a starting point for the revitalization of a very old Portland neighborhood that was the first home of many immigrant communities over the years. It has realized those hopes. Businesses around the garden are thriving, and it has spawned a $4.5 million streetscape project featuring two festival streets, with a number of other projects in the works. It is a sanctuary of elegance and nature surrounded by a busy city.

In Battery Park City, the very successful ninety-two-acre planned community described in chapter 1, a decision was made to develop the parks first. Philip Pitruzzello, president of the Battery Park City Authority from 1994 to 1996, told me that the funding for park operations was put in place in the first phases of construction in 1979, and the initial capital costs were funded with the knowledge that the investment in parks would be made back many times over when developers built. Creating the parks first "gave developers the confidence to proceed with building."[6]

What has happened in Boston is a good example of how valuable parks can be to developers and businesses. Boston, with a population of 589,000, has many lovely parks and the oldest park system in the country—the historic Emerald Necklace of connecting Olmsted-designed public greenspaces. In recent years, the city has been preoccupied with the Big Dig, a $15 billion highway replacement project. The ugly, noisy Route 93 is now below ground, and the surface has been redesigned to include a mile-long series of green spaces with benches, fountains, trees, and gardens, with four new urban parks totaling ten and a half acres. Real estate values nearby have risen dramatically—as much as 79 percent over the fifteen years the project lasted. This rise in values—which began even before the parks were constructed—is almost double the citywide increase in commercial property values during that period.

Property owners are reorienting their buildings to face the new Rose Fitzgerald Kennedy Greenway, reinvesting in their properties, and adding sidewalk cafes. Building owners who long ago sealed off windows over-looking the highway are now reopening them. New housing, shops, offices, and upscale developments are in the works. William Wheaton, an economist and director of the Center for Real Estate at the Massachusetts Institute of Technology, stated, "People looking for residential condos are willing to pay an arm and a leg more to have a park as a neighbor."[7]

The nonprofit Rose Fitzgerald Kennedy Greenway Conservancy is charged with overseeing and maintaining the one-mile greenway. This conservancy hopes to offer a useful model to other cities considering an evolution of sustainable practices. While park maintenance in Boston, as in many urban areas around the country, continues to be a challenge because of insufficient operating budgets, the late Justine Liff, commissioner of Boston's Department of Parks and Recreation, saw the importance of maintaining these urban green spaces. She said, "How we care for parks and open spaces is a reflection of who we are as a society."[8] City planners and residents alike hope that the parks will transform this area of downtown Boston, even redefine the city.

On a smaller scale, when developer Greg O'Connell generously made an attractive public landscape out of his private property on the waterfront in Red Hook, Brooklyn (see chapter 1), the new space attracted the attention of other businesses to the possibilities in the neighborhood. In 2007 a Fairway market, with 52,000 square feet of retail space, opened in one of the huge nineteenth-century brick pier buildings he owns nearby. He also created apartments for tenants who were attracted by the gorgeous views of the harbor and the lush plantings surrounding the area. This project won a Municipal Arts Society New York City Masterworks Award in 2006 as "the best neighborhood catalyst."

A spectacular beautification project undertaken by the City of Chicago together with business people along Michigan Avenue, the city's premier shopping area, has been very profitable for businesses. Beginning in 1991 with Crate & Barrel, each year individual store owners have underwritten the cost of forty-seven planted areas along the sidewalks in front of their stores. In tandem with this effort, the city constructed medians down the middle of the street, filled with colorful plantings. Since 1993, a business group, the Michigan Avenue Streetscape Association, has raised the $200,000 to pay for three distinct plantings a year. The city funds the cost of the avenue's plantings south of the Chicago River. The landscape architect Douglas Hoerr of Hoerr Schaudt Landscape Architects charges only a minimal fee for his fabulous designs,

Since 1991, private businesses working with the city have underwritten lush plantings, designed by landscape architect Douglas Hoerr, on Chicago's Michigan Avenue. This initiative has improved business in a spectacular way. Photo courtesy Hoerr Schaudt Landscape Architects.

because he believes in what these plantings do for the area. Hoerr writes, "To attract attention from passing motorists and be interesting enough to cast a spell on pedestrians, bold horticultural designs were needed."[9] He describes what the street looked like in 1989 before all this began: "The only color on Michigan Avenue in those days was the yellow stripe down the middle of the street."[10] In an article in the *Chicago Tribune Magazine*, Mayor Daley was quoted as saying: "[Michigan Avenue] needed a shot in the arm. The plantings turned it around. People started coming down there in large numbers."[11]

A national organization, the American Planning Association, reports that the beautification of Chicago has become a popular topic in planning meetings everywhere.[12] Jennifer S. Vey of the Brookings Institution's Metropolitan Policy Program says that research into census figures shows that the population of Chicago's downtown area, where

Michigan Avenue is located, has increased by 30 percent from 1990 to 2000, and its median income by 12 percent, which builds the business base and brings in more tax money.[13]

Until recently, evidence for the benefits of urban beautification was mostly anecdotal. People who worked in the field knew what a difference it made, but this was not enough to convince businesses, city governments, and individuals to get on board. Now studies all over the country are providing statistics about the positive impact of well-tended green spaces, street plantings, and public gardens.

Kathleen L. Wolf of the University of Washington's Center for Urban Horticulture conducted a study of how consumers respond to the planting of trees on streets, published in the December 2005 issue of the *Journal of Forestry*. Wolf concluded that "plantings in urban neighborhoods are a symbol of care and . . . change."[14] Respondents from all regions of the United States favor tree plantings, and her research also shows that retail customers are willing to pay up to 12 percent more in shopping areas with well-cared for trees than in those without them. How much more would they be willing to pay if the streets were embellished with lush colorful plantings of shrubs, perennials, and annuals like those on Chicago's Michigan Avenue?

The Pennsylvania Horticultural Society has a very active and widely respected program called Philadelphia Green, which has been enhancing city life there since 1974. Their work began with window box competitions and progressed to more than four hundred community gardens in inner-city areas. After more than thirty years of experience in the field, including work in many major parks, Philadelphia Green realized that they needed statistics to back up what their greening experience had taught them, more concrete evidence that could garner support for their programs from the business community and the city. In 2004 they joined with the Wharton School of Business at the University of Pennsylvania to conduct a study of one of their community development projects. Among other things, the Wharton Study found a $12 million rise in property values in Philadelphia's New Kensington neighborhood as a result of $1 million invested in various greening projects.[15] (For more on this study, see the Resource Directory.)

Philadelphia Green states on its Web site that "research consistently shows that investment in parks generates higher real estate values, economic revitalization, increased tourism, and better overall quality of life." Their studies have also demonstrated that the costs of beautification are minimal compared to building new developments and repairing infrastructure. As Blaine Bonham, executive vice president of the Pennsylvania Horticultural Society, told me, "The study of the positive returns on investments in greening took what we knew in our hearts and made it quantifiable."

❧

In a perfect world, beautiful parks and gardens would be a high priority for any city government that cares about the quality of life for its citizens. Although New Yorkers rank parks next in importance after police, fire, and education in community-board polls, too often city budgets do not reflect a commitment to good public green space, and when budgets get tight, park budgets are inevitably cut. Some funding must come from the private sector, and innovative approaches to finding and attracting private funding are often determining factors in a park's or garden's success.

The Power of Plants and Parks

When a park is neglected it affects almost all of us psychologically and perhaps spiritually. When nurtured it adds greatly to the comfort, sense of well-being, and high spirits of our citizens. . . . [They] are encouraged and enjoy a sense of pride when open spaces are well cared for.

—Arthur Ross, New York philanthropist and supporter of parks, 2005

The beauty and enchantment of public gardens . . . instill new pride in communities and change the personal and public experience of city life.

—Smith College plaque, October 1999

On the day of the World Trade Center attacks, New Yorkers went to their parks. The streets were empty, but the parks in every neighborhood were full of people. They knew instinctively that they would feel safer there and could be with others who shared their shock and grief. As so often happens in times of national disaster, strangers talked to one another. That achingly beautiful Tuesday, visitors kept arriving in the Conservatory Garden, saying how much better it made them feel to be in that peaceful spot, and that perhaps life would go on. In Wagner Park, just blocks from Ground Zero, firefighters and rescue workers used the park for breaks. Though the smoke and ashes were everywhere, the flowers kept right on blooming, conveying nature's comforting message of hope.

The next morning, I was looking out my window and thinking about what I could do to help my beloved city. I could see the plumes of smoke all the way uptown where I lived. Just three days before, there had been a successful rally in Union Square Park for additional city support

Wagner Park in early September 2001. After 9/11, firefighters and rescue workers used this park for breaks, and despite the ashes and smoke the flowers continued to bloom.

Boxes of daffodils arrived from Holland as a gift to the City of New York in memory of the victims of 9/11.

Volunteers from all over New York, and from other cities as well, came to plant daffodils in the city's parks.

for parks, particularly in the poorer areas. Now the city's thoughts would be far from such matters. I heard the fax machine buzz and found a message from Hans van Waardenburg, a Dutch bulb grower and distributor who had supplied bulbs for many of my public projects for more than twenty years. Hans wrote how distressed he was for New York and how he wished there was something he could do for us. It suddenly struck me that in years past Hans had sometimes sent free bulbs for us to distribute to people for use in their parks and gardens. Perhaps he could do this again, and we could plant them in memory of those who died. When the flowers came up the next spring, it might lift people's spirits. "Hans," I wrote back, "you don't have any extra bulbs, do you?"

After numerous messages back and forth, Hans gave the City of New York half a million daffodils as a memorial for 9/11 victims, and the City of Rotterdam gave half a million more. I met with the Parks Department and we agreed to work together, using the department's gardeners and staff and their many volunteers. New Yorkers for Parks recruited members of several parks organizations to help get the bulbs in the ground. I insisted that we plant the bulbs not in parks that had already been restored but in those that hadn't seen a flower in years, and that is what we did.

In late September, ships began to arrive in New York harbor carrying thousands of boxes of daffodil bulbs for the city. All through the fall months, as New Yorkers tried to deal with their shock and grief, people came into the city's parks and planted bulbs. About ten thousand people came out of their apartments, houses, and offices and got down on their knees in the dirt.

People from other cities came to help. A delegation from Jamestown, New York—eight hours away—drove most of the night through an early snowstorm to join us at Thomas Jefferson Park, at 112th Street and First Avenue in East Harlem. It was a sunny October Saturday in the city. My old friend Bill Steyer, who had escorted me around the Conservatory Garden so many years before, unpacked and distributed the bulbs. Eileen Remor, the enthusiastic, efficient manager of the Parks Department's volunteer events, had everything organized. Trowels and gloves were donated by Target Stores. As the cars whizzed by, we dug in the hard ground. Many of the volunteers had never planted anything before. I explained that the daffodils would look better planted in natural groupings rather than in rows, and everyone enjoyed the technique I showed them: tossing the daffodil bulbs into the air and planting them where they fall. A group of reluctant policemen who had wandered into the park were persuaded to help us. Some kids playing basketball joined in.

The same thing happened all over the city that fall. Many firefighters from Rockaway, in Queens, had lost their lives, and we planted daffodils for them along Jamaica Bay, with its view across the river to where the towers had stood against the horizon. We planted them in Dewitt Clinton Park on the West Side, near where victims' families had gone to get help from the city. One day the prime minister of Slovakia, who was in the city to run in the New York Marathon, planted daffodils with local firefighters in a little park in Greenwich Village. In Brooklyn on a vacant lot by the East River with a direct view of where the World Trade Center had once been, a group of people cleared the weeds and planted twenty thousand daffodils in the shape of the twin towers.

The next spring, yellow flowers bloomed throughout the city, memorializing those who died and reminding people that life was renewing itself, that parks are sacred places, and that nature could comfort us and make our city beautiful again. Thanks to Hans's continuing generosity and to public and private support, we still plant daffodils each fall in parks, along parkways, in housing projects, and around school yards. From a boat or a ferry in spring, you can see daffodils in a bright ring around the city. In 2007, with three million bulbs in the ground,

In the spring of 2002, one million daffodils bloomed in yellow ribbons all over New York. We have continued to plant them each spring since. Photo by Joseph de Sciose.

Beautiful places soften and civilize city life.

Mayor Bloomberg declared the daffodil the official flower of New York. We hope someday to have eight million, one for each New Yorker.

This project has all the elements necessary for successful city beautification. Government support comes from the City Council, which funds the shipping costs. The private nonprofit advocacy group New Yorkers for Parks, working with the Parks Department, continues to organize the distribution of hundreds of thousands of bulbs, involving volunteers from community parks organizations and businesses. Public and private school children plant daffodils in parks near their schools. Each year New Yorkers for Parks holds a heartwarming breakfast to raise funds for the Daffodil Project and honor those from around the city who plant these flowers to beautify their city. Private individuals, foundations, and corporations like Con Edison, which has customers in all five boroughs, support the Daffodil Project. The daffodils are an advocacy tool, calling people's attention to the importance of their parks and to what still needs to be done for them. Other places, such as Dayton, Ohio, York, Pennsylvania, Suffolk County on Long Island, Wilmington, Delaware, Detroit, Michigan, and Tupelo, Mississippi, have adopted this idea to bring people together and beautify their parks and cities.

Beautifying cities with well-planted gardens, parks, and streets is beneficial to many aspects of city life: it is good for business, tourism, and economic development; it helps reduce crime; and, perhaps most important, it soothes the souls of city dwellers. Beautiful parks like Central Park and San Francisco's Golden Gate Park, formal gardens like the Conservatory Garden and Portland's Chinese Garden, informal landscape plantings like those along the Brooklyn waterfront in Red Hook or in Seattle's Lake People Park—these landscapes both soften and strengthen the human experience for those who live in a city. A wide variety of plants that change and develop over the course of the year make nature and its rhythms more accessible to city dwellers, giving them pleasure and reassurance. This in turn makes people feel more secure, and they behave in a more civil manner toward their fellow citizens.

Well-maintained parks tell people that their city cares about them and give them a compelling reason to remain in the city. A visitor once said to me, after experiencing the Conservatory Garden for the first time, that she had intended to leave New York, but if there was a place like this in the city, she wasn't leaving. Garden cities like Chicago, with its gorgeous street plantings, become inviting urban centers where people want to live and work.

Creating successful public space requires the interplay of many factors: money (public and private), energy, and the work of trained staff and volunteers; an effective design based on a strong understanding of the elements that will attract visitors all year round; high-quality plants grown in healthy soil, with a long-term commitment to their maintenance; and a stubborn conviction that people matter.

With so much to divide us, one thing seems common to us all: everyone loves to be surrounded by something beautiful. Public parks and gardens make us feel good about ourselves and our cities, and we all benefit.

Being surrounded by beauty makes people feel good about themselves and their city. Photo by Sara Cedar Miller.

Make it gorgeous and they will come; keep it that way and they will help you.

Gorgeous plantings will fill your park with visitors.

Notes

Introduction

1. Frederick Law Olmsted, *Notes on the Plan of Franklin Park and Related Matters* (Boston: Department of Parks, 1886), 107, quoted in Charles A. Lewis, *Green Nature/Human Nature: The Meaning of Plants in Our Lives* (Chicago: University of Illinois Press, 1996), 7.
2. Enid Nemy, "New Yorkers, etc.," *New York Times*, April 19, 1987.
3. F. E. Kuo and W. C. Sullivan, "Environment and Crime in the Inner City: Does Vegetation Reduce Crime?" *Environment and Behavior* 33, no. 3 (2001): 343–67. Available at www.lhhl.uiuc.edu/all.scientific .articles.htm.
4. Frances E. Kuo, "Beyond Beauty: The Benefits of Greening Our Cities," speech given at the Second Annual Greening Symposium, Chicago, August 20, 2003. More information about these studies is available at the Web site of the Landscape and Human Health Laboratory at the University of Illinois at Urbana-Champaign (www.lhhl.uiuc.edu).
5. "Revitalizing Chicago through Parks and Public Spaces: Remarks from Mayor Richard M. Daley, City of Chicago," speech given at the Great Parks/Great Cities Conference at the Urban Parks Institute, July 31, 2001. Available at the Project for Public Spaces Web site, www.pps.org/topics/whats_new/daley_speech.

1. All Over Town: The Conservatory Garden and Other Projects

1. *New York Times*, November 8, 1988.

2. Elements of a Successful Public Space

1. William H. Whyte, *The Social Life of Small Urban Spaces* (Washington, D.C.: The Conservation Foundation, 1980), 18.
2. Paul Goldberger, foreword to *The Essential William H. Whyte* (New York: Fordham University Press, 2000), ix.
3. David Dillon, "Sage of the City, or How a Keen Observer Solves the Mysteries of Our Streets," *Preservation Magazine*, September/October 1996, 74.
4. William H. Whyte, "Revitalization of Bryant Park: Report to the Rockefeller Brothers Fund" (1979), 14.
5. William H. Whyte, *City: Rediscovering the Center* (New York: Doubleday, 1988), 156.
6. Charles A. Lewis, *Green Nature/Human Nature: The Meaning of Plants in Our Lives* (Chicago: University of Illinois Press, 1996), 64

7. Dr. Gerhard Pirner, e-mail to author, January 31, 2008.
8. Whyte, *The Social Life of Small Urban Spaces*, 31.

3. The Art of Garden Design

1. Louise Beebe Wilder, *Color in My Garden* (New York: Atlantic Monthly Press, 1990), 7.
2. Vita Sackville-West, *In Your Garden* (London: Frances Lincoln, 2004), 224.
3. Charles A. Lewis, *Green Nature/Human Nature: The Meaning of Plants in Our Lives* (Chicago: University of Illinois Press, 1996), 64.
4. Ibid., 3.
5. Quoted in Pilar Viladas, "The Constant Gardener," *New York Times Magazine*, May 16, 2004, 43.
6. The botanical names used in this book are taken from the Royal Horticultural Society's *RHS Plant Finder 2007–2008* (New York: Dorling Kindersley, 2007). The RHS also provides searchable online access to its horticultural database; see the Resource Directory for details.
7. Michael Pollan, "Against Nativism," *New York Times Magazine*, May 15, 1994, as quoted on www.michaelpollan.com/article.php?id=31.
8. *The Correspondence of Alexander Pope*, ed. George Sherburn, 5 vols. (Oxford: Clarendon Press, 1956), 4:40.
9. Gertrude Jekyll, *Colour Schemes for the Flower Garden* (1936 ed.; repr., Woodbridge, England: Baron Publishing, 1982), 17.

4. Soil

1. *Natural History*, book XVII.
2. *Elizabeth and Her German Garden* (New York and London: Macmillan, 1900), 219.

5. Maintenance

1. T. H. Everett, *The New York Botanical Garden Illustrated Encyclopedia of Horticulture*, 10 vols. (New York and London: Garland, 1982), 10:3531.
2. Michael Pollan, *Second Nature: A Gardener's Education* (New York: Atlantic Monthly Press, 1991), 48.
3. Charles A. Lewis, *Green Nature/Human Nature: The Meaning of Plants in Our Lives* (Chicago: University of Illinois Press, 1996), 105.

7. Advocacy

1. Henry Payne, "Murder City," *Wall Street Journal*, December 8, 2007.
2. Quoted in Susan Saulny, "Detroit Considers Sale of City's Small Parks," *New York Times*, December 29, 2007.
3. The population figure is a 2007 estimate taken from www.bcstats .gov.
4. Quoted in Amy Biegelsen, "In Like Flynn," *Style,* January 16, 2008, available at www.styleweekly.com.
5. Emily Le Coz, "Program to Net Big Bucks for Beautification," *Northeast Mississippi Daily Journal*, May 21, 2008.
6. See Harold M. Mayer and Richard C. Wade, *Chicago: Growth of a Metropolis* (Chicago: University of Chicago Press, 1969).
7. "Revitalizing Chicago through Parks and Public Spaces: Remarks from Mayor Richard M. Daley, City of Chicago," speech given at the Great Parks/Great Cities Conference at the Urban Parks Institute, July 31, 2001. Available at the Project for Public Spaces Web site, www.pps.org/topics/whats_new/daley_speech.
8. Quoted in Lisa Chamberlain, "Union Square Park: Planning the Final Stages of a Park's Makeover," *New York Times*, June 26, 2005.
9. Project for Public Spaces Web site, www.pps.org.
10. NYRP Web site, www.nyrp.org.

8. Private Funding and Benefits for Business

1. "Beautiful York Action Plan, 2006–2007," available at www.yccf.org/ pdf/receive/BeautifulYork.pdf.

2. Alex Mindlin, "In the Middle of Broadway, Sickness, and a Sturdy Legacy," *New York Times*, January 7, 2007, 5.
3. Tom Fox, *Urban Open Space: An Investment That Pays* (New York: The Neighborhood Open Space Coalition, 1990), 12.
4. John Charles Olmsted, *Annual Report of the Park Board*, Portland, Oregon, 1903; quoted at www.ccrh.org/comm/slough/primary /parkboard.htm.
5. From www.portlandchinesegarden.org/garden/mission.
6. Philip Pitruzzello, e-mail message to author, March 19, 2006.
7. *Real Estate Impacts of the Massachusetts Turnpike Authority and the Central Artery/Third Harbor Tunnel Project*, vol. 2 (Boston: Economic Development Research Group, 2008), 26.
8. M. R. Montgomery, "The Emerald Necklace at 100," *Boston Globe*, September 21, 1996, C5.
9 Web site of the Illinois Chapter of the American Society of Landscape Architects, www.il-asla.org/Awards/2001winners/michiganave.htm.
10. Lee Scheier, "Floral Report," *Chicago Tribune Magazine*, August 5, 2007, 18.
11. Ibid.
12. Ibid., 29.
13. Lee Scheier, "Michigan Avenue Streetscape Studies," unpublished article draft, 15.
14. Scheier, "Floral Report," 29.
15. Susan Wachter, "The Determinants of Neighborhood Transformations in Philadelphia," Wharton School, University of Pennsylvania, 2004. Available at gislab.wharton.upenn.edu/silus/Papers/ GreeninGStudy.pdf.

Resource Directory

The following selected resources are organized by chapter. Recommended plants for public spaces are listed separately in the section titled "Plant Lists," followed by a list of recommended reading.

The Web sites below are sources of good information. Mention of these sites is not an endorsement of any of their products or services.

For more information about Lynden B. Miller's gardens, including additional photos, news, and tips for successful public spaces, visit her website at www.publicgardendesign.com.

Chapter 1: All Over Town
Selected list of Lynden B. Miller's public and university garden projects

Columbia University, Morningside Campus
> Enter campus at 116th Street gates, at Broadway or Amsterdam Avenue, Manhattan.
> Open daily.

The Conservatory Garden
> Fifth Avenue and 105th Street in Central Park, Manhattan
> Open daily, 8 A.M. to dusk.
> (212) 860-1382
> www.centralparknyc.org/virtualpark/northend/conservatory garden

The Gardens in Bryant Park
> Avenue of the Americas and 42nd Street, Manhattan
> Open daily.
> (212) 768-4242
> www.bryantpark.org

Madison Square Park
> Between Madison Avenue and Fifth Avenue, 23rd to 26th streets, Manhattan
> Open daily.
> (212) 447-1805
> www.madisonsquarepark.org

The New York Botanical Garden
> Irwin Perennial Garden, Ladies Border
> 200th Street and Southern Boulevard, Bronx
> Open Tuesday–Sunday; Monday, holidays only.
> (718) 817-8700
> www.nybg.org

Pier 44 Waterfront Garden
> 290 Conover Street at Pier 44, Red Hook, Brooklyn

Princeton University, Princeton, N.J.
> Wyman House Garden, Maclean House Garden, Prospect Garden
> Open daily.

Stony Brook University, Stony Brook, N.Y.
> Plantings at the Academic Mall, Staller Amphitheater, Javits Center, Entry Drive, and Entry Circle (enter at Nichols Road)
> Open daily.
> www.sunysb.edu

Tribute Park, Rockaway, Queens
> Beach Channel Drive and 116th Street
> Open daily.

Wagner Park in Battery Park City, Manhattan
> Just north of Historic Battery Park, off Battery Place
> Open daily, dawn to dusk.
> (212) 267-9700

Chapter 2: Elements of a Successful Public Space
Video of William H. Whyte's groundbreaking work on urban spaces

Social Life of Small Urban Spaces
> Available from Direct Cinema, (310) 636-8200 or online at www.directcinema.com/dcl/title.php?id=95&list=94,95,452 &cat_id=324

National landscape beautification organizations

America in Bloom
> Columbus, Ohio
> www.americainbloom.org

American Public Gardens Association
> www.publicgardens.org (click on Garden Search to locate public gardens)

The Cultural Landscape Foundation
> www.tclf.org

Keep America Beautiful
Stamford, Connecticut
www.kab.org

National directories of landscape designers and landscape architects
American Society of Landscape Architects
www.asla.org
Association of Professional Landscape Designers
www.apld.com

Chapter 3: The Art of Garden Design

See the Recommended Reading section for many fine books on garden design.

Plant nomenclature
The Royal Horticultural Society Horticultural Database
The Royal Horticultural Society makes its *RHS Plant Finder* available online at www.rhs.org.uk/rhsplantfinder/plantfinder.asp (scroll down to Search). The same page also provides links to other material in the *Plant Finder*, including guides to plant-naming conventions, a glossary, and a bibliography.

American Horticultural Society resources
American Horticultural Society
www.ahs.org
Great Plant Guide
www.ahs.org/books/books.htm
Hardiness and Heat Zone Maps
Hardiness Map: www.ahs.org/publications/usda_hardiness_zone _map.htm
Heat Zone Map: www.ahs.org/publications/heat_zone_map.htm

Information about reliable plants in different regions of the country
Great Plant Picks for the Pacific Northwest
www.greatplantpicks.org
Long Island Gold Medal Plant Award Program brochure
www.cce.cornell.edu/suffolk/Ag/Gold Medal Plant Awards.htm
National Gardening Association
Plant Finder, searchable by hardiness zone and other criteria: www.garden.org/plantfinder
Also, click on Regional Reports for more information about plants in every region of the U.S.
Missouri Botanical Garden
Plant Finder: www.mobot.org/gardeninghelp/plantfinder/Alpha .asp.
Also lists Plants of Merit for St. Louis region
Perennial Plant of the Year
View selections from 1990 to date: www.perennialplant.org
Plant Information Online
Discover plant sources in 1,043 North American nurseries: https://plantinfo.umn.edu/arboretum/
The United States National Arboretum
www.usna.usda.gov/

Information on invasive plants and weeds
Brooklyn Botanic Garden All-Region Guides
Native Alternatives to Invasive Plants, by C. Colston Burrell
Available at www.bbg.org (click on Shop, then BBG Publications)
Center for Invasive Plant Management
www.weedcenter.org
National Gardening Association
Weed Library: www.garden.org/weedlibrary/
United States Department of Agriculture
plants.usda.gov/java/noxiousDriver

Chapter 4: Soil

General information on soil
Harvard University Facilities Maintenance Operations
The Harvard University Green Initiative: www.organiclandscaping .uos.harvard.edu
The Soil and Water Conservation Society
www.swcs.org
Soil Food Web
www.soilfoodweb.com
Soil Science Society of America
www.soils.org
USDA National Resources Conservation Service
www.ny.nrcs.usda.gov/technical/soils/ and soils.usda.gov/teachers .html

Soil testing information
Cooperative Extensions
Find your nearest cooperative extension office: www.csrees.usda.gov /Extension/index.html
University of Massachusetts Amherst
Soil & Plant Tissue Testing Laboratory: www.umass.edu/soiltest/

Making compost and compost tea
Battery Park City Conservancy
www.bpcparks.org/bpcp/bpcp/operations.php
Brooklyn Botanic Garden Urban Composting Project
www.bbg.org/compost
Handbook, "Easy Compost: The Secret to Great Soil and Spectacular Plants"
www.bbg.org/gar2/topics/sustainable/handbooks/easycompost/
International Compost Tea Council
www.intlctc.org
National Sustainable Agriculture Information Service
www.attra.org, see "Notes on Compost Teas" publication in section on Soils & Compost
US Environmental Protection Agency
www.epa.gov/osw/conserve/rrr/composting/
USDA Natural Resources Conservation Service compost information
www.ars.usda.gov/Research/docs.htm?docid=8818#Backyard%20C omposting

Chapter 5: Maintenance

Master Gardener programs
Links to all programs in the US by state and in three Canadian provinces: www.ahs.org/master_gardeners/

Battery Park City Conservancy's chemical-free
    sustainable maintenance practices
Battery Park City Conservancy
    www.bpcparks.org/bpcp/bpcp/operations.php

Resources for pest and disease management
National Gardening Association
    Pest Library for pest and disease control: www.garden.org/pestlibrary
Safer Pest Control Project
    www.spcpweb.org (for the "Integrated Pest Management for Park
        Districts" guide, click on Yards & Parks, then scroll down to Park
        District Manual)
United States Environmental Protection Agency
    Integrated Pest Management and alternative control information:
        www.epa.gov/agriculture/tipm.html

Finding an ISA-certified arborist for tree care
International Society of Arboriculture
    www.isa-arbor.com/home.aspx (click on Verify Certification to
        search for a certified arborist in your area)

Chapter 6: Volunteers
Recruiting volunteers
AmeriCorps
    www.americorps.org
VolunteerMatch
    www.volunteermatch.org

Volunteering in New York City parks
Central Park Conservancy
    www.centralparknyc.org
New York City Department of Parks and Recreation
    Volunteer Opportunities: www.nycgovparks.org/sub_opportunities
        /volunteer_opportunities.html
Partnership for Parks and It's My Park! Day
    www.partnershipforparks.org/

Additional information on the Riker's Island GreenHouse
    program
The Horticultural Society of New York
    www.hsny.org (click on Programs then Outreach)

An example of volunteer handbook materials
Central Park Conservancy Volunteer Program
    www.centralparknyc.org/site/PageNavigator/aboutcon_jobs_vol_vo
        lunteerinfo

Chapter 7: Advocacy for Parks
Selected websites of city parks and gardens making a
    difference
Chicago, Illinois
    Chicago Park District: www.chicagoparkdistrict.com
    Mayor Daley's speech on parks: www.pps.org/topics/whats_new
        /daley_speech
    Guide to Chicago Landscape Ordinance: www.newrules.org
        /environment/chiland.html

Detroit, Michigan
    Belle Isle Botanical Society: www.bibsociety.org
    Belle Isle Women's Committee: www.biwcinc.org
    Friends of Belle Isle: www.fobi.org
Minneapolis, Minnesota
    Park and Recreation Board: www.minneapolisparks.org/home.asp
Portland, Oregon
    Parks and Recreation Bureau: www.portlandonline.com/parks
Richmond, Virginia
    Department of Community Development: www.richmondgov
        .com/departments/communitydev, www.lewisginter.org
Tupelo, Mississippi
    www.livingintupelo.com
Vancouver, B.C.
    Parks and Gardens: www.vancouverparks.ca
Wilmington, Delaware
    Delaware Center for Horticulture: www.dehort.org (for Beautifica-
        tion Commision, click on What We Do, then Public Landscapes,
        Wilmington)

Selected examples of advocacy organizations
City Parks Alliance
    www.cityparksalliance.org
Friends of Olmsted Parks
    www.olmstedpark.org
Municipal Arts Society
    www.mas.org
New Yorkers for Parks
    www.ny4p.org
The New York Restoration Project
    www.nyrp.org
Project for Public Spaces
    www.pps.org
Tennessee State Parks' Friends Group
    www.tennessee.gov/environment/parks/friends.shtml
    Email requests for examples of Friends Group materials to
        ask.tnstateparks@state.tn.us
The Trust for Public Land
    www.tpl.org
    Parks for People Program (click on Conservation Initiatives, then
        Parks for People)

New Yorkers for Parks advocacy resource examples
Advocacy Day
    www.ny4p.org (click on Take Action, then Parks Advocacy Day)
Advocacy Workbook
    Read the workbook online at www.ny4p.org (click on Take Action,
        then Tools for Action)
"How Smart Parks Investment Pays Its Way," Ernst & Young report
    www.ny4p.org/index.php?option=com_content&task=view&id=54
        &Itemid=76
Report Cards, District Profiles, and Progress Reports on Parks
    www.ny4p.org (click on Resources & Publications, then NY4P
        Reports)
Report on Best Practices in Urban Parks
    Comparative Park Management Models: www.ny4p.org (click on
        Resources & Publications, then NY4P Reports)

Chapter 8: Private Funding and Benefits for Business

Information on public-private parks partnerships
Project for Public Spaces
www.pps.org/parks_plazas_squares/info/pubpriv/

Examples of park conservancies
Buffalo Olmsted Parks Conservancy
www.buffaloolmstedparks.org
Central Park Conservancy
www.centralparknyc.org
Charleston Parks Conservancy
www.charlestonparksconservancy.org
Emerald Necklace Conservancy
www.emeraldnecklace.org
Forest Park Forever
www.forestparkforever.org
Lincoln Park Conservancy
www.lincolnparkconservancy.org
The Olmsted Parks Conservancy
www.olmstedparks.org
Piedmont Park Conservancy
www.piedmontpark.org
Pittsburgh Parks Conservancy
www.pittsburghparks.org
Prospect Park Alliance
www.prospectpark.org
Rose Fitzgerald Kennedy Greenway Conservancy
www.rosekennedygreenway.org
San Francisco Golden Gate National Parks Conservancy
www.parksconservancy.org

General information on business improvement districts
New York City Small Business Services: Help for Neighborhoods
www.nyc.gov/html/sbs/html/neighborhood/bid.shtml

Examples of BIDs
Bryant Park Corporation
www.bryantpark.org/park-management/overview.php
34th Street Partnership
www.34thstreet.org
Lincoln Square BID
www.lincolnbid.org

Examples of private urban beautification organizations
Broadway Mall Association
www.broadwaymall.org
Chicago Parkways Foundation
www.parkways.org
City Parks Foundation
www.cityparksfoundation.org

Michigan Avenue Streetscape Association
www.themagnificentmile.com/StreetScape/default.cfm
Seattle Parks Foundation
www.seattleparksfoundation.org
York City Community Foundation
www.yccf.org; to access Beautiful York Action Plan, go to www.yccf
.org/pdf/receive/beautifulyork.pdf
Public-private garden partnerships mentioned in the chapter
The Abkhazi Garden
1964 Fairfield Road, Victoria
BC V8S 1H4, Canada
www.gardensvictoria.com/abkhazigardens.html
The Portland Classical Chinese Garden
239 Northwest Everett Street
Portland, Ore.
www.portlandchinesegarden.org

Studies on the effects of parks
American Planning Association
www.planning.org
Brookings Institution Metropolitan Policy Program
www.brookings.edu/METRO.ASPX
The Center for Urban Horticulture
depts.washington.edu/urbhort/cuh/index.html
Council on the Environment of New York City
www.cenyc.org
Greenmarket (212) 788-7476
Open Space Greening (212) 788-7935
Kathleen Wolf's study "Human Dimensions of Urban Forestry and Urban Greening"
University of Washington, College of Forest Resources
Seattle, WA 98195-2100
www.cfr.washington.edu/research.envmind/index.html
Landscape and Human Health Laboratory; Frances Kuo
University of Illinois at Urbana-Champaign
www.lhhl.uiuc.edu
Philadelphia Green Program
www.pennsylvaniahorticulturalsociety.org/phlgreen/index.html
Pennsylvania Horticultural Society
www.pennsylvaniahorticulturalsociety.org
Wharton School of Business Study, "The Determinants of Neighborhood Transformations in Philadelphia"
gislab.wharton.upenn.edu/silus/Papers/GreeninGStudy.pdf; also
available at www.pennsylvaniahorticulturalsociety.org

Chapter 9: The Power of Plants and Parks

Additional information on New York City's Daffodil Project
New Yorkers for Parks
www.ny4p.org (click on The Daffodil Project)

Plant Lists

The lists in this section include plants that I have found hardy, reliable, and noteworthy for public garden use in the greater New York area, generally Zones 6 and 7. Overall, these have proved to be relatively low-maintenance plants. For more information on plants for specific situations, see my Web site at www.publicgardendesign.com.

❄ = Winter and very early spring interest in the Northeast from bark, berries, evergreen foliage, or long-lasting seedheads

Deciduous Trees, Shrubs, and Vines

Once established, trees, shrubs, and vines are generally lower maintenance than perennials and annuals, unless you wish to prune them into hedges or rounds. Vines are marked with an asterisk; I generally avoid using vines, with the exception of those listed here, as many tend to be invasive.

 Acer palmatum 'Bloodgood'
 A. palmatum var. *dissectum* 'Garnet', 'Tamukeyama'
 Berberis thunbergii 'Aurea', 'Crimson Pygmy'
 B. thunbergii f. *atropurpurea* 'Rose Glow'
 Buddleja davidii 'Nanho Blue', 'Black Knight'
 Cercis canadensis
 *Clematis: small-flowered cultivars, such as *C.* 'Betty Corning',
  'Étoile Violette', 'Jackmanii', 'Rooguchi'
 C. × *durandii*
 Cornus alba 'Elegantissima' ❄
 C. kousa
 C. sanguinea 'Midwinter Fire' ❄
 C. sericea 'Silver and Gold' ❄
 Corylopsis pauciflora ❄
 Cotinus coggygria 'Royal Purple'
 Cotoneaster horizontalis
 Crataegus viridis 'Winter King'
 Edgeworthia chrysantha ❄
 Hamamelis × *intermedia* 'Jelena' ❄
 Hibiscus syriacus 'Aphrodite', BLUE BIRD, 'Blue Satin', 'Diana'
 *Hydrangea anomala subsp. *petiolaris*
 H. arborescens
 H. macrophylla 'Blue Wave', 'Enziandom', 'Glowing Embers',
  'Mariesii Variegata', 'Nikko Blue'
 H. paniculata 'Limelight', PINK DIAMOND, 'Tardiva'

 H. quercifolia ❄
 H. quercifolia SNOWFLAKE ❄
 H. serrata 'Blue Billow'
 Jasminum nudiflorum ❄
 Lagerstroemia fauriei ❄
 L. hardy cultivars, such as *L.* 'Choctaw', 'Muskogee', 'Natchez' ❄
 Lespedeza thunbergii 'Albiflora', 'Pink Fountain'
 M. × *soulangeana*
 Magnolia stellata
 Malus cultivars:
  White: *M.* 'Bob White'
  Pink: *M.* 'Coralburst'
  Dark Pink: *M.* 'Burgundy'
  Dwarf Roundtable series
 Prunus × *cistena*
 Spiraea japonica 'Golden Elf', 'Goldflame', 'White Gold'
 S. thunbergii 'Ogon'
 Stephanandra incisa 'Crispa'
 Viburnum nudum 'Earthshade', 'Winterthur'
 V. plicatum f. *tomentosum* 'Mariesii'
 Vitex agnus-castus
 Weigela 'Florida Variegata'

Evergreen Trees and Shrubs ❄

 Buxus 'Green Mountain', 'Green Velvet'
 Camellia Ackerman hybrids
 C. japonica 'Spring's Promise', 'April Snow'
 Chamaecyparis pisifera 'Golden Mop'
 Euonymus fortunei 'Coloratus', 'Emerald Gaiety'
 E. kiautschovicus 'Manhattan'
 Ilex aquifolium 'Aurea Marginata'
 I. crenata 'Sky Pencil'
 I. × *meserveae* BLUE PRINCE, BLUE PRINCESS
 I. 'Nellie R. Stevens'
 Juniperus communis 'Compressa'
 J. scopulorum 'Skyrocket', 'Wichita Blue'
 J. squamata 'Blue Star'
 Myrica pensylvanica
 Picea pungens 'Montgomery'

Pieris japonica 'Dorothy Wyckoff'
Prunus laurocerasus 'Otto Luyken'
Rhododendron 'Boule de Neige', 'Pleasant White', 'Treasure'
Sarcococca hookeriana var. *humilis*
Skimmia japonica
Taxus baccata 'Repandens'
T. × *media* 'Hatfieldii'
Thuja occidentalis 'Smaragd'

Roses

Carefree series
David Austin roses
Knock Out series
Meidiland roses
R. 'Betty Prior', 'Seafoam', SIMPLICITY (pink and white forms), TRUMPETER
R. glauca (*R. rubrifolia*)

Perennials

Achillea 'Moonshine'
Aconitum carmichaelii 'Arendsii'
Actaea simplex Atropurpurea Group
Agastache 'Black Adder'
Alcea rosea (biennial; I prefer single-flowered varieties)
Alchemilla mollis
Amsonia hubrichtii
Anemone × *hybrida* 'Honorine Jobert'
A. × *hybrida* 'Robustissima'
Artemisia ludoviciana 'Silver Queen'
Aruncus aethusifolius
A. dioicus
Asarum europaeum ✳
Aster 'Little Carlow'
A. novae-angliae 'Purple Dome'
A. tataricus 'Jindai'
Astilbe chinensis var. *taquetii* 'Superba'
Baptisia australis
Bergenia 'Bressingham Ruby' ✳
Brunnera macrophylla
Campanula lactiflora 'Prichard's Variety'
Ceratostigma plumbaginoides
Coreopsis verticillata 'Moonbeam'
Crocosmia 'Lucifer'
Cynara cardunculus (biennial)
Darmera peltata
Dicentra spectabilis 'Alba'
Digitalis purpurea and *D. p. f. albiflora* (biennial)
Echinacea purpurea
Epimedium species and cultivars
Erigeron karvinskianus
Eryngium giganteum (biennial)
Eupatorium maculatum 'Gateway'
Euphorbia amygdaloides var. *robbiae* ✳
Ferns: *Athyrium filix-femina*, *A. niponicum* var. *pictum*, *Dryopteris erythrosora* ✳
Geranium 'Brookside', 'Johnson's Blue', 'Jolly Bee'

G. macrorrhizum ✳
Geum 'Fire Opal', 'Lady Stratheden', 'Mrs. J. Bradshaw' ✳
Helianthus angustifolius
Heliopsis helianthoides var. *scabra* 'Prairie Sunset', *H.* SUMMER SUN
Helleborus foetidus ✳
H. × *hybridus* ✳
Hemerocallis 'Autumn Prince', 'Happy Returns', 'Hyperion', 'Poinsettia'
Heuchera 'Plum Pudding' ✳
Hibiscus moscheutos 'Lady Baltimore', 'Lord Baltimore'
Hosta 'Patriot'
H. plantaginea 'Aphrodite'
H. sieboldiana var. *elegans*
H. 'Sum and Substance'
Iris ensata 'Variegata'
I. pallida 'Argentea Variegata'
Kirengeshoma palmata
Kniphofia 'Alcazar', 'Little Maid', 'Percy's Pride'
Lavandula angustifolia 'Hidcote'
Ligularia 'The Rocket'
Liriope muscari 'Big Blue' ✳
Liriope SILVERY SUNPROOF ✳
Lychnis chalcedonica
Nepeta racemosa 'Walker's Low'
N. sibirica 'Souvenir d'Andre Chaudron'
N. 'Six Hills Giant'
N. subsessilis
Paeonia lactiflora 'Krinkled White'
Penstemon digitalis 'Husker Red'
Perovskia atriplicifolia
Persicaria amplexicaulis 'Firetail', 'Atrosanguinea'
P. bistorta 'Superba'
Phlox paniculata 'Bright Eyes', 'David'
Platycodon grandiflorus
Polygonatum odoratum var. *pluriflorum* 'Variegatum'
Pulmonaria saccharata 'Mrs. Moon'
Rodgersia aesculifolia
Rudbeckia laciniata 'Herbstsonne'
R. maxima
Salvia nemorosa 'Ostfriesland'
S. × *sylvestris* 'Blauhügel' ('Blue Hill'), 'Mainacht' ('May Night')
Santolina chamaecyparissus
Sedum AUTUMN JOY ✳
S. cauticola 'Lidakense'
Solidago rugosa 'Fireworks'
Stachys byzantina 'Countess Helen von Stein'
Thalictrum aquilegiifolium
T. rochebruneanum 'Lavender Mist'
Verbascum bombyciferum 'Polarsommer' (biennial)
V. 'Helen Johnson'
Vernonia noveboracensis
Veronicastrum virginicum
Vinca minor ✳
Yucca filamentosa 'Color Guard' ✳

Grasses ✳

Acorus gramineus and *A. g.* 'Ogon'
Carex elata 'Aurea'

C. oshimensis 'Evergold'
Chasmanthium latifolium
Festuca glauca 'Elijah Blue'
Hakonechloa macra 'Aureola'
Helictotrichon sempervirens
Imperata cylindrica 'Rubra'
Miscanthus 'Purpurascens'
M. sinensis 'Gracillimus', 'Morning Light', 'Variegatus'
Panicum virgatum 'Heavy Metal', 'Shenandoah'
Pennisetum alopecuroides
P. orientale 'Karley Rose'

Annuals

Abelmoschus manihot
Agapanthus species and cultivars
Ageratum houstonianum 'Blue Horizon'
Alternanthera dentata 'Rubiginosa'
Angelonia Angelface series
Artemisia 'Powis Castle'
Begonia Dragon Wing series
Bouvardia ternifolia
Browallia americana
Caladium cultivars
Canna 'Australia', 'King Humbert', 'Pretoria'
Centaurea gymnocarpa
Colocasia cultivars
Cordyline australis 'Red Sensation'
Cosmos atrosanguineus
Cuphea 'David Verity'
Cynara cardunculus
Dahlia 'Bishop of Llandaff', 'Crossfield Ebony', 'Fascination', 'Gingeroo', 'Onesta'
Euphorbia cotinifolia
E. 'Diamond Frost'
Gomphrena 'Lavender Lady', 'Strawberry Fields'
Helianthus argophyllus 'Japanese Silver Leaf'
Heliotropium arborescens 'Marine'
Hibiscus acetosella 'Red Shield'
Impatiens New Guinea Group
Ipomoea batatas 'Blackie', 'Margarita'
Lantana camara 'Confetti', 'Miss Huff'
Melampodium paludosum 'Lemon Delight'
Nicotiana alata and *N. a.* 'Daylight Sensation'
N. langsdorffii
N. mutabilis
Pennisetum setaceum 'Rubrum'
Plectranthus argentatus
P. 'Mona Lavender'
Ruellia brittoniana
Salvia coccinea 'Lady in Red'
S. guaranitica and *S. g.* 'Black and Blue'
S. 'Indigo Spires'
S. leucantha
Salvia splendens 'Van-Houttei'
Scaevola aemula 'Blue Wonder'
Solenostemon (coleus) cultivars
Tibouchina urvilleana

Tithonia rotundifolia 'Fiesta del Sol', 'Torch'
Verbena bonariensis
Viola hybrids and cultivars (especially the Sorbet series)
Zinnia linearis cultivars
Z. Profusion series

Bulbs

Allium cristophii
A. 'Gladiator', 'Globemaster'
A. hollandicum 'Purple Sensation'
Anemone blanda 'Blue Star'
Arum italicum subsp. *italicum* 'Marmoratum' ❋
Chionodoxa luciliae
Eremurus species and cultivars
Fritillaria imperialis cultivars
F. meleagris
Gladiolus murielae
Hyacinthoides hispanica
Leucojum aestivum
L. canadense
Lilium Citronella Group
L. henryi
L. speciosum var. *album*
L. speciosum var. *rubrum*
Muscari armeniacum
Narcissus—see note below
Scilla siberica
Tulipa—see note below
Tulipa species as perennials: *T. clusiana* var. *chrysantha*, *T. tarda*

Note: I use mixed daffodils to naturalize in ground covers like *Euonymus fortunei* 'Coloratus' but not in mixed borders because of their unsightly spent foliage. I do use tulips sparingly in mixed borders but remove them after flowering, although species tulips can be left in place. Generally, when you use bulbs in mixed borders, do not mix them in with perennials but place them in the spaces reserved for annuals.

Design Elements

Contrast: Big Leaves
Canna; *Colocasia*; *Darmera peltata*; *Hosta*; *Hydrangea*; *Ligularia*; *Rodgersia*

Contrast: Variegated Foliage
Athyrium niponicum var. *pictum*
Caladium cultivars
Canna 'Pretoria'
Carex oshimensis 'Evergold'
Cornus alba 'Elegantissima'
C. sericea 'Silver and Gold'
Euonymus fortunei 'Emerald Gaiety'
Hosta 'Patriot'
Hydrangea macrophylla 'Mariesii Variegata'
Ilex aquifolium 'Aurea Marginata'
Iris ensata 'Variegata'
I. pallida 'Argentea Variegata'

L. Silvery Sunproof
Miscanthus sinensis 'Variegatus'
Polygonatum odoratum var. *pluriflorum* 'Variegatum'
Pulmonaria saccharata 'Mrs. Moon'
Solenostemon (coleus) cultivars
Weigela 'Florida Variegata'
Yucca filamentosa 'Color Guard'

Form: "Minarets"

Many plants in the garden naturally form rounds, or "domes," but fewer plants serve as verticals, or "minarets." I list here some of my favorite plants to use as vertical elements in garden design.

Agastache 'Black Adder'
Allium species
Cynara cardunculus
Digitalis purpurea
Eremurus species and cultivars
Gladiolus murielae
Ilex crenata 'Sky Pencil'
Juniperus communis 'Compressa'
J. scopulorum 'Wichita Blue'
Kniphofia 'Alcazar', 'Little Maid', 'Percy's Pride'
Persicaria bistorta 'Superba'
Thuja occidentalis 'Smaragyd'
Verbascum bombyciferum 'Polarsommer' (biennial)

Color

Dark Red Foliage

Acer palmatum var. *dissectum* 'Garnet', 'Tamukeyama'
A. palmatum 'Bloodgood'
Actaea simplex Atropurpurea Group
Alternanthera dentata 'Rubiginosa'
Berberis thunbergii 'Crimson Pygmy'
Canna 'Australia', 'King Humbert'
Cordyline australis 'Red Sensation'
Cotinus coggygria 'Royal Purple'
Dahlia 'Fascination'
Euphorbia cotinifolia
Heuchera 'Plum Pudding'
Hibiscus acetosella 'Red Shield'
Imperata cylindrica 'Rubra'
Pennisetum setaceum 'Rubrum'
Penstemon digitalis 'Husker Red'
Prunus × *cistena*
Solenostemon 'Red Carpet'

Gray and Silver Foliage

Artemesia ludoviciana 'Silver Queen'
A. 'Powis Castle'
Centaurea gymnocarpa
Cynara cardunculus (biennial)
Lavandula angustifolia 'Hidcote'
Nepeta racemosa 'Walker's Low'
Perovskia atriplicifolia
Plectranthus argentatus
Santolina chamaecyparissus
Stachys byzantina 'Countess Helen Von Stein'
Verbascum bombyciferum 'Polarsommer' (biennial)

Blues

Aconitum carmichaelii
Agastache 'Black Adder'
Ageratum houstonianum 'Blue Horizon'
Anemone blanda 'Blue Star'
Baptisia australis
Browallia americana
Brunnera macrophylla
Campanula lactiflora 'Prichard's Variety'
Chionodoxa luciliae
Festuca glauca 'Elijah Blue'
Geranium 'Brookside', 'Johnson's Blue', 'Jolly Bee'
Helictotrichon sempervirens
Hibiscus syriacus BLUE BIRD, 'Blue Satin'
Hyacinthoides hispanica
Hydrangea macrophylla 'Blue Wave', 'Enziandom', 'Nikko Blue'
H. serrata 'Blue Billow'
Juniperus squamata 'Blue Star'
Muscari armeniacum
Nepeta racemosa 'Walker's Low'
N. sibirica 'Souvenir d'Andre Chaudron'
N. subsessilis
Picea pungens 'Montgomery'
Platycodon grandiflorus
Plectranthus 'Mona Lavender'
Ruellia brittoniana
Salvia guaranitica 'Black and Blue'
S. 'Indigo Spires'
S. nemorosa 'Ostfriesland'
S. × *sylvestris* 'Blauhügel' ('Blue Hill'), 'Mainacht' ('May Night')
Scaevola aemula 'Blue Wonder'
Scilla siberica
Tibouchina urvilleana
Vitex agnus-castus

Yellows

Achillea 'Moonshine'
Acorus gramineus 'Ogon'
Amsonia hubrichtii (fall foliage color)
Berberis thunbergii 'Aurea'
Carex elata 'Aurea'
Chamaecyparis pisifera 'Golden Mop'
Coreopsis verticillata 'Moonbeam'
Corylopsis pauciflora
Euphorbia amygdaloides var. *robbiae*
Geum 'Lady Stratheden'
Helianthus argophyllus 'Japanese Silver Leaf'
Helianthus augustifolius
Heliopsis helianthoides var. *scabra* 'Prairie Sunset', *H.* SUMMER SUN
Hemerocallis 'Happy Returns', 'Hyperion'
Jasminum nudiflorum
Kirengeshoma palmata
Kniphofia 'Little Maid', 'Percy's Pride'
Lilium Citronella Group
Melampodium paludosum 'Lemon Delight'
Nicotiana langsdorffii
Rudbeckia lacinata 'Herbstsonne'

R. maxima
Solidago rugosa 'Fireworks'
Spiraea japonica 'Golden Elf', 'White Gold'
S. thunbergii 'Ogon'
Yucca filamentosa 'Color Guard'

Reds and Oranges

Begonia 'Bonfire'
Begonia Dragon Wing series
Bouvardia ternifolia
Crocosmia 'Lucifer'
Cuphea 'David Verity'
Geum 'Fire Opal', 'Mrs. J. Bradshaw'
Gomphrena 'Strawberry Fields'
Hemerocallis 'Poinsettia'
Hibiscus moscheutos 'Lord Baltimore'
Kniphofia 'Alcazar'
Lantana camara 'Miss Huff'
Lilium canadense
L. henryi
Lychnis chalcedonica
Persicaria amplexicaulis 'Firetail', 'Atrosanguinea'
Salvia coccinea 'Lady in Red'
Spiraea japonica 'Goldflame' (orange spring foliage)
Tithonia rotundifolia 'Fiesta del Sol', 'Torch'

Pinks

Allium cristophii
Anemone hybrida 'Robustissima'
Astilbe chinensis var. *taquetii* 'Superba'
Dahlia 'Fascination', 'Onesta'
Digitalis purpurea (biennial)
Echinacea purpurea
Eupatorium maculatum 'Gateway'
Geranium macrorrhizum
Gomphrena 'Lavender Lady'
Helleborus × *hybridus*
Hibiscus moscheutos 'Lady Baltimore'
Lespedeza thunbergii 'Pink Fountain'
Lilium speciosum var. *rubrum*
Magnolia × *soulangeana*
Nicotiana mutabilis
Pennisetum alopecuroides 'Karley Rose'
Persicaria bistorta 'Superba'
Phlox paniculata 'Bright Eyes'
Rosa 'Betty Prior', SIMPLICITY (pink form)
R. glauca (*R. rubrifolia*)
Salvia splendens 'Van-Houttei'
Sedum AUTUMN JOY
S. cauticola 'Lidakense'
Thalictrum rochebruneanum 'Lavender Mist'

Recommended Reading

American Horticultural Society Great Plant Guide. Grand Rapids, Mich.: Dorling Kindersley, 2004.

Berner, Nancy, and Susan Lowry. *Garden Guide: New York City.* New York: Little Bookroom, 2002.

Beveridge, Charles, Paul Rocheleau, and David Larkin. *Frederick Law Olmsted: Designing the American Landscape.* New York: Universe, 1998.

Bowles, John Paul, and Barbara B. Pesch. *Soils.* Plants & Gardens Series, *Brooklyn Botanic Garden Records*, vol. 42, no. 2. Brooklyn: Brooklyn Botanic Garden, 1986.

Brown, Jane. *Beatrix: The Gardening Life of Beatrix Jones Farrand, 1872–1959.* New York: Viking, 1995.

Burrell, C. Colston. *Native Alternatives to Invasive Plants.* Edited by Janet Marinelli and Bonnie Harper-Lore. Brooklyn: Brooklyn Botanic Garden, 2006.

Caro, Robert A. *The Power Broker: Robert Moses and the Fall of New York.* New York: Vintage, 1975.

Chatto, Beth. *Garden Notebook.* North Mankato, Minn.: Orion Media, 2004.

Craul, Phillip J. *Urban Soil in Landscape Design.* New York: Wiley, 1992.

Crowe, Sylvia. *Garden Design.* 3rd. ed. Wappingers' Falls, N.Y.: Garden Art Press, 1994.

Darke, Rick. *The American Woodland Garden: Capturing the Spirit of the Deciduous Forest.* Portland, Ore.: Timber Press, 2002.

———. *The Encyclopedia of Grasses for Livable Landscapes.* Portland, Ore.: Timber Press, 2007.

Dirr, Michael A. *Dirr's Hardy Trees and Shrubs: An Illustrated Encyclopedia.* Portland, Ore.: Timber Press, 1997.

———. *Manual of Woody Landscape Plants: Their Identification, Ornamental Characteristics, Culture, Propagation and Uses.* Champaign, Ill.: Stipes, 1998.

DiSabato-Aust, Tracy. *The Well-Tended Perennial Garden: Planting and Pruning Techniques.* Portland, Ore.: Timber Press, 2006.

Dunnett, Nigel, and Noel Kingsbury. *Planting Green Roofs and Living Walls.* Portland, Ore.: Timber Press, 2004.

Eck, Joe. *Elements of Garden Design.* New York: Henry Holt, 1996.

Eck, Joe, and Wayne Winterrowd. *A Year at North Hill: Four Seasons in a Vermont Garden.* New York: Owl Books, 1996.

Eddison, Sydney. *The Self Taught Gardener: Lessons from a Country Garden.* New York: Viking, 1997.

———. *The Unsung Season: Gardens and Gardeners in Winter.* New York: Houghton Mifflin, 1995.

Everett, T. H. *New York Botanical Garden Illustrated Encyclopedia of Horticulture.* 10 vols. Grand Rapids, Mich: Garland, 1982.

Farrand, Beatrix. *Beatrix Farrand's Plant Book for Dumbarton Oaks.* Edited by Diane K. McGuire. Washington, D.C.: Dumbarton Oaks, 1980.

Flint, Harrison L. *Landscape Plants for Eastern North America: Exclusive of Florida and the Immediate Gulf Coast.* New York: Wiley, 1997.

Garden Club of America, Horticultural Committee. *Plants That Merit Attention.* Vol. 1, *Trees*; vol. 2, *Shrubs.* Edited by Janet M. Poor and Nancy P. Brewster. Portland, Ore.: Timber Press, 1985.

Garvin, Alexander, and Gayle Berens. *Urban Parks and Open Space.* Washington, D.C.: Urban Land Institute, 1997.

Geneve, Robert. *A Book of Blue Flowers.* Portland, Ore.: Timber Press, 2000.

Gerlach-Spriggs, Nancy, Richard E. Kaufman, and Sam Bass Warner. *Restorative Gardens: The Healing Landscape.* New Haven: Yale University Press, 1999.

Gordon, David L. *Battery Park City: Planning and Politics on the New York Waterfront.* Vol. 1. New York: Gordon and Breach, 1997.

Harnik, Peter. *Inside City Parks.* Washington, D.C.: Urban Land Institute, 2000.

Hayes, Virginia, et al. "Lessons from Lotusland: Sustainability in the Garden." *Pacific Horticulture*, Apr/May/June 2003, 22–28.

Hobbs, Thomas. *Shocking Beauty.* London: Periplus Editions, 1999.

Hobhouse, Penelope. *Colour in Your Garden.* Boston: Little, Brown, 1985.

———. *Garden Style.* New York: Willow Creek Press, 1997.

———. *On Gardening.* New York: Wiley, 1994.

Hyland, Bob. *Designing Borders for Sun and Shade.* Brooklyn: Brooklyn Botanic Garden, 2006.

Jacobs, Jane. *The Death and Life of Great American Cities.* New York: Random House, 1997.

Jekyll, Gertrude. *Colour Schemes for the Flower Garden.* 1936 ed. Reprinted, Woodbridge, England: Baron Publishing, 1982.

Jiler, James. *Doing Time in the Garden: Life Lessons through Prison Horticulture.* New York: New Village Press, 2006.

Karson, Robin. *Fletcher Steele, Landscape Architect: An Account of the Gardenmaker's Life, 1885–1971.* Rev. ed. Amherst, Mass: Library of American Landscape History, 2003.

Kelly, Bruce, Gail T. Guillet, and Mary E. W. Hern. *Art of the Olmsted*

Landscape. New York: New York City Landmarks Preservation Commission, 1981.

Larson, Erik. *The Devil in the White City: Murder, Magic, and Madness at the Fair That Changed America.* New York: Vintage, 2004.

Lawrence, Elizabeth. *A Southern Garden: A Handbook for the Middle South.* Rev. ed. Chapel Hill: University of North Carolina Press, 1984.

Lewis, Charles A. *Green Nature/Human Nature: The Meaning of Plants in Our Lives.* Chicago: University of Illinois Press, 1996.

Lloyd, Christopher. *Succession Planting for Year-Round Pleasure.* Portland, Ore.: Timber Press, 2005.

Lowenfels, Jeff, and Wayne Lewis. *Teaming with Microbes: A Gardener's Guide to the Soil Food Web.* Portland, Ore.: Timber Press, 2006.

Miller, Sara Cedar. *Central Park, An American Masterpiece: A Comprehensive History of the Nation's First Urban Park.* New York: Harry N. Abrams in association with the Central Park Conservancy, 2003.

Nardi, James B. *Life in the Soil: A Guide for Naturalists and Gardeners.* Chicago: University of Chicago Press, 2007. See especially Part 3.

Olmsted, Frederick L. *Forty Years of Landscape Architecture: Central Park.* Cambridge: MIT Press, 1973.

Page, Russell. *The Education of a Gardener.* New York: Random House, 1983.

Phillips, Roger, and Martyn Rix. *The Random House Book of Perennials.* Vol. 1, *Early Perennials*; vol. 2, *Late Perennials.* New York: Random House, 1991.

———. *The Random House Book of Shrubs.* New York: Random House, 1989.

Pollan, Michael. *The Botany of Desire: A Plant's-Eye View of the World.* New York: Random House, 2001.

———. *Second Nature: A Gardener's Education.* New York: Atlantic Monthly Press, 1991.

Rogers, Elizabeth Barlow. *Landscape Design: A Cultural and Architectural History.* New York: Harry N. Abrams, 2001.

Royal Horticultural Society. *RHS Plant Finder 2007–2008.* New York: Dorling Kindersley, 2007.

Rybczynski, Witold. *A Clearing in the Distance: Frederick Law Olmsted and America in the 19th Century.* New York: Scribner, 1999.

Schinz, Marina, and Gabrielle van Zuylen. *The Gardens of Russell Page.* London: Frances Lincoln, 2008.

Scully, Vincent. *American Architecture and Urbanism.* New York: Praeger, 1969.

Simpson, Jeffrey. *Art of the Olmsted Landscape: His Works in New York City.* New York: New York City Landmarks Preservation Commission, 1981.

Trustees' Garden Club. *Garden Guide to the Lower South.* Savannah, Ga.: Trustees' Garden Club, 2006.

Verey, Rosemary. *The Art of Planting.* Boston: Little, Brown, 1990.

Von Arnim, Elizabeth. *Elizabeth and Her German Garden.* London: Macmillan, 1900. Reprinted, with an introduction by Jane Howard, London: Virago, 2006.

Walliser, Jessica. *Good Bug, Bad Bug: Who's Who, What They Do, and How to Manage Them Organically: All You Need to Know about the Insects in Your Garden.* New York: Saint Lynn's Press, 2008.

Whyte, William H. *The City: Rediscovering the Center.* New York: Doubleday, 1988.

———. *The Essential William H. Whyte.* Edited by Albert LaFarge. New York: Fordham University Press, 2000.

———. *The Last Landscape.* Garden City, N.Y.: Doubleday, 1968.

———. *The Social Life of Small Urban Spaces.* Chicago: World Wildlife Fund, 1980.

Wiland, Harry, Dale Bell, and Joseph D'Agnese. *Edens Lost and Found: How Ordinary Citizens Are Restoring Our Great American Cities.* New York: Chelsea Green, 2006.

Wilder, Louise Beebe. *Color in My Garden.* 1918. Reprint, New York: Atlantic Monthly Press, 1990.

Wood-Roper, Laura. *F.L.O.: A Biography of Frederick Law Olmsted.* Baltimore: Johns Hopkins University Press, 1974.

Yoch, James J. *Landscaping the American Dream: The Gardens and Film Sets of Florence Yoch: 1890–1972.* New York: Abrams, 1989.

Index